the

Gay Talese

reader

Other Gay Talese Books by Walker & Company

The Bridge

the

Gay Talese

reader

portraits & encounters

Introduction by Barbara Lounsberry

Walker & Company
New York

First published in the United States of America in 2003
by Walker Publishing Company, Inc.

Published simultaneously in Canada by Fitzhenry and Whiteside,
Markham, Ontario L3R 4T8

For information about permission to reproduce selections from this book, write to
Permissions, Walker & Company, 104 Fifth Avenue, New York, New York 10011

"New York Is a City of Things Unnoticed" was originally published in *New York: A Serendipiter's Journey*, New York: Harper & Brothers, 1961. The following essays first appeared in
Esquire magazine: "Frank Sinatra Has a Cold" (1966); "The Loser" (1964); "The Silent Season of a Hero" (1966); "Peter O'Toole on the Ould Sod" (1963); "*Vogueland*" (1961); "Looking for Hemingway" (1960); "Joe Louis: The King as a Middle-Aged Man" (1962); "Mr. Bad
News" (1966); "Ali in Havana" (1996); and "The Brave Tailors of Maida" (1989). They
were later reprinted in *Fame and Obscurity*, Cleveland: World Publishing, 1970. "Peter
O'Toole on the Ould Sod," "Looking for Hemingway," and "Joe Louis: The King as a
Middle-Aged Man" were also reprinted in *The Overreachers*, New York: Harper & Row,
1965. "Ali in Havana" was also reprinted in *The Best American Essays 1997*, New York:
Houghton Mifflin Company, 1997. "The Brave Tailors of Maida" was also reprinted in *The
Best American Essays 1989*, Boston: Ticknor & Fields, 1989. "Origins of a Nonfiction Writer"
was originally published in *Writing Creative Nonfiction: The Literature of Reality*, with Barbara
Lounsberry. Boston: Addison-Wesley, 1997. "When I Was Twenty-five" first appeared in
P.O.V. magazine (1997). "Walking My Cigar" first appeared in *Cigar Aficionado* (1992).

Library of Congress Cataloging-in-Publication Data

Talese, Gay.
The Gay Talese reader : portraits & encounters / introduction by
Barbara Lounsberry.
p.   cm.
ISBN 0-8027-7675-2 (alk. paper)
1. Journalism—United States.   2. Reportage literature, American.   I. Title.
PN4725.T35   2003
071'.3—dc22   2003055579

Visit Walker & Company's Web site at www.walkerbooks.com

Book design by Maura Fadden Rosenthal/*mspace*

Printed in the United States of America

2   4   6   8   10   9   7   5   3   1

Contents

Introduction *Barbara Lounsberry*   vii

New York Is a City of Things Unnoticed   1

Frank Sinatra Has a Cold   18

The Loser   64

The Silent Season of a Hero   88

Peter O'Toole on the Ould Sod   114

*Vogue*land   125

Looking for Hemingway   136

Joe Louis: The King as a Middle-Aged Man   157

Mr. Bad News   172

Ali in Havana   187

The Brave Tailors of Maida   213

Origins of a Nonfiction Writer   227

When I Was Twenty-five   258

Walking My Cigar   261

Introduction

Barbara Lounsberry

For more than half a century Gay Talese has told real American stories—stories of bridge builders and the men and women who built the *New York Times*; of gangsters and *Vogue* editors; of overlooked Americans like the man who rang the bell at Madison Square Garden prizefights and the diplomatic barber who cut hair at the United Nations—stories, as he told *Playboy*, not of "the mythology of fame and success but the real *soul* of success and the bitterness of attaining [it] and the heartbreak of not attaining it." He broke the Mafia's "code of silence"; dared to report on American adultery; and has painted indelible portraits of Joe DiMaggio and Joe Louis, Frank Sinatra and Floyd Patterson and Muhammad Ali—portraits from unusual angles and of singular depth. He reframes the famous and celebrates the unnoticed in prose as lovingly crafted as the works of his immigrant Italian-American forebears—his father, Joseph, a tailor, and his namesake grandfather, Gaetano, a stonemason. Works created from fine materials, made to last.

A reporter's reporter who is revered by fellow writers, Talese possesses a long standing coterie of loyal and admiring readers. His stories are told with seamless artistry, reading almost like fiction, so that readers lose sight of the extraordinary daring and persistent effort required to obtain them. Admired though he is, Talese has not always been adequately recognized for extending the boundaries of nonfiction *subject matter*—as well as style—to enlarge our understanding of the human condition.

The Kingdom and the Power, the first of Talese's four consecutive best-sellers, is a case in point. When the thirty-five-year-old writer first proposed his "human history" of the *New York Times* to New York publishers, he was told that no one was interested in reporters. When the book became an unexpected best-seller in 1969, journalists' lives suddenly were of great interest to many, as seen in the plethora of inside-the-media books that followed: among them, Brendan Gill's *Here at the* New Yorker and Carl Bernstein and Bob Woodward's *All the President's Men.* In like manner, fans of today's television Mafia family, the Sopranos, probably do not realize that in the late 1960s, when Talese embarked on the story of real family life in the Mafia, which became *Honor Thy Father* in 1971, journalistic consensus was that the Mafia's "code of silence" was impenetrable and enduring. "They will not talk to you," was the general opinion. Nonetheless, Talese managed to enter and live for months with the Bonanno family, to ride unarmed with Bill Bonanno's bodyguards, and to write about them all, opening the door this time to a flood of nonfiction life-in-the-Mafia books, including chieftain Joseph Bonanno's 1983 autobiography, *A Man of Honor.*

Talese turned to sexual taboos for his third and most controversial book, the 1980 best-seller *Thy Neighbor's Wife,* which chronicled sex and censorship in the United States from the Puritans to modern-day Americans. Here Talese reported from within the bedroom using real names and with the permission of the participants. An extraordinary financial success—film rights alone sold for a then-record $2.5 million—*Thy Neighbor's Wife* became the first Talese work to outrage reviewers, many of whom were shocked at his opening the doors of sexual privacy, at his hinting at the social benefits of massage parlors, and at his widely publicized participatory research methods.

Next he abandoned the biggest story of his career, that of Lee Iacocca and Chrysler, to write about his father's life as an Italian-American in his 1992 *Unto the Sons*. It was of a piece for a writer who has always turned away from the "big story" to report the unnoticed one.

Gay Talese was born February 7, 1932, on the small island of Ocean City, New Jersey, a resort town just south of Atlantic City. The boy was a minority within a minority, an Italian-American Catholic in an Irish Catholic parish on an island settled as a Methodist religious retreat in 1879. He was neither Irish nor Methodist, neither blue-eyed nor fair-skinned, and he did poorly in school. Talese stood apart from his classmates in more than just his visage, his name, and his miserable grades. He was the only student who came to class wearing a jacket and tie, a walking advertisement for his father's tailoring prowess in his small beautifully hand-stitched suits. An immigrant's son raised with impeccable "store manners"—his parents owned the Talese Town Shop, which grew to include a dry cleaning business, fur storage, and a fashionable women's dress boutique when men's custom tailoring proved insufficiently profitable—he was ever respectful but shy and isolated from his classmates.

Talese's profound identification with the *unnoticed* and his cele-bration of "losers" throughout his writing career are rooted in his own sense of failure as a grade-school and high-school student. Journalism provided an escape and the first success for the undervalued but always curious Talese. He chanced to become a high-school reporter, wherein he found a role for himself on the sidelines. Too shy to date, he could attend the dances as a journalist, lingering gracefully around the perimeter in his custom-tailored suits—the position where, even today, he feels most at ease. But Talese was no ordinary high-school reporter. From his first article, written at the age of fifteen in June 1947, until his "Swan Song" column in September 1949, when he left the island to attend the University of Alabama, Talese wrote 311 articles and columns for the weekly *Ocean City Sentinel-Ledger*—often more than two articles per week. His "High School Highlights" column allowed him to become the Balzac of his own microcosmic culture.

"Origins of a Nonfiction Writer," which appears in this volume, tells the story of Talese's escape to Alabama. "I chose journalism as my college major because that is what I knew," he recalls, "but I really became a student of history." At Alabama, Talese turned his high-school "Sportopics" column into a more experimental and literary college column titled "Sports Gay-zing," a conscious play on his own name and unconscious confession of his continuing outsider, voyeur role. Talese was a nineteen-year-old college sophomore when he attempted his first scene in a feature story. This was 1951, a year before Lillian Ross's famous *Picture* and a half-decade before Truman Capote's "The Muses Are Heard." The young writer turned to the short stories and novels of F. Scott Fitzgerald, Irwin Shaw, John O'Hara, Carson McCullers, and Ernest Hemingway as models for what he sought to do with *nonfiction*. He had noticed that while journalists forever focused on "winners"—the highest scorers, the big men and women on campus, the achievers—fiction writers (and playwrights like Arthur Miller and Tennessee Williams) were writing about ordinary people and their lives, subject matter highly congenial to Talese. His genius was to believe that he could do with nonfiction what Shaw and company were doing with fiction, that he could write "stories with real names." He wanted to write about "the overlooked nonnewsworthy population that is everywhere, but rarely taken into account by journalists and other chroniclers of reality."

After Talese joined the *New York Times* following his graduation in 1953, he spent the next twelve years trying to slip this kind of writing into the "paper of record." Talese introduced scenes and dialogue to a journalistic establishment wedded to facts and substantiating quotations. He was even able to insert dialogue designed to reveal mood—

not just information. He experimented with a diary structure in one *Times* boxing story and with James Joyce's stream-of-consciousness style in an article on bare-knuckle fighter Billy Ray.

Talese further expanded traditional journalistic practice in his effort always to delay a story's "news peg," the factor that makes the story "news," until as late in a story as he could. This was the reverse of standard journalistic teaching, which calls for the peg to be as near to the beginning as possible to justify the story. Talese was happiest when he found a way to dispense with the news peg altogether. He did this, just as he eased notable names into the background, defying the venerable journalism maxim "names sell newspapers," because he sought to make his stories universal rather than specific. Talese had no determination to be timely; he was writing for eternity. His "Portrait of a Young Prize Fighter"—another piece in the fine tradition of James Joyce—represented a special triumph over newspaper convention, for he managed to withhold José Torres's name until the story's twenty-first, and final, paragraph.

Talese's stylish writing did not go unnoticed, and in 1960 Harold Hayes, editor of *Esquire* magazine, offered him more space and freedom for his writing than the close (and closely guarded) columns of the *Times* could oblige. The first selection of *The Gay Talese Reader*, the opening section of Talese's first book, *New York: A Serendipiter's Journey*, was Talese's first article for *Esquire*. The piece was different from anything he had written before. He composed it by stitching together the leads of dozens of *Times* articles he had written on the unnoticed to create this now-famous opening:

> *New York is a city of things unnoticed. It is a city with cats sleeping under parked cars, two stone armadillos crawling up St. Patrick's Cathedral, and thousands of ants creeping on top of the Empire State Building. The*

> *ants probably were carried there by wind or birds, but nobody is sure; no-*
> *body in New York knows any more about the ants than they do about the*
> *panhandler who takes taxis to the Bowery; or the dapper man who picks*
> *trash out of Sixth Avenue trash cans; or the medium in the West Seventies*
> *who claims, "I'm clairvoyant, clairaudient, and clairsensuous."*

In "When I Was 25," a 1997 reminiscence reprinted here for the first time, Talese looks back at those early *Times* days when his twenty-fifth birthday was spent chasing stray cats around Manhattan so he could document their lives.

Talese followed his auspicious *Esquire* debut with a series of profiles from 1961 to 1966 today considered classics of magazine journalism. In 1965, in perhaps the first use of the term "The New Journalism," Pete Hamill lauded the grace and style of these profiles, citing them as "examples of how really good the magazine article can be." "Frank Sinatra Has a Cold," included in this collection, is one of the most famous magazine profiles of all time. Here Talese faced a reporter's nightmare—and turned it into reporter's gold. The problem was simple: Sinatra, suffering from a cold, had canceled their interview. Many writers would have postponed or abandoned the story. Not Talese, who has perfected what he calls the "fine art of hanging out." Denied direct access to his subject, Talese shifted his lens to the entourage surrounding the star and wrote of Sinatra by capturing how drivers and agents, orchestra conductors and studio executives, wives, ex-wives, and children are unsettled when The Voice falls victim to the common cold.

Sinatra was an Italian-American icon. So, too, was Joe DiMaggio, the Yankee Clipper whom Talese unveils in "The Silent Season of a Hero," a profile recently called the greatest sports article of the twentieth century in *The Best American Sports Writing of the Century*, an anthology edited by

David Halberstam and Glenn Stout. Here Talese penetrates the formidable façade of the baseball legend to disclose a man struggling with his personal demons within the glare of media adoration.

Equally intimate is Talese's account of his travels with Irish actor Peter O'Toole, presented here in "Peter O'Toole on the Ould Sod." On planes and across the Irish Sea, Talese follows O'Toole's escape to Eire, where he returns periodically from London to refresh his spirit at the Dublin pubs and horse races and "to spend some solitary hours thinking" away from the burden of his acting projects and his ascending fame.

Also preserved in this volume, in "*Vogue*land" and "Looking for Hemingway," is a rarely shown side of Talese's talent: that of Talese the deft social satirist. "*Vogue*land" traces the history of *Vogue* magazine and its editors, "a group of suave and wrinkle-proof women, who call one another 'dear' and 'dahling,' and can speak in italics and curse in French." "Looking for Hemingway," in turn, hints that George Plimpton and the *Paris Review* set were playing at life (with the safety net of wealth) in imitation of what was serious (and poverty-ridden) for the young Hemingway of the 1920s. Talese retains to this day a file of letters from Plimpton, challenging one facet of this article or another. Talese's tour of New York publications is completed in *The Gay Talese Reader* by "Mr. Bad News," a behind-the-scenes portrait of the *New York Times*'s head obituary writer in 1965, the man charged with the sober task of writing obituaries of the famous before they die.

A special wing of Talese's portrait gallery is reserved for boxers, for of the many sports figures and celebrities he has immortalized, prizefighters have most suited his human and literary pursuits. Boxing is an individual sport offering dramatic, potentially life-threatening, scenes. Fighters also have tended to be minorities, outsiders often derided by polite society—as is boxing itself. Journalists rarely write more than one feature story on a given celebrity; three or four articles over a span of years might seem excessive to some. In 1957, Talese wrote the first of thirty-eight separate articles on heavyweight champion Floyd Patterson that culminated in the classic 1964 *Esquire* profile "The Loser," included here. In this ironically titled article, Patterson reveals what it feels like to be knocked out, and Talese provides a rich psychological portrait of a man who is a success in life though haunted by his failures in the ring. Nearly all Talese's profiles present the star's life after reaching the pinnacle of fame, for his interest is in success and failure as they are genuinely lived—behind and after, as well as before, the spotlight. "Joe Louis: The King as a Middle-Aged Man" offers just such a portrait. Tom Wolfe acknowledged he learned to write scenes from the opening of this 1962 *Esquire* profile: " 'Hi, sweetheart!' Joe Louis called to his wife, spotting her waiting for him at the Los Angeles airport." Thirty-four years later, in "Ali In Havana," Talese recreates the 1996 encounter in Cuba between an aging Fidel Castro and an ailing, but still vital, Muhammad Ali.

Two recent and very personal pieces conclude *The Gay Talese Reader*. "The Brave Tailors of Maida," part of the charming ninth chapter of *Unto the Sons*, reprises a fateful moment in 1911 when a band of tailors—Talese's own father among them—faced down a Mafiosi in the southern Italian village of Maida. "Walking My Cigar," which concludes the volume, offers Talese at his Establishment-defying best. Here we join the writer at sixty-four, walking his Australian terriers each evening as he smokes his single cigar, lamenting ruefully the "neo-Puritanism and negativism that has . . . in the name of health and virtue and fairness, reduced options and pleasures" in America.

The Gay Talese Reader collects for the first time Talese's writing from the 1960s through the 1990s. What next for the durable author? What "stories with real names" remain to be told? Since 1992 Talese has continued his memoir writing, pressing forward with the sequel to *Unto the Sons* (which ends in 1944, when he is only twelve). It will chronicle Talese's subsequent life—and American culture—in the second half of the twentieth century. It will include his college days at the University of Alabama (then still segregated) and his years with the *New York Times*. He may tell us of his nights at the Sandstone free-love colony in California and of his days behind the wheel with Lee Iacocca in Detroit—all of this an American narrative never before shared.

Beyond his own American story, Talese has pursued other subjects during the 1990s in his patented, patient fashion. He continues to seek strong story lines and wait for compelling characters to emerge. His new work will feature more women: Jackie Ho, a Chinese-American success story, and Liu Ying, the Chinese soccer player who missed the penalty kick at the Rose Bowl bringing victory to the U.S. women's soccer team and failure to herself and her Chinese teammates.

In 1999, Pulitzer Prize–winning writer David Halberstam called Talese "the most important nonfiction writer of his generation, the person whose work most influenced at least two generations of other reporters." In the final analysis, Talese's dedication—his willingness to return again and again to his subjects—may be his most enduring legacy. Whatever "stories with real names" Gay Talese chooses to tell next, his reputation for exhaustive research, for unlocking forbidden subjects, and for respectful celebration of the unnoticed is secure.

the

Gay Talese

reader

New York Is a City of Things Unnoticed

NEW YORK IS A CITY of things unnoticed. It is a city with cats sleeping under parked cars, two stone armadillos crawling up St. Patrick's Cathedral, and thousands of ants creeping on top of the Empire State Building. The ants probably were carried up there by wind or birds, but nobody is sure; nobody in New York knows any more about the ants than they do about the panhandler who takes taxis to the Bowery; or the dapper man who picks trash out of Sixth Avenue trash cans; or the medium in the West Seventies who claims, "I am clairvoyant, clairaudient, and clairsensuous."

New York is a city for eccentrics and a center for odd bits of information. New Yorkers blink twenty-eight times a minute, but forty when tense. Most popcorn chewers at Yankee Stadium stop chewing momentarily just before the pitch. Gum chewers on Macy's escalators stop chewing momentarily just before they get off—to concentrate on the last step. Coins, paper clips, ballpoint pens, and little girls' pocketbooks are found by workmen when they clean the sea lions' pool at the Bronx Zoo.

Each day New Yorkers guzzle 460,000 gallons of beer, swallow 3,500,000 pounds of meat, and pull 21 miles of dental floss through their teeth. Every day in New York about 250 people die, 460 are born, and 150,000 walk through the city wearing eyes of glass or plastic.

A Park Avenue doorman has parts of three bullets in his head—there since World War I. Several young gypsy daughters, influenced by television and literacy, are running away from home because they do not want to grow up and become fortune-tellers. Each month 100 pounds of hair are delivered to Louis Feder at 545 Fifth Avenue, where

1

blonde hairpieces are made from German women's hair; brunette hairpieces from French and Italian women's hair; but no hairpieces from American women's hair, which, says Mr. Feder, is weak from too-frequent rinses and permanents.

Some of New York's best-informed men are elevator operators, who rarely talk but always listen—like doormen. Sardi's doorman listens to the comments made by Broadway's first-nighters walking by after the last act. He listens closely. He listens carefully. Within ten minutes of the curtain's fall he can tell you which shows will flop and which will be hits.

On Broadway in the evening, a big, dark 1948 Rolls-Royce pulls in—and out hops a little lady armed with a Bible and a sign reading "The Damned Shall Perish." She proceeds to stand on the corner screaming at the multitudes of Broadway sinners sometimes until 3 A.M., when the chauffeur-driven Rolls picks her up and drives her back to Westchester.

By this time Fifth Avenue is deserted by all but a few strolling insomniacs, some cruising cabdrivers, and a group of sophisticated females who stand in store windows all night and day wearing cold, perfect smiles—smiles formed by lips of clay, eyes of glass, and cheeks that will glow until the paint wears off. Like sentries, they line Fifth Avenue—these window mannequins who gaze onto the quiet street with tilted heads and pointed toes and long, rubber fingers reaching for cigarettes that aren't there. At 4 A.M., some store windows become a strange fairyland of gangling goddesses, all of them frozen in the act of dashing to a party, diving into a swimming pool, or sashaying skyward in a billowy blue negligee.

While this wild illusion is partly due to the runaway imagination, it is also partly due to the incredible skill of mannequin makers, who have endowed mannequins with certain individual characteristics—the theory being that no two females, not even plastic or plaster females, are quite alike. As a result, the mannequins at Peck & Peck are made to look young and prim, while at Lord & Taylor they seem wiser and wind-blown. At Saks they are demure but mature, while at Bergdorf's they look agelessly elegant and quietly rich. The profiles of Fifth Avenue's mannequins have been fashioned after some of the world's most allur-ing women—women like Suzy Parker, who posed for the Best & Co. mannequins, and Brigitte Bardot, who inspired some mannequins at Saks. The preoccupation with making mannequins almost human, and equipping them with curves, is perhaps responsible for the rather strange fascination so many New Yorkers have for these synthetic vir-gins. This is why some window decorators frequently talk to man-nequins and give them pet names, and why naked mannequins in windows inevitably attract men, disgust women, and are banned in New York City. This is why some mannequins are attacked by perverts, and why the svelte mannequin in a White Plains shop was discovered in the basement not long ago with her clothes torn off, her makeup smeared, and her body possessing evidence of attempted rape. The police laid a trap one night and caught the attacker—a shy little man: the porter.

When street traffic dwindles and most people are sleeping, some New York neighborhoods begin to crawl with cats. They move quickly through the shadows of buildings; night watchmen, policemen, garbage collectors, and other nocturnal wanderers see them—but never for very long. A majority of them hang around the fish markets, in Greenwich Village, and in the East and West Side neighborhoods where garbage cans abound. No part of the city is without its strays, however, and all-night garage attendants in such busy neighborhoods as Fifty-fourth Street have counted as many as twenty of them around the Ziegfeld Theatre early in the morning. Troops of cats patrol the waterfront piers at night searching for rats. Subway trackwalkers have discovered cats living in the darkness. They seem never to get hit by trains, though some are occasionally liquidated by the third rail. About twenty-five cats live seventy-five feet below the west end of Grand Central Terminal, are fed by the underground workers, and never wander up into the daylight.

The roving, independent, self-laundering cats of the streets live a life strangely different from New York's kept, apartment-house cats. Most are flea-bitten. Many die of food poisoning, exposure, and malnutrition; their average life span is two years, whereas the stay-at-home cats live ten to twelve years or more. Each year the ASPCA kills about 100,000 New York street cats for whom no homes can be found.

Social climbing among the stray cats of Gotham is not common. They rarely acquire a better mailing address out of choice. They usually die within the blocks of their birth, although one flea-bitten specimen picked up by the ASPCA was adopted by a wealthy woman; it now lives in a luxurious East Side apartment and spends the summer at the lady's estate on Long Island. The American Feline Society once moved two strays into the headquarters of the United Nations after having heard that some rodents had infested UN filing cabinets. "The cats took care of 'em," says Robert Lothar Kendell, society president. "And they seemed happy at the UN. One of the cats used to sleep on a Chinese dictionary."

In every New York neighborhood the strays are dominated by a "boss"—the largest, strongest tomcat. But, except for the boss, there is not much organization in the street cat's society. Within the society, however, there are three "types" of cats—wild cats, Bohemians, and part-time grocery store (or restaurant) cats.

The wild cats rely on an occasional loose garbage lid or on rats for food and will have little or nothing to do with people—even those who would feed them. These most unkempt of strays have a recognizable haunted look, a wide-eyed, wild expression, and they usually are found around the waterfront.

The Bohemian, however, is more tractable. It does not run from people. Often, it is fed in the streets daily by sensitive cat lovers (mostly women) who call the strays "little people," "angels," or "darlings" and are indignant when the objects of their charity are referred to as "alley cats." So punctual are most Bohemians at feeding time that one cat lover has advanced the theory that cats can tell time. He cited a gray tabby that appears five days a week, precisely at 5:30 P.M., in an office building at Broadway and Seventeenth Street, where the elevator men feed it. But the cat never shows up on Saturday or Sundays; it seems to know people don't work on those days.

The part-time grocery store (or restaurant) cat, often a reformed Bohemian, eats well and keeps rodents away, but it usually uses the store as a hotel and prefers to spend the nights prowling in the streets. Despite its liberal working schedule, it still assumes most of the privileges of a related breed—the full-time, or wholly nonstray, grocery store cat—including the right to sleep in the window. A reformed Bohemian at a Bleecker Street delicatessen hides behind the door and chases away all other Bohemians looking for handouts.

The number of full-time cats, incidentally, has diminished greatly since the decline of the small food store and the rise of supermarkets in New York. With better rat-proofing methods, improved packaging of foods, and more sanitary conditions, such chain stores as the A&P rarely keep a cat full-time.

On the waterfront, however, the great need for cats remains unchanged. Once a longshoreman who was allergic to cats poisoned them. Within a day rats were all over the place. Every time the men turned around, they would find rats on crates. And on Pier 95 the rats began stealing the longshoremen's lunch and even attacking the men. So the street cats were recruited from nearby neighbors, and now most of the rats are controlled.

"But cats don't get much sleep around here," said one longshoreman. "They can't. Rats would overrun them. We've had cases here where the rat has torn up the cat. But it doesn't happen often. Most waterfront cats are mean bastards."

At 5 A.M. Manhattan is a town of tired trumpet players and homeward-bound bartenders. Pigeons control Park Avenue and strut unchallenged in the middle of the street. This is Manhattan's mellowest hour. Most *night* people are out of sight—but the *day* people have not yet appeared. Truck drivers and cabs are alert, yet they do not disturb the mood. They do not disturb the abandoned Rockefeller Center, or the motionless night watchmen in the Fulton Fish market, or the gas-station attendant sleeping next to Sloppy Louie's with the radio on.

At 5 A.M. the Broadway regulars have gone home or to all-night coffee shops where, under the glaring light, you see their whiskers and wear. And on Fifty-first Street a radio press car is parked at the curb with a photographer who has nothing to do. So he just sits there for a few nights, looks through the windshield, and soon becomes a keen observer of life after midnight.

"At 1 A.M.," he says, "Broadway is filled with wise guys and with kids coming out of the Astor Hotel in white dinner jackets—kids who drive to dances in their fathers' cars. You also see cleaning ladies going home, always wearing kerchiefs. By 2 A.M., some of the drinkers are getting out of hand, and this is the hour for bar fights. At 3 A.M. the last show is over in the nightclubs, and most of the tourists and out-of-town buyers are back in hotels. At 4 A.M., after the bars close, you see the drunks come out—and also the pimps and prostitutes who take advantage of drunks. At 5 A.M., though, it is mostly quiet. New York is an entirely different city at 5 A.M."

At 6 A.M. the early workers begin to push up from the subways. The traffic begins to move down Broadway like a river. And Mrs. Mary

Woody jumps out of bed, dashes to her office, and phones dozens of sleepy New Yorkers to say in a cheerful voice, rarely appreciated: "Good morning. Time to get up." For twenty years, as an operator of Western Union's Wake-Up Service, Mrs. Woody has gotten millions out of bed.

At 7 A.M. a floridly robust little man, looking very Parisian in a blue beret and turtleneck sweater, moves in a hurried step along Park Avenue visiting his wealthy lady friends—making certain that each is given a brisk, before-breakfast rubdown. The uniformed doormen greet him warmly and call him either "Biz" or "Mac" because he is Biz Mackey, a ladies' masseur extraordinaire.

Mr. Mackey is spry and straight-spined, and always carries a black leather grip containing liniments, creams, and the towels of his trade. Up the elevator he goes; then, half an hour later, he is down again, and off to another lady—an opera singer, a movie actress, a lady police lieutenant.

Biz Mackey, a former featherweight prizefighter, started rubbing women the right way in Paris, in the twenties. He had lost a fight during a European tour and decided he'd had enough. A friend suggested he go to a school for masseurs, and six months later he had his first customer—Claire Luce, the actress then starring in the Folies-Bergère. She liked him, and sent him more clients—Pearl White, Mary Pickford, and a beefy Wagnerian soprano. It took World War II to get Biz out of Paris.

When he returned to Manhattan, his European clientele continued to patronize him when they visited here, and though he is now pushing seventy, he is still going strong. Biz handles about seven women a day. His muscular fingers and thick arms have a miraculously soothing touch. He is discreet, and that is why New York ladies prefer him. He visits each of them in her apartment and has special keys to the bedrooms; he is often the first man they see in the morning, and they lie in bed waiting for him. He never reveals the names of his customers, but most of them are middle-aged and rich.

"Women don't want other women to know their business," Biz explains. "You know women," he adds, offhandedly, leaving no doubt that he does.

The doormen that Biz passes each morning are generally an obliging, endlessly articulate group of sidewalk diplomats who list among their friends some of Manhattan's most powerful men, most beautiful women, and snootiest poodles. More often than not the doormen are big, slightly Gothic in design, and possessors of eyes sharp enough to spot big tippers a block away in the year's thickest fog.

Some East Side doormen are as proud as grandees, and their uniforms, heavily festooned, seem to have come from the same tailor who outfitted Marshal Tito. Most hotel doormen are superb at small talk, big talk, and back talk, at remembering names and appraising luggage leather. (They size up a guest's wealth by the luggage he has, not by the clothes he wears.)

In Manhattan today there are 650 apartment-house doormen, 325 hotel doormen (14 at the Waldorf-Astoria), and an unknown, but formidable, number of restaurant and theater doormen, nightclub doormen, barking doormen, and doorless doormen.

Doorless doormen, who are nonunion vagabonds, usually without uniforms (but with rented hats), pussyfoot about town opening car doors when traffic is thick—on nights of the opera, concerts, championship fights, and conventions. The Brass Rail doorman, Christos Efthimiou, says that doorless doormen know when he is off (Mondays and Tuesdays) and that on these days they freelance off his spot on Seventh Avenue at Forty-ninth Street.

Barking doormen, who sometimes wear rented uniforms (but own their hats), post themselves in front of jazz clubs with floor shows, such as along Fifty-second Street. In addition to opening doors and lassoing cabdrivers, the barking doormen might whisper to passing pedestrians, softly but distinctly, "Psssst! No cover charge—girls inside . . . the new Queen of Alaska!"

Though there is hardly a doorman in town who does not swear up and down that he is underpaid and underrated, many hotel doormen admit that on some good, rainy weeks they have made close to $200 in tips alone. (More people desire cabs when it is raining, and doormen who provide umbrellas and cabs rarely go untipped.)

When it rains in Manhattan, automobile traffic is slow, dates are broken, and, in hotel lobbies, people slump behind newspapers or walk aimlessly about with no place to sit, nobody to talk to, nothing to do. Taxis are harder to get; department stores do between 15 to 25 percent less business; and the monkeys in the Bronx Zoo, having no audience, slouch grumpily in their cages looking more bored than the lobby loungers.

While some New Yorkers become morose with rain, others prefer it, like to walk in it, and say that on rainy days the city's buildings seem somehow cleaner—washed in an opalescence, like a Monet painting. There are fewer suicides in New York when it rains; but when the sun is shining, and New Yorkers seem happy, the depressed person sinks deeper into depression and Bellevue Hospital gets more attempted suicides.

Yet a rainy day in New York is a bright day for umbrella and raincoat salesmen, for hatcheck girls, bellhops, and for members of the British Consulate General's office, who say rain reminds them of home. Consolidated Edison claims New Yorkers burn $120,000 worth more electricity than they do on bright days; thousands of trouser creases lose their sharpness in rain, and Norton Cleaners on Forty-fifth Street presses an average of 125 more pants on such days.

Rain ruins the mascara on the eyes of fashion models who cannot find cabs; and rain makes it a lonely day for Times Square's recruiting sergeants, demonstrators, bootblacks, and burglars—who all tend to lose their enthusiasm when wet.

Shortly after 7:30 each morning, while most New Yorkers still are in a bleary-eyed slumber, hundreds of people are lined along Forty-second Street waiting for the 8 A.M. opening of the ten movie houses that stand almost shoulder to shoulder between Times Square and Eighth Avenue.

Who are these people who go to the movies at 8 A.M.? They are the city's night watchmen, derelicts, or people who can't sleep, can't go home, or have no home. They are truck drivers, homosexuals, cops, hacks, cleaning ladies, and restaurant men who have worked all night. They are also alcoholics who are waiting at 8 A.M. to pay forty cents to get a soft seat and sleep in the cool, dark, smoky theater.

And yet, aside from being smoky, each Times Square theater has a special quality, or lack of quality, about it. At the Victory Theatre one finds only horror films, while at the Times Square Theatre they feature only cowboy films. There are first-run films for forty cents at the Lyric, while at the Selwyn there are always second-run films for thirty cents. At both the Liberty and the Empire are reissues, and at the Apollo they run only foreign films. Foreign films have been making money at the Apollo for twenty years, and William Brandt, one of the owners, never could understand why. "So one day I investigated the place," he said, "and saw people in the lobby talking with their hands. I realized they were mostly deaf and dumb. They patronize the Apollo because they read the subtitles that go with foreign films; the Apollo probably has the biggest deaf-and-dumb movie audience in the world."

New York is a town of 8,485 telephone operators, 1,364 Western Union messenger boys, and 112 newspaper copyboys. An average baseball crowd at Yankee Stadium uses over ten gallons of liquid soap per game—an unofficial high mark for cleanliness in the major leagues; the stadium also has the league's top number of ushers (360), sweepers (72), and men's rooms (34).

In New York there are 500 mediums, from semitrance to trance to deep-trance types. Most of them live in New York's West Seventies, Eighties, and Nineties, and on Sundays some of these blocks are communicating with the dead, vibrating to trumpets, and solving all problems.

In New York the Fifth Avenue Lingerie Shop is on Madison Avenue, the Madison Pet Shop is on Lexington Avenue, the Park Avenue Florist is on Madison Avenue, and the Lexington Hand Laundry is on Third Avenue. New York is the home of 120 pawnbrokers, and it is where Bishop Sheen's brother, Dr. Sheen, shares an office with one Dr. Bishop.

Within a serene brownstone on Lexington Avenue, on the corner of Eighty-second Street, a pharmacist named Frederick D. Lascoff for years has been selling leeches to battered prizefighters, catnip oil to lion hunters, and thousands of strange potions to people in exotic places around the world.

Within a somber West Side factory each month a long, green line of cardboard crawls like an endless reptile up and down a printing press until it is chopped into thousands of little, annoying pieces. Each piece is designed to fit into a policeman's pocket, decorate the windshield of an illegally parked car, and relieve a motorist of fifteen dollars. About 500,000 fifteen-dollar tickets are printed for New York's police each year on West Nineteenth Street by the May Tag and Label Corp., whose employees sometimes see their workmanship boomerang on their own windshields.

New York is a city of 200 chestnut vendors, 300,000 pigeons, and 600 statues and monuments. When the equestrian statue of a general has both front hoofs off the ground, it means the general died in battle; if one hoof is off the ground, he died of wounds received in battle; if all four hoofs are on the ground, the general probably died in bed.

In New York from dawn to dusk to dawn, day after day, you can hear the steady rumble of tires against the concrete span of the George Washington Bridge. The bridge is never completely still. It trembles with traffic. It moves in the wind. Its great veins of steel swell when hot and contract when cold; its span often is ten feet closer to the Hudson River in summer than in winter. It is an almost restless structure of graceful beauty which, like an irresistible seductress, withholds secrets from the romantics who gaze upon it, the escapists who jump off it, the chubby girl who lumbers across its 3,500-foot span trying to reduce, and the 100,000 motorists who each day cross it, smash into it, shortchange it, get jammed up on it.

Few of the New Yorkers and tourists who breeze across it are aware of the workmen riding elevators through the twin towers 612 feet above, and few people know that wandering drunks occasionally have climbed blithely to the top and fallen asleep up there. In the morning they are petrified and have to be carried down by emergency crews.

Few people know that the bridge was built in an area where Indians used to roam, battles were fought, and where, during early colonial times, pirates were hanged along the river as a warning to other adventurous sailors. The bridge now stands where Washington's troops fell back before the British invaders who later captured Fort Lee, New Jersey, and who found kettles still on the fire, the cannon abandoned, and clothing strewn along the path of Washington's retreating garrison.

The roadway at the George Washington Bridge is more than 100 feet above the little red lighthouse that became obsolete when the bridge went up in 1931; its Jersey approach is two miles from where Albert Anastasia lived behind a high wall guarded by Doberman pinschers; its Jersey tollage is twenty feet from where a truck driver without a license tried to drive four elephants across in his trailer—and would have if one elephant hadn't fallen out. The upper span is 220 feet from where a Port Authority guard once climbed up to tell an aspiring suicide, "Listen, you SOB, if you don't come down, I'm going to shoot you down"—and the man crawled quickly down.

Around the clock the bridge guards stay alert. They have to. At any moment there may be an accident, breakdown, or a suicide. Since 1931, 100 people have jumped from the bridge. More than twice that number have been stopped. Bridge jumpers intent on committing suicide go quickly and quietly. On the edge of the roadway they leave automobiles, jackets, eyeglasses, and sometimes a note reading, "I wish to take the blame for everything" or "I don't want to live anymore."

A lonely out-of-town buyer who'd had a few drinks checked into a Broadway hotel near Sixty-fourth Street one night, went to bed, and awoke in the middle of the night to a shocking view. He saw, floating past his window, the shimmering image of the Statue of Liberty.

Immediately he imagined himself shanghaied—sailing past Liberty Island toward certain disaster on the high seas. But then, after a closer look, he found that he was actually seeing New York's *second*

Statue of Liberty—the obscure, almost unnoticed statue that stands on top of the Liberty-Pac warehouse at 43 West Sixty-fourth Street.

This reasonable facsimile, erected in 1902 at the request of William H. Flattau, a patriotic warehouse owner, stands 55 feet high above its pedestal as compared with Bartholdi's 151-footer on Liberty Island. This smaller Liberty also had a lighted torch, a spiral staircase, and a hole in the head through which Broadway could be seen. But in 1912 the staircase became weakened, the torch blew off in a storm, and schoolchildren were no longer permitted to run up and down inside. Mr. Flattau died in 1931, and with him went much of the information on the history of this statue.

From time to time, however, employees in the warehouse, as well as people in the neighborhood, are asked by tourists about the statue. "People usually come over and say, 'Hey, what's *that* doing up *there?*'" said a Kinney parking-lot attendant who works across from the statue. "The other day a Texan pulls in, looks up, and says, 'I thought that statue was supposed to be in the water somewhere.' But some people are really interested in the statue and take pictures of it. I consider it a privilege to work under it, and when tourists come I always remind them that this is the 'Second Largest Statue of Liberty in the World.'"

But most neighborhood folks pay no attention to the statue. The gypsy fortune-tellers who work to the left of it do not; the habitués of Mrs. Stern's tavern below it do not; the soup slurpers in Bickford's restaurant across the street do not. A New York cabby, David Zickerman (Cab No. 2865), has whizzed by the statue hundreds of times and never knew it existed. "Who the hell looks up in this town?" he asks.

For decades this statue has carried a burned-out torch over this neighborhood of punchball players, short-order cooks, and warehouse watchmen; over undertipped bellhops and cops and high-heeled transvestites who leave their fire-escaped walls after midnight and stroll through this town of perhaps too much liberty.

New York is a city of movement. Artists and beatniks live in Greenwich Village, where the Negroes first settled. Negroes live in Harlem, where the Jews and Germans once lived. The wealth has moved from the West to the East Side. Puerto Ricans cluster everywhere. Only the Chinese have stability in their enclave around the ancient angle of Doyer Street.

To some people, New York is best remembered by the smile of an airline stewardess at LaGuardia, or the patience of a shoe salesman on Fifth Avenue; to others the city represents the smell of garlic in the rear of a Mulberry Street church, or a hunk of "turf" for juvenile gangs to fight over, or a chunk of real estate to be bought and sold by Zeckendorf.

But beyond the New York City guidebooks and the chamber of commerce, New York is no summer festival. For most New Yorkers it is a town of hard work, too many cars, too many people. Many of the people are anonymous, like busmen, charwomen, and those creepy pornographers who mark up advertising posters and are never caught. Many New Yorkers seem to have only one name, like barbers, doormen, bootblacks. Some New Yorkers go through life with the wrong name—like Jimmy Buns, who lives across from Police Headquarters on Centre Street. When Jimmy Buns, whose real surname is Mancuso, was a little boy, the cops sitting across the street would yell to him, "Hey, kid, how 'bout going down the corner and getting us some coffee and buns?" Jimmy always obliged, and soon they called him "Jimmy Buns" or just "Hey Buns." Now Jimmy is a white-haired, elderly man with a daughter named Jeannie. But Jeannie never had a maiden name; everybody just calls her "Jeannie Buns."

———————————

New York is the city of Jim Torpey, who has been flashing headlines around Times Square's electric sign since 1928 without burning a bulb for himself; and of George Bannan, Madison Square Garden's official timekeeper, who has held up like an imperishable grandfather's clock through 7,000 prizefights and has rung the bell 2 million times. It is the city of Michael McPadden, who sits behind a microphone in a subway booth near the Times Square shuttle train yelling in a voice wavering between futility and frustration, "Watch your step getting off, please, watch your step." He delivers this advice 500 times a day and sometimes would like to ad-lib. Yet he rarely tries. He has long been convinced that his is a forgotten voice lost in the clamor of slamming doors and pushing bodies; and before he can think of anything witty to say, another train has arrived from Grand Central, and Mr. McPadden must say (one more time!), "Watch your step getting off, please, watch your step."

When it begins to get dark in New York, and all the shoppers have left Macy's, ten black Doberman pinschers begin to tip-tap up and down the aisles sniffing for prowlers who may be hiding behind counters or lurking in clothes racks. They wander through all twenty floors of the big store and are trained to climb ladders, jump through window frames, leap over hurdles, and bark at anything unusual—a leaky radiator, broken steamline, smoke, or a thief. Should a thief try to escape, the dogs can easily overtake him, run between his legs—and trip him. Their barks have alerted Macy's guards to many minor hazards but never to a thief—none has dared remain in the store after closing hours since the dogs arrived in 1952.

New York is a city in which large, cliff-dwelling hawks cling to skyscrapers and occasionally zoom to snatch a pigeon over Central Park, or Wall Street, or the Hudson River. Bird watchers have seen these peregrine falcons circling lazily over the city. They have seen them perched atop tall buildings, even around Times Square.

About twelve of these hawks patrol the city, some with a wingspan of thirty-five inches. They have buzzed women on the roof of the St. Regis Hotel, have attacked repairmen on smokestacks, and, in August 1947, two hawks jumped women residents in the recreation yard of the Home of the New York Guild for the Jewish Blind. Maintenance men at the Riverside Church have seen hawks dining on pigeons in the bell tower. The hawks remain there for only a little while. And then they fly out to the river, leaving pigeons' heads for the Riverside maintenance men to clean up. When the hawks return, they fly in quietly—*unnoticed*, like the cats, the ants, the doorman with three bullets in his head, the ladies' masseur, and most of the other offbeat wonders in this town without time.

Frank Sinatra Has a Cold

FRANK SINATRA, HOLDING A GLASS of bourbon in one hand and a cigarette in the other, stood in a dark corner of the bar between two attractive but fading blondes who sat waiting for him to say something. But he said nothing; he had been silent during much of the evening, except now in this private club in Beverly Hills he seemed even more distant, staring out through the smoke and semidarkness into a large room beyond the bar where dozens of young couples sat huddled around small tables or twisted in the center of the floor to the clamorous clang of folk-rock music blaring from the stereo. The two blondes knew, as did Sinatra's four male friends who stood nearby, that it was a bad idea to force conversation upon him when he was in this mood of sullen silence, a mood that had hardly been uncommon during this first week of November, a month before his fiftieth birthday.

Sinatra had been working on a film that he now disliked, could not wait to finish; he was tired of all the publicity attached to his dating the twenty-year-old Mia Farrow, who was not in sight tonight; he was angry that a CBS television documentary of his life, to be shown in two weeks, was reportedly prying into his privacy, even speculating on his possible friendship with Mafia leaders; he was worried about his starring role in an hour-long NBC show entitled *Sinatra—A Man and His Music,* which would require that he sing eighteen songs with a voice that at this particular moment, just a few nights before the taping was to begin, was weak and sore and uncertain. Sinatra was ill. He was the victim of an ailment so common that most people would consider it trivial. But when it gets to Sinatra, it can plunge him into a state of anguish, deep depression, panic, even rage. Frank Sinatra had a cold.

Sinatra with a cold is Picasso without paint, Ferrari without fuel—only worse. For the common cold robs Sinatra of that uninsurable jewel, his voice, cutting into the core of his confidence, and it not only affects his own psyche but also seems to cause a kind of psychosomatic nasal drip within dozens of people who work for him, drink with him, love him, depend on him for their own welfare and stability. A Sinatra with a cold can, in a small way, send vibrations through the entertainment industry and beyond as surely as a president of the United States, suddenly sick, can shake the national economy.

For Frank Sinatra was now involved with many things involving many people—his own film company, his record company, his private airline, his missile-parts firm, his real-estate holdings across the nation, his personal staff of seventy-five—which are only a portion of the power he is and has come to represent. He seemed now to be also the embodiment of the fully emancipated male, perhaps the only one in America, the man who can do anything he wants, *anything*, can do it because he has the money, the energy, and no apparent guilt. In an age when the very young seem to be taking over, protesting and picketing and demanding change, Frank Sinatra survives as a national phenomenon, one of the few prewar products to withstand the test of time. He is the champ who made the big comeback, the man who had everything, lost it, then got it back, letting nothing stand in his way, doing what few men can do: He uprooted his life, left his family, broke with everything that was familiar, learning in the process that one way to hold a woman is not to hold her. Now he has the affection of Nancy and Ava and Mia, the fine female produce of three generations, and still has the adoration of his children, the freedom of a bachelor, he does not feel old, he makes old men feel young, makes them think that if Frank Sinatra can do it, it can be done; not that *they* could do it, but it is still nice for other men to know, at fifty, that it can be done.

But now, standing at this bar in Beverly Hills, Sinatra had a cold, and he continued to drink quietly and he seemed miles away in his private world, not even reacting when suddenly the stereo in the other room switched to a Sinatra song, "In the Wee Small Hours of the Morning."

It is a lovely ballad that he first recorded ten years ago, and it now inspired many young couples who had been sitting, tired of twisting, to get up and move slowly around the dance floor, holding one another very close. Sinatra's intonation, precisely clipped, yet full and flowing, gave a deeper meaning to the simple lyrics—"In the wee small hours of the morning/while the whole wide world is fast asleep/you lie awake, and think about the girl . . ."*—it was, like so many of his classics, a song that evoked loneliness and sensuality, and when blended with the dim light and the alcohol and nicotine and late-night needs, it became a kind of airy aphrodisiac. Undoubtedly the words from this song, and others like it, had put millions in the mood, it was music to make love by, and doubtless much love had been made by it all over America at night in cars, while the batteries burned down, in cottages by the lake, on beaches during balmy summer evenings, in secluded parks and exclusive penthouses and furnished rooms; in cabin cruisers and cabs and cabanas—in all places where Sinatra's songs could be heard were these words that warmed women, wooed and won them, snipped the final thread of inhibition, and gratified the male egos of ungrateful lovers; two generations of men had been the beneficiaries of such ballads, for which they were eternally in his debt, for which they may eternally hate him. Nevertheless, here he was, the man himself, in the early hours of the morning in Beverly Hills, out of range.

The two blondes, who seemed to be in their middle thirties, were preened and polished, their matured bodies softly molded within tight dark suits. They sat, legs crossed, perched on the high bar stools. They listened to the music. Then one of them pulled out a Kent, and

*© *Redd Evans Music Corp.*

Sinatra quickly placed his gold lighter under it, and she held his hand, looked at his fingers: they were nubby and raw, and the pinkies protruded, being so stiff from arthritis that he could barely bend them. He was, as usual, immaculately dressed. He wore an oxford-gray suit with a vest, a suit conservatively cut on the outside but trimmed with flamboyant silk within; his shoes, British, seemed to be shined even on the bottom of the soles. He also wore, as everybody seemed to know, a remarkably convincing black hairpiece, one of sixty that he owns, most of them under the care of an inconspicuous little gray-haired lady who, holding his hair in a tiny satchel, follows him around whenever he performs. She earns $400 a week. The most distinguishing thing about Sinatra's face are his eyes, clear blue and alert, eyes that within seconds can go cold with anger, or glow with affection, or, as now, reflect a vague detachment that keeps his friends silent and distant.

Leo Durocher, one of Sinatra's closest friends, was now shooting pool in the small room behind the bar. Standing near the door was Jim Mahoney, Sinatra's press agent, a somewhat chunky young man with a square jaw and narrow eyes who would resemble a tough Irish plain-clothesman if it were not for the expensive continental suits he wears and his exquisite shoes often adorned with polished buckles. Also nearby was a big, broad-shouldered 200-pound actor named Brad Dexter who seemed always to be thrusting out his chest so that his gut would not show.

Brad Dexter has appeared in several films and television shows, displaying fine talent as a character actor, but in Beverly Hills he is equally known for the role he played in Hawaii two years ago when he swam a few hundred yards and risked his life to save Sinatra from drowning in a riptide. Since then Dexter has been one of Sinatra's constant companions and has been made a producer in Sinatra's film company. He occupies a plush office near Sinatra's executive suite. He

is endlessly searching for literary properties that might be converted
into new starring roles for Sinatra. Whenever he is among strangers
with Sinatra, he worries because he knows that Sinatra brings out the
best and worst in people—some men will become aggressive, some
women will become seductive, others will stand around skeptically
appraising him, the scene will be somehow intoxicated by his mere
presence, and maybe Sinatra himself, if feeling as badly as he was
tonight, might become intolerant or tense, and then: headlines. So
Brad Dexter tries to anticipate danger and warn Sinatra in advance.
He confesses to feeling very protective of Sinatra, admitting in a recent moment of self-revelation: "I'd kill for him."

While this statement may seem outlandishly dramatic, particularly when taken out of context, it nonetheless expresses a fierce fidelity that is quite common within Sinatra's special circle. It is a
characteristic that Sinatra, without admission, seems to prefer: *All the
Way; All or Nothing at All.* This is the Sicilian in Sinatra; he permits his
friends, if they wish to remain that, none of the easy Anglo-Saxon
outs. But if they remain loyal, there is nothing Sinatra will not do in
turn—fabulous gifts, personal kindnesses, encouragement when
they're down, adulation when they're up. They are wise to remember,
however, one thing. He is Sinatra. The boss. *Il Padrone.*

I had seen something of this Sicilian side of Sinatra last summer
at Jilly's saloon in New York, which was the only other time I'd gotten
a close view of him prior to this night in this California club. Jilly's,
which is on West Fifty-second Street in Manhattan, is where Sinatra
drinks whenever he is in New York, and there is a special chair reserved for him in the back room against the wall that nobody else may
use. When he is occupying it, seated behind a long table flanked by
his closest New York friends—who include the saloonkeeper, Jilly
Rizzo, and Jilly's azure-haired wife, Honey, who is known as the
"Blue Jew"—a rather strange ritualistic scene develops. That night

dozens of people, some of them casual friends of Sinatra's, some mere acquaintances, some neither, appeared outside of Jilly's saloon. They approached it like a shrine. They had come to pay respect. They were from New York, Brooklyn, Atlantic city, Hoboken. They were old actors, young actors, former prizefighters, tired trumpet players, politicians, a boy with a cane. There was a fat lady who said she remembered Sinatra when he used to throw the *Jersey Observer* onto her front porch in 1933. There were middle-aged couples who said they had heard Sinatra sing at the Rustic Cabin in 1938 and "We knew then that he really had it!" Or they had heard him when he was with Harry James's band in 1939, or with Tommy Dorsey in 1941 ("Yeah, that's the song, "I'll Never Smile Again"—he sang it one night in this dump near Newark and we danced . . ."); or they remembered that time at the Paramount with the swooners, and him with those bow ties, the voice; and one woman remembered that awful boy she knew then—Alexander Dorogokupetz, an eighteen-year-old heckler who had thrown a tomato at Sinatra, and the bobby-soxers in the balcony had tried to flail him to death. What ever became of Alexander Dorogokupetz? The lady did not know.

And they remembered when Sinatra was a failure and sang trash like "Mairzy Doats," and they remembered his comeback, and on this night they were all standing outside Jilly's saloon, dozens of them, but they could not get in. So some of them left. But most of them stayed, hoping that soon they might be able to push or wedge their way into Jilly's between the elbows and backsides of the men drinking three-deep at the bar, and they might be able to peek through and *see* him sitting back there. This is all they really wanted; they wanted to see him. And for a few moments they gazed in silence through the smoke, and they stared. Then they turned, fought their way out of the bar, went home.

Some of Sinatra's close friends, all of whom are known to the men

guarding Jilly's door, do manage to get an escort into the back room.
But once they are there, they too must fend for themselves. On the
particular evening, Frank Gifford, the former football player, got only
seven yards in three tries. Others who had somehow been close
enough to shake Sinatra's hand did *not* shake it; instead they just
touched him on the shoulder or sleeve, or they merely stood close
enough for him to see them, and, after he'd given them a wink of
recognition or a wave or a nod or called out their names (he has a fan-
tastic memory for first names), they would then turn and leave. They
had checked in. They had paid their respects. And as I watched this
ritualistic scene, I got the impression that Frank Sinatra was dwelling
simultaneously in two worlds that were not contemporary.

On the one hand, he is the swinger—as he is when talking and jok-
ing with Sammy Davis, Jr., Richard Conte, Liza Minelli, Bernice Massi,
or any of the other show-business people who get to sit at *the* table; on
the other, as when he is nodding or waving to his *paisanos* who are close
to him (Al Silvani, a boxing manager who works with Sinatra's film
company; Dominic Di Bona, his wardrobe man; Ed Pucci, a 300-
pound former football lineman who is his aide-de-camp), Frank Sinatra is *Il Padrone*. Or, better still, he is what in traditional Sicily have
long been called *uomini rispettati*—men of respect: men who are both
majestic and humble, men who are loved by all and are very generous
by nature, men whose hands are kissed as they walk from village to village, men who would *personally* go out of their way to redress a wrong.

Frank Sinatra does things *personally*. At Christmastime, he will
personally pick dozens of presents for his close friends and family,
remembering the type of jewelry they like, their favorite colors, the
sizes of their shirts and dresses. When a musician friend's house was
destroyed and his wife was killed in a Los Angeles mud slide a little
more than a year ago, Sinatra personally came to his aid, finding the
musician a new home, paying whatever hospital bills were left unpaid

by the insurance, then personally supervising the furnishing of the new home down to the replacing of the silverware, the linen, the purchase of new clothing.

The same Sinatra who did this can, within the same hour, explode in a towering rage of intolerance should a small thing be incorrectly done for him by one of his *paisanos*. For example, when one of his men brought him a frankfurter with catsup on it, which Sinatra apparently abhors, he angrily threw the bottle at the man, splattering catsup all over him. Most of the men who work around Sinatra are big. But this never seems to intimidate Sinatra nor curb his impetuous behavior with them when he is mad. They will never take a swing back at him. He is *Il Padrone*.

At other times, aiming to please, his men will overreact to his desires: When he casually observed that his big orange desert jeep in Palm Springs seemed in need of a new painting, the word was swiftly passed down through channels, becoming ever more urgent as it went, until finally it was a *command* that the jeep be painted *now*, immediately, yesterday. To accomplish this would require the hiring of a special crew of painters to work all night, at overtime rates; which, in turn, meant that the order had to be bucked back up the line for further approval. When it finally got back to Sinatra's desk, he did not know what it was all about; after he had figured it out, he confessed, with a tired look on his face, that he did not care when the hell they painted his jeep.

Yet it would have been unwise for anyone to anticipate his reaction, for he is a wholly unpredictable man of many moods and great dimension, a man who responds instantaneously to instinct—suddenly, dramatically, wildly he responds, and nobody can predict what will follow. A young lady named Jane Hoag, a reporter at *Life*'s Los Angeles bureau who had attended the same school as Sinatra's daughter, Nancy, had once been invited to a party at Mrs. Sinatra's California home at which

Frank Sinatra, who maintains very cordial relations with his former wife, acted as host. Early in the party Miss Hoag, while leaning against a table, accidentally with her elbow knocked over one of a pair of alabaster birds to the floor, smashing it to pieces. Suddenly, Miss Hoag recalled, Sinatra's daughter cried, "Oh, that was one of Mother's favorite . . ."—but before she could complete the sentence, Sinatra glared at her, cutting her off, and while forty other guests in the room all stared in silence, Sinatra walked over, quickly with his finger flicked the *other* alabaster bird off the table, smashing it to pieces, and then put an arm gently around Jane Hoag and said, in a way that put her completely at ease, "That's okay, kid."

Now Sinatra said a few words to the blondes. Then he turned from the bar and began to walk toward the poolroom. One of Sinatra's other men friends moved in to keep the girls company. Brad Dexter, who had been standing in the corner talking to some other people, now followed Sinatra.

The room cracked with the clack of billiard balls. There were about a dozen spectators in the room, most of them young men who were watching Leo Durocher shoot against two other aspiring hustlers who were not very good. This private drinking club has among its membership many actors, directors, writers, models, nearly all of them a good deal younger than Sinatra or Durocher and much more casual in the way they dress for the evening. Many of the young women, their long hair flowing loosely below their shoulders, wore tight, fanny-fitting Jax pants and very expensive sweaters; and a few of the young men wore blue or green velour shirts with high collars, and narrow tight pants and Italian loafers.

It was obvious from the way Sinatra looked at these people in the poolroom that they were not his style, but he leaned back against a high stool that was against the wall, holding his drink in his right hand, and said nothing, just watched Durocher slam the billiard balls back and forth. The younger men in the room, accustomed to seeing Sinatra at this club, treated him without deference, although they said nothing offensive. They were a cool young group, very California-cool and casual, and one of the coolest seemed to be a little guy, very quick of movement, who had a sharp profile, pale blue eyes, light brown hair, and squared eyeglasses. He wore a pair of brown corduroy slacks, a green shaggy-dog Shetland sweater, a tan suede jacket, and Game Warden boots, for which he had recently paid sixty dollars.

Frank Sinatra, leaning against the stool, sniffling a bit from his cold, could not take his eyes off the Game Warden boots. Once, after gazing at them for a few moments, he turned away; but now he was focused on them again. The owner of the boots, who was just standing in them watching the pool game, was named Harlan Ellison, a writer who had just completed work on a screenplay, *The Oscar*.

Finally, Sinatra could not contain himself.

"Hey," he yelled in his slightly harsh voice that still had a soft, sharp edge. "Those Italian boots?"

"No," Ellison said.

"Spanish?"

"No."

"Are they *English* boots?"

"Look, I donno, man," Ellison shot back, frowning at Sinatra, then turning away again.

Now the poolroom was suddenly silent. Leo Durocher, who had been poised behind his cue stick and was bent low, just froze in that position for a second. Nobody moved. Then Sinatra moved away from the stool and walked with that slow, arrogant swagger of his toward Ellison, the hard tap of Sinatra's shoes the only sound in the room.

Then, looking down at Ellison with a slightly raised eyebrow and a tricky little smile, Sinatra asked, "You expecting a *storm?*"

Harlan Ellison moved a step to the side. "Look, is there any reason why you're talking to me?"

"I don't like the way you're dressed," Sinatra said.

"Hate to shake you up," Ellison said, "but I dress to suit myself."

Now there was some rumbling in the room, and somebody said, "Com'on, Harlan, let's get out of here," and Leo Durocher made his pool shot and said, "Yeah, com'on."

But Ellison stood his ground.

Sinatra said, "What do you do?"

"I'm a plumber," Ellison said.

"No, no, he's not," another man quickly yelled from across the table. "He wrote *The Oscar.*"

"Oh, yeah," Sinatra said, "well I've seen it, and it's a piece of crap."

"That's strange," Ellison said, "because they haven't even released it yet."

"Well, I've seen it," Sinatra repeated, "and it's a piece of crap."

Now Brad Dexter, very anxious, very big opposite the small figure of Ellison, said, "Com'on, kid, I don't want you in this room."

"*Hey,*" Sinatra interrupted Dexter, "can't you see I'm talking to this guy?"

Dexter was confused. Then his whole attitude changed, and Dexter's voice went soft and he said to Ellison, almost with a plea, "*Why do you persist in tormenting me?*"

The whole scene was becoming ridiculous, and it seemed that Sinatra was only half-serious, perhaps just reacting out of sheer boredom or inner despair; at any rate, after a few more exchanges Harlan Ellison left the room. By this time the word had gotten out to those on the dance floor about the Sinatra-Ellison exchange, and somebody went to look for the manager of the club. But somebody else said that the manager had already heard about it—and had quickly gone out the door, hopped in his car, and drove home. So the assistant manager went into the poolroom.

"I don't want anybody in here without coats and ties," Sinatra snapped.

The assistant manager nodded and walked back to his office.

It was the morning after. It was the beginning of another nervous day for Sinatra's press agent, Jim Mahoney. Mahoney had a headache, and he was worried but not over the Sinatra-Ellison incident of the night before. At the time Mahoney had been with his wife at a table in the other room, and possibly he had not even been aware of the little drama. The whole thing had lasted only about three minutes. And three minutes after it was over, Frank Sinatra had probably forgotten about it for the rest of his life—as Ellison will probably remember it for the rest of *his* life: He had had, as hundreds of others before him, at an unexpected moment between darkness and dawn, a scene with Sinatra.

It was just as well that Mahoney had not been in the poolroom; he had enough on his mind today. He was worried about Sinatra's cold and worried about the controversial CBS documentary that, despite Sinatra's protests and withdrawal of permission, would be shown on television in less than two weeks. The newspapers this morning were full of hints that Sinatra might sue the network, and Mahoney's phones were ringing without pause, and now he was plugged into New York talking to the *Daily News*'s Kay Gardella, saying: "That's right, Kay . . . they made a gentleman's agreement to not ask certain questions about Frank's private life, and then Cronkite went right ahead: 'Frank, tell me about those associations.' *That* question, Kay—*out!* That question should never have been asked."

As he spoke, Mahoney leaned back in his leather chair, his head shaking slowly. He is a powerfully built man of thirty-seven; he has a round, ruddy face, a heavy jaw, and narrow pale eyes, and he might appear pugnacious if he did not speak with such clear, soft sincerity and if he were not so meticulous about his clothes. His suits and shoes are superbly tailored, which was one of the first things Sinatra noticed about him, and in his spacious office opposite the bar is a red-muff electrical shoe polisher and a pair of brown wooden shoulders on a stand over which Mahoney can drape his jackets. Near the bar is an autographed photograph of President Kennedy and a few pictures of Frank Sinatra, but there are none of Sinatra in any other rooms in Mahoney's public-relations agency; there once was a large photograph of him hanging in the reception room, but this apparently bruised the egos of some of Mahoney's other movie-star clients and, since Sinatra never shows up at the agency anyway, the photograph was removed.

Still, Sinatra seems ever present, and if Mahoney did not have legitimate worries about Sinatra, as he did today, he could invent them—and, as worry aids, he surrounds himself with little mementos of moments in the past when he did worry. In his shaving kit there is a two-year-old box of sleeping tablets dispensed by a Reno druggist—the date on the bottle marks the kidnapping of Frank Sinatra, Jr. There is on a table in Mahoney's office a mounted wood reproduction of Frank Sinatra's ransom note written on the aforementioned occasion. One of Mahoney's mannerisms, when he is sitting at his desk worrying, is to tinker with the tiny toy train he keeps in front of him—the train is a souvenir from the Sinatra film *Von Ryan's Express*; it is to men who are close to Sinatra what the PT-109 tie clasps are to men who were close to Kennedy—and Mahoney then proceeds to roll the little train back and forth on the six inches of track; back and forth, back and forth, click-*clack* click-*clack*. It is his Queeg-thing.

Now Mahoney quickly put aside the little train. His secretary told him there was a *very* important call on the line. Mahoney picked it up, and his voice was even softer and more sincere than before. "Yes, Frank," he said. "Right . . . right . . . yes, Frank . . ."

When Mahoney put down the phone, quietly, he announced that Frank Sinatra had left in his private jet to spend the weekend at his home in Palm Springs, which is a sixteen-minute flight from his home in Los Angeles. Mahoney was now worried again. The Lear jet that Sinatra's pilot would be flying was identical, Mahoney said, to the one that had just crashed in another part of California.

On the following Monday, a cloudy and unseasonably cool California day, more than 100 people gathered inside a white television studio, an enormous room dominated by a white stage, white walls, and with dozens of lights and lamps dangling; it rather resembled a gigantic operating room. In this room, within an hour or so, NBC was scheduled to begin taping a one-hour show that would be televised in color on the night of November 24 and would highlight, as much as it could in the limited time, the twenty-five-year career of Frank Sinatra as a public entertainer. It would not attempt, to probe, as the forthcoming CBS *Sinatra* documentary allegedly would, that area of Sinatra's life that he regards as private. The NBC show would be mainly an hour of Sinatra singing some of the hits that carried him from Hoboken to Hollywood, a show that would be interrupted only now and then by a few film clips and commercials for Budweiser beer. Prior to his cold, Sinatra had been very excited about this show; he saw here an opportunity not only to appeal to those who were nostalgic but also to communicate his talent to some rock-and-rollers—in a sense, he was battling the Beatles. The press releases being prepared by Mahoney's agency stressed this, reading: "If you happen to be tired of kid singers wearing mops of hair thick enough to hide a crate of melons . . . it should be refreshing to consider the entertainment value of a video special titled *Sinatra—A Man and His Music.*"

But now in this NBC studio in Los Angeles, there was an atmosphere of anticipation and tension because of the uncertainty of the Sinatra voice. The forty-three musicians in Nelson Riddle's orchestra had already arrived, and some were up on the white platform warming up. Dwight Hemion, a youthful sandy-haired director who had won praise for his television special on Barbra Streisand, was seated in the glass-enclosed control booth that overlooked the orchestra and stage. The camera crews, technical teams, security guards, Budweiser ad men were also standing between the floor lamps and cameras, waiting, as were a dozen or so ladies who worked as secretaries in other parts of the building but had sneaked away so they could watch this.

A few minutes before eleven o'clock, word spread quickly through the long corridor into the big studio that Sinatra was spotted walking through the parking lot and was on his way, and was looking fine. There seemed great relief among the group that was gathered; but when the lean, sharply dressed figure of the man got closer, and closer, they saw to their dismay that it was not Frank Sinatra. It was his double, Johnny Delgado.

Delgado walks like Sinatra, has Sinatra's build, and from certain facial angles does resemble Sinatra. But he seems a rather shy individual. Fifteen years ago, early in his acting career, Delgado applied for a role in *From Here to Eternity.* He was hired, finding out later that he was to be Sinatra's double. In Sinatra's latest film, *Assault on a Queen*, a story in which Sinatra and some fellow conspirators attempt to hijack the *Queen Mary*, Johnny Delgado doubles for Sinatra in some water scenes; and now, in this NBC studio, his job was to stand under the hot television lights marking Sinatra's spots on the stage for the camera crews.

Five minutes later, the real Frank Sinatra walked in. His face was pale; his blue eyes seemed a bit watery. He had been unable to rid himself of the cold, but he was going to try to sing anyway because the schedule was tight and thousands of dollars were involved at this moment in the assembling of the orchestra and crews and the rental of the studio. But when Sinatra, on his way to his small rehearsal room to warm up his voice, looked into the studio and saw that the stage and orchestra's platform were not close together, as he had specifically requested, his lips tightened and he was obviously very upset. A few moments later, from his rehearsal room, could be heard the pounding of his fist against the top of the piano and the voice of his accompanist, Bill Miller, saying, softly, "Try not to upset yourself, Frank."

Later Jim Mahoney and another man walked in, and there was talk of Dorothy Kilgallen's death in New York earlier that morning. She had been an ardent foe of Sinatra for years, and he became equally uncomplimentary about her in his nightclub act, and now, though she was dead, he did not compromise his feelings. "Dorothy Kilgallen's dead," he repeated, walking out of the room toward the studio. "Well, guess I got to change my whole act."

When he strolled into the studio, the musicians all picked up their instruments and stiffened in their seats. Sinatra cleared his throat a few times and then, after rehearsing a few ballads with the orchestra, he sang "Don't Worry About Me" to his satisfaction and, being uncertain of how long his voice could last, suddenly became impatient.

"Why don't we tape this mother?" he called out, looking up toward the glass booth where the director, Dwight Hemion, and his staff were sitting. Their heads seemed to be down, focusing on the control board.

"Why don't we tape this mother?" Sinatra repeated.

The production stage manager, who stands near the camera wearing a headset, repeated Sinatra's words exactly into his line to the control room: "Why don't we tape this mother?"

Hemion did not answer. Possibly his switch was off. It was hard to know because of the obscuring reflections the lights made against the glass booth.

"Why don't we put on a coat and tie," said Sinatra, then wearing a high-necked yellow pullover, "and tape this . . ."

Suddenly, Hemion's voice came over the sound amplifier, very calmly: "Okay, Frank, would you mind going back over . . ."

"Yes, I *would* mind going back," Sinatra snapped.

The silence from Hemion's end, which lasted a second or two, was then again interrupted by Sinatra saying, "When we stop doing things around here the way we did them in 1950, maybe we . . . ," and Sinatra continued to tear into Hemion, condemning as well the lack of modern techniques in putting such shows together; then, possibly not wanting to use his voice unnecessarily, he stopped. And Dwight Hemion, very patient, so patient and calm that one would assume he had not heard anything that Sinatra had just said, outlined the opening part of the show. And Sinatra a few minutes later was reading his opening remarks, words that would follow "Without a Song," off the large idiot-cards being held near the camera. Then, this done, he prepared to do the same thing on camera.

"Frank Sinatra Show, Act I, Page 10, Take 1," called a man with a clapboard, jumping in front of the camera—*clap*—then jumping away again.

"Did you ever stop to think," Sinatra began, "what the world would be like without a song? . . . It would be a pretty dreary place. . . . Gives you something to think about, doesn't it?"

Sinatra stopped.

"Excuse me," he said, adding, "*Boy*, I need a drink."

They tried it again.

"Frank Sinatra Show, Act I, Page 10, Take 2," yelled the jumping guy with the clapboard.

"Did you ever stop to think what the world would be like without a song? . . ." Frank Sinatra read it through this time without stopping. Then he rehearsed a few more songs, once or twice interrupting the orchestra when a certain instrumental sound was not quite what he wanted. It was hard to tell how well his voice was going to hold up, for this was early in the show; up to this point, however, everybody in the room seemed pleased, particularly when he sang an old sentimental favorite written more than twenty years ago by Jimmy Van Heusen and Phil Silvers—"Nancy," inspired by the first of Sinatra's three children when she was just a few years old.

> *If I don't see her each day*
> *I miss her. . . .*
> *Gee what a thrill*
> *Each time I kiss her.*

As Sinatra sang these words, though he had sung them hundreds and hundreds of times in the past, it was suddenly obvious to everybody in the studio that something quite special must be going on inside the man, because something quite special was coming out. He was singing now, cold or no cold, with power and warmth; he was letting himself go; the public arrogance was gone; the private side was in this song about the girl, who, it is said, understands him better than anybody else and is the only person in front of whom he can be unashamedly himself.

Nancy is twenty-five. She lives alone, her marriage to singer Tommy Sands having ended in divorce. Her home is in a Los Angeles suburb, and she is now making her third film and is recording for her father's record company. She sees him every day; or, if not, he telephones, no matter if it be from Europe or Asia. When Sinatra's singing first became popular on radio, stimulating the swooners, Nancy would listen at home and cry. When Sinatra's first marriage broke up in 1951 and he left

home, Nancy was the only child old enough to remember him as a father. She also saw him with Ava Gardner, Juliet Prowse, Mia Farrow, and
many others, has gone on double dates with him. . . .

> *She takes the winter*
> > *And makes it summer. . . .*
> *Summer could take*
> > *Some lessons from her.*

Nancy now also sees him visiting at home with his first wife, the
former Nancy Barbato, a plasterer's daughter from Jersey City whom
he married in 1939 when he was earning twenty–five dollars a week
singing at the Rustic Cabin near Hoboken.

The first Mrs. Sinatra, a striking woman who has never remarried
("When you've been married to Frank Sinatra . . . ," she once explained to a friend), lives in a magnificent home in Los Angeles with
her younger daughter, Tina, who is seventeen. There is no bitterness,
only great respect and affection between Sinatra and his first wife,
and he has long been welcome in her home and has even been known
to wander in at odd hours, stoke the fire, lie on the sofa, and fall
asleep. Frank Sinatra can fall asleep anywhere, something he learned
when he used to ride bumpy roads with band buses; he also learned at
that time, when sitting in a tuxedo, how to pinch the trouser creases in
the back and tuck the jacket under and out, and fall asleep perfectly
pressed. But he does not ride buses anymore, and his daughter Nancy,
who in her younger days felt rejected when he slept on the sofa instead
of giving attention to her, later realized that the sofa was one of the few
places left in the world where Frank Sinatra could get any privacy,
where his famous face would neither be stared at nor cause an abnor-
mal reaction in others. She realized, too, that things normal have always eluded her father; his childhood was one of loneliness and a

drive toward attention, and since attaining it he has never again been certain of solitude. Upon looking out the window of a home he once owned in Hasbrouck Heights, New Jersey, he would occasionally see the faces of teenagers peeking in; and in 1944, after moving to California and buying a home behind a ten-foot fence on Lake Toluca, he discovered that the only way to escape the telephone and other intrusions was to board his paddleboat with a few friends, a card table, and a case of beer, and stay afloat all afternoon. But he has tried, insofar as it has been possible, to be like everyone else, Nancy says. He wept on her wedding day; he is very sentimental and sensitive. . . .

"What the hell are you doing up there, Dwight?"

Silence from the control booth.

"Got a party or something going on up there, *Dwight?*"

Sinatra stood on the stage, arms folded, glaring up across the cameras toward Hemion. Sinatra had sung "Nancy" with probably all he had in his voice on this day. The next few numbers contained raspy notes, and twice his voice completely cracked. But now Hemion was in the control booth out of communication; then he was down in the studio walking over to where Sinatra stood. A few minutes later they both left the studio and were on the way up to the control booth. The tape was replayed for Sinatra. He watched only about five minutes of it before he started to shake his head. Then he said to Hemion: "Forget it, just forget it. You're wasting your time. What you got there," Sinatra said, nodding to the singing image of himself on the television screen, "is a man with a cold." Then he left the control booth, ordering that the whole day's performance be scrubbed and future taping postponed until he had recovered.

———————

Soon the word spread like an emotional epidemic down through Sinatra's staff, then fanned out through Hollywood, then was heard across the nation in Jilly's saloon, and also on the other side of the Hudson River in the homes of Frank Sinatra's parents and his other relatives and friends in New Jersey.

When Frank Sinatra spoke with his father on the telephone and said he was feeling awful, the elder Sinatra reported that *he* was also feeling awful: that his left arm and fist were so stiff with a circulatory condition he could barely use them, adding that the ailment might be the result of having thrown too many left hooks during his days as a bantamweight almost fifty years ago.

Martin Sinatra, a ruddy and tattooed little blue-eyed Sicilian born in Catania, boxed under the name "Marty O'Brien." In those days, in those places, with the Irish running the lower reaches of city life, it was not uncommon for Italians to wind up with such names. Most of the Italians and Sicilians who migrated to America just prior to the 1900s were poor and uneducated, were excluded from the building-trades unions dominated by the Irish, and were somewhat intimidated by the Irish police, Irish priests, Irish politicians.

One notable exception was Frank Sinatra's mother, Dolly, a large and very ambitious woman who was brought to this country at two months of age by her mother and father, a lithographer from Genoa. In later years Dolly Sinatra, possessing a round red face and blue eyes, was often mistaken for being Irish, and surprised many at the speed with which she swung her heavy handbag at anyone uttering "Wop."

By playing skillful politics with North Jersey's Democratic machine, Dolly Sinatra was to become, in her heyday, a kind of Catherine de Medici of Hoboken's third ward. She could always be counted upon to deliver 600 votes at election time from her Italian neighborhood, and this was her base of power. When she told one of the politicians that she wanted her husband to be appointed to the Hoboken Fire Department, and was told, "But, Dolly, we don't have an opening," she snapped, "*Make* an opening."

They did. Years later she requested that her husband be made a captain, and one day she got a call from one of the political bosses that began, "Dolly, congratulations!"

"For what?"

"*Captain* Sinatra."

"Oh, you finally made him one—thank you very much."

Then she called the Hoboken Fire Department.

"Let me speak to *Captain* Sinatra," she said. The fireman called Martin Sinatra to the phone, saying, "Marty, I think your wife has gone nuts." When he got on the line, Dolly greeted him: "Congratulations, *Captain* Sinatra!"

Dolly's only child, christened Francis Albert Sinatra, was born and nearly died on December 12, 1915. It was a difficult birth, and during his first moment on Earth he received marks he will carry till death—the scars on the left side of his neck being the result of a doctor's clumsy forceps, and Sinatra has chosen not to obscure them with surgery.

After he was six months old, he was reared mainly by his grand-mother. His mother had a full-time job as a chocolate dipper with a large firm and was so proficient at it that the firm once offered to send her to the Paris office to train others. While some people in Hoboken remember Frank Sinatra as a lonely child, one who spent many hours on the porch gazing into space, Sinatra was never a slum kid, never in jail, always well dressed. He had so many pants that some people in Hoboken called him "Slacksey O'Brien."

Dolly Sinatra was not the sort of Italian mother who could be ap-peased merely by a child's obedience and good appetite. She made many demands on her son, was always very strict. She dreamed of his becoming an aviation engineer. When she discovered Bing Crosby pictures hanging on his bedroom walls one evening, and learned that her son wished to become a singer too, she became infuriated and threw a shoe at him. Later, finding she could not talk him out of it—"he takes after me"—she encouraged his singing.

Many Italian-American boys of his generation were then shooting for the same star—they were strong with song, weak with words, not a big novelist among them: no O'Hara, no Bellow, no Cheever, no Shaw; yet they could communicate *bel canto*. This was more in their tradition, no need for a diploma; they could, with a song, someday see their names in lights . . . *Perry Como* . . . *Frankie Laine* . . . *Tony Bennett* . . . *Vic Damone* . . . but none could see it better than *Frank Sinatra*.

Though he sang through much of the night at the Rustic Cabin, he was up the next day singing without a fee on New York radio to get more attention. Later he got a job singing with Harry James's band, and it was there in August of 1939 that Sinatra had his first recording hit: "All or Nothing at All." He became very fond of Harry James and the men in the band, but when he received an offer from Tommy Dorsey, who in those days had probably the best band in the country, Sinatra took it; the job paid $125 a week, and Dorsey knew how to feature a vocalist. Yet Sinatra was very depressed at leaving James's band, and the final night with them was so memorable that, twenty years later, Sinatra could recall the details to a friend: "The bus pulled out with the rest of the boys at about half-past midnight. I'd said good-bye to them all, and it was snowing, I remember. There was nobody around and I stood alone with my suitcase in the snow and watched the taillights disappear. Then the tears started and I tried to run after the bus. There was such spirit and enthusiasm in that band, I hated leaving it."

But he did—as he would leave other warm places, too, in search of something more, never wasting time, trying to do it all in one generation, fighting under his *own* name, defending underdogs, terrorizing top dogs. He threw a punch at a musician who said something anti-

Semitic, espoused the Negro cause two decades before it became fashionable. He also threw a tray of glasses at Buddy Rich when he played the drums too loud.

Sinatra gave away $50,000 worth of gold cigarette lighters before he was thirty, was living an immigrant's wildest dream of America. He arrived suddenly on the scene when DiMaggio was silent, when *paisanos* were mournful, were quietly defensive about Hitler in their homeland. Sinatra became, in time, a kind of one-man Anti-Defamation League for Italians in America, the sort of organization that would be unlikely for them because, as the theory goes, they rarely agreed on anything, being extreme individualists: fine as soloists, but not so good in a choir; fine as heroes, but not so good in a parade.

When many Italian names were used in describing gangsters on a television show, *The Untouchables*, Sinatra was loud in his disapproval. Sinatra and many thousands of other Italian-Americans were resentful as well when a small-time hoodlum, Joseph Valachi, was brought by Bobby Kennedy into prominence as a Mafia expert, when indeed, from Valachi's testimony on television, he seemed to know less than most waiters on Mulberry Street. Many Italians in Sinatra's circle also regard Bobby Kennedy as something of an Irish cop, more dignified than those in Dolly's day, but no less intimidating. Together with Peter Lawford, Bobby Kennedy is said to have suddenly gotten "cocky" with Sinatra after John Kennedy's election, forgetting the contribution Sinatra had made in both fund-raising and in influencing many anti-Irish Italian votes. Lawford and Bobby Kennedy are both suspected of having influenced the late president's decision to stay as a houseguest with Bing Crosby instead of Sinatra, as originally planned, a social setback Sinatra may never forget. Peter Lawford has since been drummed out of Sinatra's "summit" in Las Vegas.

"Yes, my son is like me," Dolly Sinatra says, proudly. "You cross him, he never forgets." And while she concedes his power, she quickly points out, "He can't make his mother do anything she doesn't want to do," adding, "Even today, he wears the same brand of underwear I used to buy him."

Today Dolly Sinatra is seventy-one years old, a year or two younger than Martin, and all day long people are knocking on the back door of her large home asking her advice, seeking her influence. When she is not seeing people and not cooking in the kitchen, she is looking after her husband, a silent but stubborn man, and telling him to keep his sore left arm resting on the sponge she has placed on the armrest of a soft chair. "Oh, he went to some terrific fires, this guy did," Dolly said to a visitor, nodding with admiration toward her husband in the chair.

Though Dolly Sinatra has eighty-seven godchildren in Hoboken, and still goes to that city during political campaigns, she now lives with her husband in a beautiful sixteen-room house in Fort Lee, New Jersey. This home was a gift from their son on their fiftieth wedding anniversary three years ago. The home is tastefully furnished and is filled with a remarkable juxtaposition of the pious and the worldly—photographs of Pope John and Ava Gardner, of Pope Paul and Dean Martin; several statues of saints and holy water, a chair autographed by Sammy Davis, Jr., and bottles of bourbon. In Mrs. Sinatra's jewelry box is a magnificent strand of pearls she had just received from Ava Gardner, whom she liked tremendously as a daughter-in-law and still keeps in touch with and talks about; and hung on the wall is a letter addressed to Dolly and Martin: "The sands of time have turned to gold, yet love continues to unfold like the petals of a rose, in God's garden of life . . . may God love you thru all eternity. I thank Him, I thank you for the being of one. Your loving son, Francis."

Mrs. Sinatra talks to her son on the telephone about once a week, and recently he suggested that, when visiting Manhattan, she make use of his apartment on East Seventy-second Street on the East River. This is an expensive neighborhood of New York even though there is a small factory on the block, but this latter fact was seized upon by Dolly Sinatra as a means of getting back at her son for some unflattering descriptions of his childhood in Hoboken.

"What—you want me to stay in *your* apartment, in *that* dump?" she asked. "You think I'm going to spend the night in *that* awful neighborhood?"

Frank Sinatra got the point, and said, "Excuse *me*, Mrs. Fort Lee."

After spending the week in Palm Springs, his cold much better, Frank Sinatra returned to Los Angeles, a lovely city of sun and sex, a Spanish discovery of Mexican misery, a star land of little men and lithe women sliding in and out of convertibles in tense tight pants.

Sinatra returned in time to see the long-awaited CBS documentary with his family. At about 9 P.M. he drove to the home of his former wife, Nancy, and had dinner with her and their two daughters. Their son, whom they rarely see these days, was out of town.

Frank, Jr., who is twenty-two, was touring with a band and moving cross country toward a New York engagement at Basin Street East with the Pied Pipers, with whom Frank Sinatra sang when he was with Dorsey's band in the 1940s. Today Frank Sinatra, Jr., whom his father says he named after Franklin D. Roosevelt, lives mostly in hotels, dines each evening in his nightclub dressing room, and sings until 2 A.M., accepting graciously, because he has no choice, the inevitable comparisons. His voice is smooth and pleasant, and improving with work, and while he is very respectful of his father, he discusses him with objectivity and in an occasional tone of subdued cockiness.

Concurrent with his father's early fame, Frank Jr. said, was the creation of a "press-release Sinatra" designed to "set him apart from the common man, separate him from the realities: It was suddenly Sinatra, the electric magnate, Sinatra who is supernormal, not super*human*, but super*normal*. And here," Frank Jr. continued, "is the great fallacy, the great bullshit, for Frank Sinatra *is* normal, *is* the guy whom you'd meet on a street corner. But this other thing, the supernormal guise, has affected Frank Sinatra as much as anybody who watches one of his television shows or reads a magazine article about him. . . .

"Frank Sinatra's life in the beginning was so normal," he said, "that nobody would have guessed in 1934 that this little Italian kid with the curly hair would become the giant, the monster, the great living legend. . . . He met my mother one summer on the beach. She was Nancy Barbato, daughter of Mike Barbato, a Jersey City plasterer. And she meets the fireman's son, Frank, one summer day on the beach at Long Branch, New Jersey. Both are Italian, both Roman Catholic, both lower-middle-class summer sweethearts—it is like a million bad movies starring Frankie Avalon. . . .

"They have three children. The first child, Nancy, was the most normal of Frank Sinatra's children. Nancy was a cheerleader, went to summer camp, drove a Chevrolet, had the easiest kind of development centered around the home and family. Next is me. My life with the family is very, very normal up until September of 1958 when, in complete contrast to the rearing of both girls, I am put into a college-preparatory school. I am now away from the inner family circle, and my position within has never been remade to this day. . . . The third child, Tina. And to be dead honest, I really couldn't say what her life is like."

The CBS show, narrated by Walter Cronkite, began at 10 P.M. A minute before that, the Sinatra family, having finished dinner, turned their chairs around and faced the camera, united for whatever disaster might follow. Sinatra's men in other parts of town, in other parts of the nation, were doing the same thing. Sinatra's lawyer, Milton A. Rudin, smoking a cigar, was watching with a keen eye, an alert legal mind. Other sets were watched by Brad Dexter, Jim Mahoney, Ed Pucci; Sinatra's makeup man, "Shotgun" Britton; his New York representative, Henri Giné; his haberdasher, Richard Carroll; his insurance broker, John Lillie; his valet, George Jacobs, a handsome

Negro who, when entertaining girls in *his* apartment, plays records by Ray Charles.

And like so much of Hollywood's fear, the apprehension about the CBS show all proved to be without foundation. It was a highly flattering hour that did not deeply probe, as rumors suggested it would, into Sinatra's love life, or the Mafia, or other areas of his private province. While the documentary was not authorized, wrote Jack Gould in the next day's *New York Times*, "it could have been."

Immediately after the show, the telephones began to ring throughout the Sinatra system conveying words of joy and relief—and from New York came Jilly's telegram: "WE RULE THE WORLD!"

The next day, standing in the corridor of the NBC building where he was about to resume taping his show, Sinatra was discussing the CBS show with several of his friends, and he said, "Oh, it was a gas."

"Yeah, Frank, a helluva show."

"But I think Jack Gould was right in the *Times* today," Sinatra said. "There should have been more on the *man*, not so much on the music."

They nodded, nobody mentioning the past hysteria in the Sinatra world when it seemed CBS was zeroing in on the *man;* they just nodded, and two of them laughed about Sinatra's apparently having gotten the word *bird* on the show—this being a favorite Sinatra word. He often inquires of his cronies, "How's your bird?"; and when he nearly drowned in Hawaii, he later explained, "Just got a little water on my bird"; and under a large photograph of him holding a whiskey bottle, a photo that hangs in the home of an actor friend named Dick Bakalyan, the inscription reads: "Drink, Dickie! It's good for your bird." In the song "Come Fly with Me," Sinatra sometimes alters the lyrics—"just say the words and we'll take our birds down to Acapulco Bay."

Ten minutes later Sinatra, following the orchestra, walked into the

NBC studio, which did not resemble in the slightest the scene here of eight days ago. On this occasion Sinatra was in fine voice; he cracked jokes between numbers; nothing could upset him. Once, while he was singing "How Can I Ignore the Girl Next Door," standing on the stage next to a tree, a television camera mounted on a vehicle came rolling in too close and plowed against the tree.

"Kee-rist!" yelled one of the technical assistants.

But Sinatra seemed hardly to notice it.

"We've had a slight accident," he said, calmly. Then he began the song all over from the beginning.

When the show was over, Sinatra watched the rerun on the monitor in the control room. He was very pleased, shaking hands with Dwight Hemion and his assistants. Then the whiskey bottles were opened in Sinatra's dressing room. Pat Lawford was there, and so were Andy Williams and a dozen others. The telegrams and telephone calls continued to be received from all over the country with praise for the CBS show. There was even a call, Mahoney said, from the CBS producer, Don Hewitt, with whom Sinatra had been so angry a few days before. And Sinatra was *still* angry, feeling that CBS had betrayed him, though the show itself was not objectionable.

"Shall I drop a line to Hewitt?" Mahoney asked.

"Can you send a fist through the mail?" Sinatra asked.

He has everything, he cannot sleep, he gives nice gifts, he is not happy, but he would not trade, even for happiness, what he is. . . .

He is a piece of our past—but only we have aged, he hasn't . . . we are dogged by domesticity, he isn't . . . we have compunctions, he doesn't . . . it is our fault, not his . . .

He controls the menus of every Italian restaurant in Los Angeles; if you want North Italian cooking, fly to Milan. . . .

Men follow him, imitate him, fight to be near him . . . there is something of the locker room, the barracks about him . . . bird . . . bird. . . .

He believes you must play it big, wide, expansively—the more open you are, the more you take in, your dimensions deepen, you grow, you become more what you are—bigger, richer . . .

He is better than anybody else, or at least they think he is, and he has to live up to it.

—NANCY SINATRA, JR.

He is calm on the outside—inwardly a million things are happening to him.

—DICK BAKALYAN

He has an insatiable desire to live every moment to its fullest because, I guess, he feels that right around the corner is extinction.

—BRAD DEXTER

All I ever got out of any of my marriages was the two years Artie Shaw financed on an analyst's couch.

—AVA GARDNER

We weren't mother and son—we were buddies.

—DOLLY SINATRA

I'm for anything that gets you through the night, be it prayer, tranquilizers, or a bottle of Jack Daniel's.

—FRANK SINATRA

Frank Sinatra was tired of all the talk, the gossip, the theory—tired of reading quotes about himself, of hearing what people were saying about him all over town. It had been a tedious three weeks, he said, and now he just wanted to get away, go to Las Vegas, let off some steam. So he hopped in his jet, soared over the California hills across the Nevada flats, then over miles and miles of desert to the Sands and the Clay-Patterson fight.

On the eve of the fight he stayed up all night and slept through most of the afternoon, though his recorded voice could be heard singing in the lobby of the Sands, in the gambling casino, even in the toilets, being interrupted every few bars, however, by the paging public address: "Telephone call for Mr. Ron Fish, Mr. Ron Fish . . . *with a ribbon of gold in her hair.* . . . Telephone call for Mr. Herbert Rothstein, Mr. Herbert Rothstein . . . *memories of a time so bright, keep me sleepless through dark endless nights.*"

Standing around in the lobby of the Sands and other hotels up and down the strip on this afternoon before the fight were the usual prefight prophets: the gamblers, the old champs, the little cigar butts from Eighth Avenue, the sportswriters who knock the big fights all year but would never miss one, the novelists who seem always to be identifying with one boxer or another, the local prostitutes assisted by some talent in from Los Angeles, and also a young brunette in a wrinkled black cocktail dress who was at the bell captain's desk crying, "But I want to speak to Mr. Sinatra."

"He's not here," the bell captain said.

"Won't you put me through to his room?"

"There are *no* messages going through, Miss," he said, and then she turned, unsteadily, seeming close to tears, and walked through the lobby into the big noisy casino crowded with men interested only in money.

Shortly before 7 P.M., Jack Entratter, a big gray-haired man who operates the Sands, walked into the gambling room to tell some men around the blackjack table that Sinatra was getting dressed. He also said that he had been unable to get front-row seats for everybody, and so some of the men—including Leo Durocher, who had a date, and Joey Bishop, who was accompanied by his wife—would not be able to fit in Frank Sinatra's row but would have to take seats in the third row. When Entratter walked over to tell this to Joey Bishop, Bishop's face fell. He did not seem angry; he merely looked at Entratter with an empty silence, seeming somewhat stunned.

"Joey, I'm *sorry*," Entratter said when the silence persisted, "but we couldn't get more than six together in the front row."

Bishop still said nothing. But when they all appeared at the fight, Joey Bishop was in the front row, his wife in the third.

The fight, called a holy war between Muslims and Christians, was preceded by the introduction of three balding ex-champions, Rocky Marciano, Joe Louis, Sonny Liston—and then there was "The Star-Spangled Banner," sung by another man from out of the past, Eddie Fisher. It had been more than fourteen years ago, but Sinatra could still remember every detail: Eddie Fisher was then the new king of the baritones, with Billy Eckstine and Guy Mitchell right with him, and Sinatra had been long counted out. One day he remembered walking into a broadcasting studio past dozens of Eddie Fisher fans waiting outside the hall, and when they saw Sinatra they began to jeer, "Frankie, Frankie, I'm *swooning*, I'm *swooning*." This was also the time when he was selling only about 30,000 records a year, when he was dreadfully miscast as a funny man on his television show, and when he recorded such disasters as "Mama Will Bark," with Dagmar.

"I growled and barked on the record," Sinatra said, still horrified by the thought. "The only good it did me was with the dogs."

His voice and his artistic judgment were incredibly bad in 1952, but even more responsible for his decline, say his friends, was his pursuit of Ava Gardner. She was the big movie queen then, one of the most beautiful women in the world. Sinatra's daughter Nancy recalls seeing Ava swimming one day in her father's pool, then climbing out of the water with that fabulous body, walking slowly to the fire, leaning over it for a few moments, and then it suddenly seemed that her long dark hair was all dry, miraculously and effortlessly back in place.

With most women Sinatra dates, his friends say, he never knows whether they want him for what he can do for them now—or will do for them later. With Ava Gardner, it was different. He could do nothing for her later. She was on top. If Sinatra learned anything from his experience with her, he possibly learned that when a proud man is down, a woman cannot help. Particularly a woman on top.

Nevertheless, despite a tired voice, some deep emotion seeped into his singing during this time. One particular song that is well remembered even now is "I'm A Fool to Want You," and a friend who was in the studio when Sinatra recorded it recalled: "Frank was really worked up that night. He did the song in one take, then turned around and walked out of the studio, and that was that."

Sinatra's manager at that time, a former song plugger named Hank Sanicola, said, "Ava loved Frank, but not in the way he loved her. He needs a great deal of love. He wants it twenty-four hours a day; he must have people around—Frank is that kind of guy." Ava Gardner, Sanicola said, "was very insecure. She feared she could not really hold a man . . . twice he went chasing her to Africa, wasting his own career."

"Ava didn't want Frank's men hanging around all the time," another friend said, "and this got him mad. With Nancy he used to be able to bring the whole band home with him, and Nancy, the good Italian wife, would never complain—she'd just make everybody a plate of spaghetti."

In 1953, after almost two years of marriage, Sinatra and Ava Gardner were divorced. Sinatra's mother reportedly arranged a reconciliation, but if Ava was willing, Frank Sinatra was not. He was seen with other women. The balance had shifted. Somewhere during this period

Sinatra seemed to change from the kid singer, the boy actor in the sailor suit, to a man. Even before he had won the Oscar in 1953 for his role in *From Here to Eternity*, some flashes of his old talent were coming through—in his recording of "The Birth of the Blues," in his Riviera-nightclub appearance that jazz critics enthusiastically praised; and there was also a trend now toward LPs and away from the quick three-minute deal, and Sinatra's concert style would have capitalized on this with or without an Oscar.

In 1954, totally committed to his talent once more, Frank Sinatra was selected Metronome's "Singer of the Year," and later he won the UPI disc-jockey poll, unseating Eddie Fisher—who now, in Las Vegas, having sung "The Star-Spangled Banner," climbed out of the ring, and the fight began.

Floyd Patterson chased Clay around the ring in the first round, but was unable to reach him, and from then on he was Clay's toy, the bout ending in a technical knockout in the twelfth round. A half hour later, nearly everybody had forgotten about the fight and was back at the gambling tables or lining up to buy tickets for the Dean Martin-Sinatra-Bishop nightclub routine on the stage of the Sands. This routine, which includes Sammy Davis, Jr., when he is in town, consists of a few songs and much cutting up, all of it very informal, very special, and rather ethnic—Martin, a drink in hand, asking Bishop: "Did you ever see a Jew jitsu?"; and Bishop, playing a Jewish waiter, warning the two Italians to watch out "because I got my own group—the *Matzia.*"

Then after the last show at the Sands, the Sinatra crowd, which now numbered about twenty—and included Jilly, who had flown in from New York; Jimmy Cannon, Sinatra's favorite sports columnist; Harold Gibbons, a Teamster official expected to take over if Hoffa goes to jail—all got into a line of cars and headed for another club. It was three o'clock. The night was young.

They stopped at the Sahara, taking a long table near the back, and listened to a baldheaded little comedian named Don Rickles, who is probably more caustic than any comic in the country. His humor is so rude, in *such* bad taste, that it offends no one—it is *too* offensive to be offensive. Spotting Eddie Fisher among the audience, Rickles proceeded to ridicule him as a lover, saying it was no wonder that he could not handle Elizabeth Taylor; and when two businessmen in the audience acknowledged that they were Egyptians, Rickles cut into them for their country's policy toward Israel; and he strongly suggested that the woman seated at one table with her husband was actually a hooker.

When the Sinatra crowd walked in, Don Rickles could not be more delighted. Pointing to Jilly, Rickles yelled: "How's it feel to be Frank's tractor? . . . Yeah, Jilly keeps walking in front of Frank clearing the way." Then, nodding to Durocher, Rickles said, "Stand up, Leo, show Frank how you slide." Then he focused on Sinatra, not failing to mention Mia Farrow, nor that he was wearing a toupee, nor to say that Sinatra was washed up as a singer, and when Sinatra laughed, everybody laughed, and Rickles pointed toward Bishop: "Joey Bishop keeps checking with Frank to see what's funny."

Then, after Rickles told some Jewish jokes, Dean Martin stood up and yelled, "Hey, you're always talking about the Jews, never about the Italians," and Rickles cut him off with, "What do we need the Italians for?—all they do is keep the flies off our fish."

Sinatra laughed, they all laughed, and Rickles went on this way for nearly an hour until Sinatra, standing up, said, "All right, com'on, get this thing over with. I gotta go."

"Shaddup and sit down!" Rickles snapped. "I've had to listen to you sing."

"Who do you think you're talking to?" Sinatra yelled back.

"Dick Haymes," Rickles replied, and Sinatra laughed again, and then Dean Martin, pouring a bottle of whiskey over his head, entirely drenching his tuxedo, pounded the table.

"Who would ever believe that staggering would make a star?" Rickles said, but Martin called out, "Hey, I wanna make a speech."

"Shaddup."

"No, Don, I wanna tell ya," Dean Martin persisted, "that I think you're a great performer."

"Well, thank you, Dean," Rickles said, seeming pleased.

"But don't go by me," Martin said, plopping down into his seat, "I'm drunk."

"I'll buy that," Rickles said.

By 4 A.M. Frank Sinatra led the group out of the Sahara, some of them carrying their glasses of whiskey with them, sipping it along the sidewalk and in the cars; then, returning to the Sands, they walked into the gambling casino, It was still packed with people, the roulette wheels spinning, the crapshooters screaming in the far corner.

Frank Sinatra, holding a shot glass of bourbon in his left hand, walked through the crowd. He, unlike some of his friends, was perfectly pressed, his tuxedo tie precisely pointed, his shoes unsmudged. He never seems to lose his dignity, never lets his guard completely down no matter how much he has drunk, nor how long he has been up. He never sways when he walks, like Dean Martin, nor does he ever dance in the aisles or jump up on tables, like Sammy Davis.

A part of Sinatra, no matter where he is, is never there. There is always a part of him, though sometimes a small part, that remains *Il Padrone*. Even now, resting his shot glass on the blackjack table, facing the dealer, Sinatra stood a bit back from the table, not leaning against it. He reached under his tuxedo jacket into his trouser pocket and came up with a thick but *clean* wad of bills. Gently he peeled off a $100 bill and placed it on the green-felt table. The dealer dealt him two cards. Sinatra called for a third card, overbid, lost the hundred.

Without a change of expression, Sinatra put down a second $100 bill. He lost that. Then he put down a third and lost that. Then he placed two $100 bills on the table and lost those. Finally, putting his sixth $100 bill on the table, and losing it, Sinatra moved away from the table, nodding to the man, and announcing, "Good dealer."

The crowd that had gathered around him now opened up to let him through. But a woman stepped in front of him, handing him a piece of paper to autograph. He signed it and then *he* said, "Thank you."

In the rear of the Sands's large dining room was a long table reserved for Sinatra. The dining room was fairly empty at this hour, with perhaps two dozen other people in the room, including a table of four unescorted young ladies sitting near Sinatra. On the other side of the room, at another long table, sat seven men shoulder-to-shoulder against the wall, two of them wearing dark glasses, all of them eating quietly, speaking hardly a word, just sitting and eating and missing nothing.

The Sinatra party, after getting settled and having a few more drinks, ordered something to eat. The table was about the same size as the one reserved for Sinatra whenever he is at Jilly's in New York; and the people seated around this table in Las Vegas were many of the same people who are often seen with Sinatra at Jilly's or at a restaurant in California, or in Italy, or in New Jersey, or wherever Sinatra happens to be. When Sinatra sits to dine, his trusted friends are close; and no matter where he is, no matter how elegant the place may be, there is something of the neighborhood showing because Sinatra, no matter how far he has come, is still something of the boy from the neighborhood—only now he can take his neighborhood with him.

In some ways, this quasi-family affair at a reserved table in a public place is the closest thing Sinatra now has to home life. Perhaps, having had a home and left it, this approximation is as close as

he cares to come; although this does not seem precisely so because
he speaks with such warmth about his family, keeps in close touch
with his first wife, and insists that she make no decision without
first consulting him. He is always eager to place his furniture or
other mementos of himself in her home or his daughter Nancy's,
and he also is on amiable terms with Ava Gardner. When he was in
Italy making *Von Ryan's Express*, they spent some time together,
being pursued wherever they went by the paparazzi. It was reported
then that the paparazzi had made Sinatra a collective offer of
$16,000 if he would pose with Ava Gardner; Sinatra was said to have
made a counter offer of $32,000 if he could break one paparazzi arm
and leg.

While Sinatra is often delighted that he can be in his home completely without people, enabling him to read and think without inter-
ruption, there are occasions when he finds himself alone at night, and
not by choice. He may have dialed a half-dozen women, and for one
reason or another they are all unavailable. So he will call his valet,
George Jacobs.

"I'll be coming home for dinner tonight, George."

"How many will there be?"

"Just myself," Sinatra will say. "I want something light; I'm not
very hungry."

George Jacobs is a twice-divorced man of thirty-six who resembles Billy Eckstine. He has traveled all over the world with Sinatra and
is devoted to him. Jacobs lives in a comfortable bachelor's apartment
off Sunset Boulevard around the corner from Whiskey à Go Go, and he
is known around town for the assortment of frisky California girls he
has as friends—a few of whom, he concedes, were possibly drawn to
him initially because of his closeness to Frank Sinatra.

When Sinatra arrives, Jacobs will serve him dinner in the dining
room. Then Sinatra will tell Jacobs that he is free to go home. If Sinatra,

on such evenings, should ask Jacobs to stay longer, or to play a few hands of poker, he would be happy to do so. But Sinatra never does.

This was his second night in Las Vegas, and Frank Sinatra sat with friends in the Sands' dining room until nearly 8 A.M. He slept through much of the day, then flew back to Los Angeles, and on the following morning he was driving his little golf cart through the Paramount Pictures movie lot. He was scheduled to complete two final scenes with the sultry blonde actress Virna Lisi in the film *Assault on a Queen*. As he maneuvered the little vehicle up the road between the big studio buildings, he spotted Steve Rossi, who, with his comedy partner Marty Allen, was making a film in an adjoining studio with Nancy Sinatra.

"Hey, Dag," he yelled to Rossi, "stop kissing Nancy."

"It's part of the film, Frank," Rossi said, turning as he walked.

"In the garage?"

"It's my Dago blood, Frank."

"Well, cool it," Sinatra said, winking, then cutting his golf cart around a corner and parking it outside a big drab building within which the scenes for *Assault* would be filmed.

"Where's the fat director?" Sinatra called out, striding into the studio that was crowded with dozens of technical assistants and actors all gathered around cameras. The director, Jack Donohue, a large man who has worked with Sinatra through twenty-two years on one production or other, has had headaches with this film. The script had been chopped, the actors seemed restless, and Sinatra had become bored. But now there were only two scenes left—a short one to be filmed in the pool, and a longer and passionate one featuring Sinatra and Virna Lisi to be shot on a simulated beach.

The pool scene, which dramatizes a situation where Sinatra and his hijackers fail in their attempt to sack the *Queen Mary*, went quickly and well. After Sinatra had been kept in the water shoulder-high for a few minutes, he said, "Let's move it, fellows—it's cold in this water, and I've just gotten over one cold."

So the camera crews moved in closer, Virna Lisi splashed next to Sinatra in the water, and Jack Donohue yelled to his assistants operating the fans, "Get the waves going," and another man gave the command, *"Agitate!"* and Sinatra broke out in song. "Agitate in rhythm," then quieted down just before the cameras started to roll.

Frank Sinatra was on the beach in the next situation, supposedly gazing up at the stars, and Virni Lisi was to approach him, toss one of her shoes near him to announce her presence, then sit near him and prepare for a passionate session. Just before beginning, Miss Lisi made a practice toss of her shoe toward the prone figure of Sinatra sprawled on the beach. As she tossed her shoe, Sinatra called out, "Hit me in my bird, and I'm going home."

Virni Lisi, who understands little English and certainly none of Sinatra's special vocabulary, looked confused, but everybody behind the camera laughed. She threw the shoe toward him. It twirled in the air, landed on his stomach.

"Well, that's about three inches too high," he announced. She again was puzzled by the laughter behind the camera.

Then Jack Donohue had them rehearse their lines, and Sinatra, still very charged from the Las Vegas trip, and anxious to get the cameras rolling, said, "Let's try one." Donohue, not certain that Sinatra and Lisi knew their lines well enough, nevertheless said okay, and an assistant with a clapboard called, "419, Take 1," and Virna Lisi approached with the shoe, tossed it at Frank lying on the beach. It fell short of his thigh, and Sinatra's right eyebrow raised almost imperceptibly, but the crew got the message, smiled.

"What do the stars tell you tonight?" Miss Lisi said, delivering her first line, and sitting next to Sinatra on the beach.

"The stars tell me tonight I'm an idiot," Sinatra said, "a gold-plated idiot to get mixed up in this thing."

"Cut," Donohue said. There were some microphone shadows on the sand, and Virna Lisi was not sitting in the proper place near Sinatra.

"419, Take 2," the clapboard man called.

Miss Lisi again approached, threw the shoe at him, this time falling short—Sinatra exhaling only slightly—and she said, "What do the stars tell you tonight?"

"The stars tell me I'm an idiot, a gold-plated idiot to get mixed up in this thing." Then, according to the script, Sinatra was to continue, "Do you know what we're getting into? The minute we step on the deck of the *Queen Mary*, we've just tattooed ourselves," but Sinatra, who often improvises on lines, recited them: "Do you know what we're getting into? The minute we step on the deck of that mother's-ass ship—"

"*No*, no," Donohue interrupted, shaking his head, "I don't think that's right."

The cameras stopped, some people laughed, and Sinatra looked up from his position in the sand as if he had been unfairly interrupted.

"I don't see why that can't work," he began, but Richard Conte, standing behind the camera, yelled, "It won't play in London."

Donohue pushed his hand through his thinning gray hair and said, but not really in anger, "You know, that scene was pretty good until somebody blew the line."

"Yeah," agreed the cameraman, Billy Daniels, his head popping out from around the camera, "it was a pretty good piece—"

"Watch your language," Sinatra cut in. Then Sinatra, who has a genius for figuring out ways of not reshooting scenes, suggested a way in which the film could be used and the "mother" line could be rere-corded later. This met with approval. Then the cameras were rolling again, Virna Lisa was leaning toward Sinatra in the sand, and then he pulled her down close to him. The camera now moved in for a close-up of their faces, ticking away for a few long seconds, but Sinatra and Lisi did not stop kissing; they just lay together in the sand wrapped in one another's arms, and then Virna Lisi's left leg just slightly began to rise a bit, and everybody in the studio now watched in silence, not saying anything until Donohue finally called out: "If you ever get through, let me know. I'm running out of film."

Then Miss Lisi got up, straightened out her white dress, brushed back her blonde hair, and touched up her lipstick, which was smeared. Sinatra got up, a little smile on his lips, and headed for his dressing room.

Passing an older man who stood near a camera, Sinatra asked, "How's your Bell & Howell?"

The older man smiled.

"It's fine, Frank."

"Good."

In his dressing room Sinatra was met by an automobile designer who had the plans for Sinatra's new custom-built model to replace the $25,000 Ghia he has been driving for the last few years. He also was awaited by his secretary, Tom Conroy, who had a bag full of fan mail, including a letter from New York's Mayor John Lindsay; and by Bill Miller, Sinatra's pianist, who would rehearse some of the songs that would be recorded later in the evening for Sinatra's newest album, *Moonlight Sinatra*.

While Sinatra does not mind hamming it up a bit on a movie set, he is extremely serious about his recording sessions; as he explained to a British writer, Robin Douglas-Home: "Once you're on that record singing, it's you and you alone. If it's bad and gets you criticized, it's you who's to blame—no one else. If it's good, it's also you. With a film it's never like that; there are producers and scriptwriters, and hundreds of men in offices and the thing is taken right out of your hands. With a record, you're *it.*"

> But now the days are short
>   I'm in the autumn of the year
> And now I think of my life
>   As vintage wine
> From fine old kegs.

It no longer matters what song he is singing, or who wrote the words—they are all *his* words, *his* sentiments, they are chapters from the lyrical novel of his life.

> Life is a beautiful thing
>   As long as I hold the string.

When Frank Sinatra drives to the studio, he seems to dance out of the car across the sidewalk into the front door; then, snapping his fingers, he is standing in front of the orchestra in an intimate, airtight room, and soon he is dominating every man, every instrument, every sound wave. Some of the musicians have accompanied him for twenty-five years, have gotten old hearing him sing "You Make Me Feel So Young."

When his voice is on, as it was tonight, Sinatra is in ecstasy, the room becomes electric, there is an excitement that spreads through the orchestra and is felt in the control booth, where a dozen men, Sinatra's friends, wave at him from behind the glass. One of the men is the Dodgers' pitcher Don Drysdale ("Hey, Big D," Sinatra calls out, "*hey,* baby!"); another is the professional golfer Bo Wininger; there are also numbers of pretty women standing in the booth behind the engineers, women who smile at Sinatra and softly move their bodies to the mellow mood of his music:

Will this be moon love
    Nothing but moon love
Will you be gone when the dawn
    Comes stealing through.

After he is finished, the record is played back on tape, and Nancy Sinatra, who has just walked in, joins her father near the front of the orchestra to hear the playback. They listen silently, all eyes on them, the king, the princess; and when the music ends, there is applause from the control booth, Nancy smiles, and her father snaps his fingers and says, kicking a foot, *"Ooba-deeba-boobe-do!"*

Then Sinatra calls to one of his men. "Hey, Sarge, think I can have a half-a-cup of coffee?"

Sarge Weiss, who had been listening to the music, slowly gets up.

"Didn't mean to wake ya, Sarge," Sinatra says, smiling

Then Weiss brings the coffee, and Sinatra looks at it, smells it, then announces, "I thought he'd be nice to me, but it's *really* coffee."

There are more smiles, and then the orchestra prepares for the next number. And one hour later, it is over.

The musicians put their instruments into their cases, grab their coats, and begin to file out, saying good night to Sinatra. He knows them all by name, knows much about them personally, from their bachelor days, through their divorces, through their ups and downs, as they know him. When a French-horn player, a short Italian named Vincent DeRosa, who has played with Sinatra since the Lucky Strike "Hit Parade" days on radio, strolled by, Sinatra reached out to hold him for a second.

"Vicenzo," Sinatra said, "how's your little girl?"

"She's fine, Frank."

"Oh, she's not a *little* girl anymore," Sinatra corrected himself, "she's a big girl now."

"Yes, she goes to college now. USC."

"That's great."

"She's also got a little talent, I think, Frank, as a singer."

Sinatra was silent for a moment, then said, "Yes, but it's very good for her to get her education first, Vicenzo."

Vincent DeRosa nodded.

"Yes, Frank," he said, and then he said, "Well, good night, Frank."

"Good night, Vicenzo."

After the musicians had all gone, Sinatra left the recording room and joined his friends in the corridor. He was going to go out and do some drinking with Drysdale, Wininger, and a few other friends, but first he walked to the other end of the corridor to say good night to Nancy, who was getting her coat and was planning to drive home in her own car.

After Sinatra had kissed her on the cheek, he hurried to join his friends at the door. But before Nancy could leave the studio, one of Sinatra's men, Al Silvani, a former prizefight manager, joined her.

"Are you ready to leave yet, Nancy?"

"Oh, thanks, Al," she said, "but I'll be all right."

"Pope's orders," Silvani said, holding his hands up, palms out.

Only after Nancy had pointed to two of her friends who would escort her home, and only after Silvani recognized them as friends, would he leave.

The rest of the month was bright and balmy. The record session had gone magnificently, the film was finished, the television shows were out of the way, and now Sinatra was in his Ghia driving out to his office to begin coordinating his latest projects. He had an engagement at the Sands, a new spy film called *The Naked Runner* to be shot in England, and a couple more albums to do in the immediate months ahead. And within a week he would be fifty years old.

Life is a beautiful thing
  As long as I hold the string
I'd be a silly so-and-so
  If I should ever let go.

Frank Sinatra stopped his car. The light was red. Pedestrians passed quickly across his windshield, but, as usual, one did not. It was a girl in her twenties. She remained at the curb staring at him. Through the corner of his left eye he could see her, and he knew, because it happens almost every day, that she was thinking, *It looks like him, but is it?*

Just before the light turned green, Sinatra turned toward her, looked directly into her eyes, waiting for the reaction he knew would come. It came, and he smiled. She smiled, and he was gone.

The Loser

AT THE FOOT OF A mountain in upstate New York, about sixty miles from Manhattan, there is an abandoned country clubhouse with a dusty dance floor, upturned bar stools, and an untuned piano; and the only sounds heard around the place at night come from the big white house behind it—the clanging sounds of garbage cans being toppled by raccoons, skunks, and stray cats making their nocturnal raids down from the mountain.

The white house seems deserted, too; but occasionally, when th animals become too clamorous, a light will flash on, a window wi open, and a Coke bottle will come flying through the darkness an smash against the cans. But mostly the animals are undisturbed unti daybreak, when the rear door of the white house swings open and broad-shouldered Negro appears in gray sweat clothes with a white towel around his neck.

He runs down the steps, quickly passes the garbage cans, and proceeds at a trot down the dirt road beyond the country club toward the highway. Sometimes he stops along the road and throws a flurry of punches at imaginary foes, each jab punctuated by hard gasps of his breathing—*"hegh-hegh-hegh"*—and then, reaching the highway, he turns and soon disappears up the mountain.

At this time of morning farm trucks are on the road, and the drivers wave at the runner. And later in the morning other motorists see him, and a few stop suddenly at the curb and ask, "Say, aren't *you* Floyd Patterson?"

"No," says Floyd Patterson, "I'm his brother, Raymond."

The motorists move on, but recently a man on foot, a disheveled

64

man who seemed to have spent the night outdoors, staggered behind
the runner along the road and yelled, "Hey, Floyd Patterson!"

"No, I'm his brother, Raymond."

"Don't tell *me* you're not Floyd Patterson. I know what Floyd Patterson looks like."

"Okay," Patterson said, shrugging, "if you want me to be Floyd
Patterson, I'll be Floyd Patterson."

"So let me have your autograph," said the man, handing him a
rumpled piece of paper and a pencil.

He signed it—"Raymond Patterson."

One hour later Floyd Patterson was jogging his way back down the dirt
path toward the white house, the towel over his head absorbing the
sweat from his brow. He lives alone in a two-room apartment in the
rear of the house and has remained there in almost complete seclu-
sion since getting knocked out a second time by Sonny Liston.

In the smaller room is a large bed he makes up himself, several
record albums he rarely plays, a telephone that seldom rings. The
larger room has a kitchen on one side and, on the other, adjacent to a
sofa, is a fireplace from which are hung boxing trunks and T-shirts to
dry, and a photograph of him when he was the champion, and also a
television set. The set is usually on except when Patterson is sleeping,
or when he is sparring across the road inside the clubhouse (the ring is
rigged over what was once the dance floor), or when, in a rare moment
of painful honesty, he reveals to a visitor what it is like to be the loser.

"Oh, I would give up anything to just be able to work with Liston,
to box with him somewhere where nobody would see us, and to see if
I could get past three minutes with him," Patterson was saying, wiping his face with the towel, pacing slowly around the room near the
sofa. "I *know* I can do better. . . . Oh, I'm not talking about a rematch.

Who would pay a nickel for another Patterson-Liston fight? I know *I*
wouldn't. . . . But all I want to do is get past the first round."

Then he said, "You have no idea how it is in the first round. You're
out there with all those people around you, and those cameras, and the
whole world looking in, and all that movement, that excitement, and
"The Star-Spangled Banner," and the whole nation hoping you'll win,
including the president. And do you know what all this does? It blinds
you, just blinds you. And then the bell rings, and you go at Liston and
he's coming at you, and you're not even aware that there's a referee in
the ring with you.

"Then you can't remember much of the rest, because you don't
want to. . . . All you recall is, all of a sudden you're getting up, and the
referee is saying, 'You all right?' and you say, 'Of *course* I'm all right,'
and he says, 'What's your name?' and you say, 'Patterson.'

"And then, suddenly, with all this screaming around you, you're
down again, and you know you have to get up, but you're extremely
groggy, and the referee is pushing you back, and your trainer is in
there with a towel, and people are all standing up, and your eyes focus
directly at no one person—you're sort of floating.

"It is not a *bad* feeling when you're knocked out," he said. "It's a
good feeling, actually. It's not painful, just a sharp grogginess. You
don't see angels or stars; you're on a pleasant cloud. After Liston hit
me in Nevada, I felt, for about four or five seconds, that everybody in
the arena was actually in the ring with me, circled around me like a
family, and you feel warmth toward all the people in the arena after
you're knocked out. You feel lovable to all the people. And you want to
reach out and kiss everybody—men and women—and after the Liston
fight somebody told me I actually blew a kiss to the crowd from the
ring. I don't remember that. But I guess it's true because that's the way
you feel during the four or five seconds after a knockout.

"But then," Patterson went on, still pacing, "this good feeling leaves you. You realize where you are, and what you're doing there, and what has just happened to you. And what follows is a hurt, a confused hurt—not a physical hurt—it's a hurt combined with anger; it's a what-will-people-think hurt; it's an ashamed-of-my-own-ability hurt . . . and all you want then is a hatch door in the middle of the ring—a hatch door that will open and let you fall through and land in your dressing room instead of having to get out of the ring and face those people. The worst thing about losing is having to walk out of the ring and face those people."

Then Patterson walked over to the stove and put on the kettle for tea. He remained silent for a few moments. Through the walls could be heard the footsteps and voices of the sparring partners and the trainer who live in the front of the house. Soon they would be in the clubhouse getting things ready should Patterson wish to spar. In two days he was scheduled to fly to Stockholm and fight an Italian named Amonti, Patterson's first appearance in the ring since the last Liston fight.

Next he hoped to get a fight in London against Henry Cooper. Then, if his confidence was restored, his reflexes reacting, Patterson hoped to start back up the ladder in this country, fighting all the leading contenders, fighting often, and not waiting so long between each fight as he had done when he was a champion in the 90 percent tax bracket.

His wife, whom he finds little time to see, and most of his friends think he should quit. They point out that he does not need the money. Even he admits that, from investments alone on his $8-million gross earnings, he should have an annual income of about $35,000 for the next twenty-five years. But Patterson, who is only twenty-nine years old and barely scratched, cannot believe that he is finished. He cannot help but think that it was something more than Liston that destroyed him—a strange, psychological force was also involved, and unless he can fully understand what it was, and learn to deal with it in the boxing ring, he may never be able to live peacefully anywhere but under this mountain. Nor will he ever be able to discard the false whiskers and mustache that, ever since Johansson beat him in 1959, he has carried with him in a small attaché case into each fight so he can slip out of the stadium unrecognized should he lose.

"I often wonder what other fighters feel, and what goes through their minds when they lose," Patterson said, placing the cups of tea on the table. "I've wanted so much to talk to another fighter about all this, to compare thoughts, to see if he feels some of the same things I've felt. But who can you talk to? Most fighters don't talk much anyway. And I can't even look another fighter in the eye at a weigh-in, for some reason.

"At the Liston weigh-in, the sportswriters noticed this, and said it showed I was afraid. But that's not it. I can never look *any* fighter in the eye because . . . well, because we're going to fight, which isn't a nice thing, and because . . . well, once I actually did look a fighter in the eye. It was a long, long time ago. I must have been in the amateurs then. And when I looked at this fighter, I saw he had such a nice face . . . and then he looked at *me* . . . and *smiled* at me . . . and *I* smiled back! It was strange, very strange. When a guy can look at another guy and smile like that, I don't think they have any business fighting.

"I don't remember what happened in that fight, and I don't re- member what the guy's name was. I only remember that, ever since, I have never looked another fighter in the eye."

The telephone rang in the bedroom. Patterson got up to answer it. It was his wife, Sandra. So he excused himself, shutting the bedroom door behind him.

Sandra Patterson and their four children live in a $100,000 home in an upper-middle-class white neighborhood in Scarsdale, New York.

Floyd Patterson feels uncomfortable in this home surrounded by a manicured lawn and stuffed with furniture, and, since losing his title to Liston, he has preferred living full-time at his camp, which his children have come to know as "daddy's house." The children, the eldest of whom is a daughter named Jeannie, now seven years old, do not know exactly what their father does for a living. But Jeannie, who watched the last Liston-Patterson fight on closed-circuit television, accepted the explanation that her father performs in a kind of game where the men take turns pushing one another down; he had his turn pushing them down, and now it is their turn.

The bedroom door opened again, and Floyd Patterson, shaking his head, was very angry and nervous.

"I'm not going to work out today," he said. "I'm going to fly down to Scarsdale. Those boys are picking on Jeannie again. She's the only Negro in this school, and the older kids give her a rough time, and some of the older boys tease her and lift up her dress all the time. Yesterday she went home crying, and so today I'm going down there and plan to wait outside the school for those boys to come out, and . . ."

"How old are they?" he was asked.

"Teenagers," he said. "Old enough for a left hook."

Patterson telephoned his pilot friend Ted Hanson, who stays at the camp and does public-relations work for him, and has helped teach Patterson to fly. Five minutes later Hanson, a lean white man with a crew cut and glasses, was knocking on the door; and ten minutes later both were in the car that Patterson was driving almost recklessly over the narrow, winding country roads toward the airport, about six miles from the camp.

"Sandra is afraid I'll cause trouble; she's worried about what I'll do to those boys; she doesn't want trouble!" Patterson snapped, swerving around a hill and giving his car more gas. "She's just not firm enough! She's afraid . . . and she was afraid to tell me about that groceryman who's been making passes at her. It took her a long time before she told me about that dishwasher repairman who comes over and calls her 'baby.' They all know I'm away so much. And that dishwasher repairman's been to my home about four, five times this month already. That machine breaks down every week. I guess he fixes it so it breaks down every week. Last time, I laid a trap. I waited forty-five minutes for him to come, but then he didn't show up. I was going to grab him and say, 'How would you like it if I called *your* wife *baby?* You'd feel like punching me in the nose, wouldn't you? Well, that's what I'm going to do—if you ever call her *baby* again. You call her Mrs. Patterson; or Sandra, if you know her. But you don't know her, so call her Mrs. Patterson.' And then I told Sandra that these men, this type of white man, he just wants to have some fun with colored women. He'll never marry a colored woman, just wants to have some fun."

Now he was driving into the airport's parking lot. Directly ahead, roped to the grass airstrip, was the single-engine green Cessna that Patterson bought and learned to fly before the second Liston fight. Flying was a thing Patterson had always feared—a fear shared by, maybe inherited from, his manager, Cus D'Amato, who still will not fly.

D'Amato, who took over training Patterson when the fighter was seventeen or eighteen years old and exerted a tremendous influence over his psyche, is a strange but fascinating man of fifty-six who is addicted to Spartanism and self-denial and is possessed by suspicion and fear: He avoids subways because he fears someone might push him onto the tracks; never has married; never reveals his home address.

"I must keep my enemies confused," D'Amato once explained. "When they are confused, then I can do a job for my fighters. What I do not want in life, however, is a sense of security; the moment a person knows security, his senses are dulled—and he begins to die. I also do not want many pleasures in life; I believe the more pleasures you get out of living, the more fear you have of dying."

Until a few years ago, D'Amato did most of Patterson's talking, and ran things like an Italian *padrone*. But later Patterson, the maturing son, rebelled against the father image. After losing to Sonny Liston the first time—a fight D'Amato had urged Patterson to resist—Patterson took flying lessons. And before the second Liston fight, Patterson had conquered his fear of height, was master at the controls, was filled with renewed confidence—and knew, too, that even if he lost, he at least possessed a vehicle that could get him out of town, fast.

But it didn't. After the fight, the little Cessna, weighed down by too much luggage, became overheated ninety miles outside of Las Vegas. Patterson and his pilot companion, having no choice but to turn back, radioed the airfield and arranged for the rental of a larger plane. When they landed, the Vegas air terminal was filled with people leaving town after the fight. Patterson hid in the shadows behind a hangar. His beard was packed in the trunk. But nobody saw him.

Later the pilot flew Patterson's Cessna back to New York alone. And Patterson flew in the larger, rented plane. He was accompanied on this flight by Hanson, a friendly, forty-two-year-old, thrice divorced Nevadan who once was a crop duster, a bartender, and a cabaret hoofer; later he became a pilot instructor in Las Vegas, and it was there that he met Patterson. The two became good friends. And when Patterson asked Hanson to help fly the rented plane back to New York, Hanson did not hesitate, even though he had a slight hangover that night—partly due to being depressed by Liston's victory, partly due to being slugged in a bar by a drunk after objecting to some unflattering things the drunk had said about the fight.

Once in the airplane, however, Ted Hanson became very alert. He had to, because, after the plane had cruised awhile at 10,000 feet, Floyd Patterson's mind seemed to wander back to the ring, and the plane would drift off course, and Hanson would say, "Floyd, Floyd, how's about getting back on course?" and then Patterson's head would snap up and his eyes would flash toward the dials. And everything would be all right for a while. But then he was back in the arena, reliving the fight, hardly believing that it had really happened.

And I kept thinking, as I flew out of Vegas that night, of all those months of training before the fight, all the roadwork, all the sparring, all the months away from Sandra . . . thinking of the time in camp when I wanted to stay up until 11:15 P.M. to watch a certain movie on The Late Show. *But I didn't because I had roadwork the next morning. . . .*

And I was thinking about how good I'd felt before the fight, as I lay on the table in the dressing room. I remember thinking, 'You're in excellent physical condition, you're in good mental condition—but are you vicious?' But you tell yourself, 'Viciousness is not important now, don't think about it now; a championship fight's at stake, and that's important enough and—who knows?—maybe you'll get vicious once the bell rings.' . . .

And so you lay there trying to get a little sleep . . . but you're only in a twilight zone, half asleep, and you're interrupted every once in a while by voices out in the hall, some guy's yelling 'Hey, Jack,' or 'Hey, Al,' or 'Hey, get those four-rounders into the ring.' And when you hear that, you think, 'They're not ready for you yet.' So you lay there . . . and wonder, 'Where will I be tomorrow? Where will I be three hours from now?' Oh, you think all kinds of thoughts, some thoughts completely unrelated to the fight . . . you wonder whether you ever paid your mother-in-law back for all those stamps she bought a year ago . . . and you remember that time at 2 A.M. when Sandra tripped on the steps while bringing a bottle up to the baby . . . and then you get mad and ask, 'What am I thinking about these things for?' . . . and you try to sleep . . . but then the door opens, and somebody says to somebody else, 'Hey, is somebody gonna go to Liston's dressing room to watch 'em bandage up?' . . .

And so then you know it's about time to get ready. . . . You open your eyes. You get off the table. You glove up, you loosen up. Then Liston's trainer walks in. He looks at you; he smiles. He feels the bandages, and later he says, 'Good luck, Floyd,' and you think, 'He didn't have to say that; he must be a nice guy.' . . .

And then you go out, and it's the long walk, always a long walk, and you think, 'What am I gonna be when I come back this way?' Then you climb into the ring. You notice Billy Eckstine at ringside leaning over to talk to somebody, and you see the reporters—some you like, some you don't like—and then it's "The Star-Spangled Banner," and the cameras are rolling, and the bell rings. . . .

How could the same thing happen twice? How? That's all I kept thinking after the knockout. . . . Was I fooling these people all these years? . . . Was I ever the champion? . . . And then they lead you out of the ring . . . and up the aisle you go, past those people, and all you want is to get to your dressing room, fast . . . but the trouble was in Las Vegas they made a wrong turn along the aisle, and when we got to the end, there was no dressing room there . . . and we had to walk all the way back down the aisle, past the same people, and they must have been thinking, 'Patterson's not only knocked out, but he can't even find his dressing room.' . . .

In the dressing room I had a headache. Liston didn't hurt me physically—a few days later I only felt a twitching nerve in my teeth—it was nothing like some fights I've had: like that Dick Wagner fight in '53 when he beat my body so bad I was urinating blood for days. After the Liston fight, I just went into the bathroom, shut the door behind me, and looked at myself in the mirror. I just looked at myself, and asked, 'What happened?" and then they started pounding on the door, and saying, 'Com'on out, Floyd, com'on out; the press is here, Cus is here, com'on out, Floyd.' . . .

And so I went out, and they asked questions, but what can you say? What you're thinking about is all those months of training, all the conditioning, all the depriving; and you think, 'I didn't have to run that extra mile, didn't have to spar that day; I could have stayed up that night in camp and watched The Late Show. . . . *I could have fought this fight tonight in no condition.' . . .*

"Floyd, Floyd," Hanson had said, "let's get back on course."

Again Patterson would snap out of his reverie and refocus on the omniscope and get his flying under control. After landing in New Mexico, and then in Ohio, Floyd Patterson and Ted Hanson brought the little plane into the New York airstrip near the fight camp. The green Cessna that had been flown back by the other pilot was already there, roped to the grass at precisely the same spot it was on this day five months later when Floyd Patterson was planning to fly it toward perhaps another fight—this time a fight with some schoolboys in Scarsdale who had been lifting up his little daughter's dress.

Patterson and Ted Hanson untied the plane, and Patterson got a rag and wiped from the windshield the splotches of insects. Then he walked around behind the plane, inspected the tail, checked under the fuselage, then peered down between the wing and the flaps to make sure all the screws were tight. He seemed suspicious of something. D'Amato would have been pleased.

"If a guy wants to get rid of you," Patterson explained, "all he has to do is remove these little screws here. Then, when you try to come in for a landing, the flaps fall off, and you crash."

Then Patterson got into the cockpit and started the engine. A few moments later, with Hanson beside him, Patterson was racing the little plane over the grassy field, then soaring over the weeds, then flying high above the gentle hills and trees. It was a nice takeoff.

Since it was only a forty-minute flight to the Westchester airport, where Sandra Patterson would be waiting with a car, Floyd Patterson did all the flying. The trip was uneventful until, suddenly behind a cloud, he flew into heavy smoke that hovered above a forest fire. His visibility gone, he was forced to the instruments. And at this precise moment, a fly that had been buzzing in the back of the cockpit flew up front and landed on the instrument panel in front of Patterson. He glared at the fly, watched it crawl slowly up the windshield, then shot a quick smash with his palm against the glass. He missed. The fly buzzed safely past Patterson's ear, bounced off the back of the cockpit, circled around.

"This smoke won't keep up," Hanson assured. "You can level off."

Patterson leveled off.

He flew easily for a few moments. Then the fly buzzed to the front again, zigzagging before Patterson's face, landed on the panel, and proceeded to crawl across it. Patterson watched it, squinted. Then he slammed down at it with a quick right hand. Missed.

Ten minutes later, his nerves still on edge, Patterson began the descent. He picked up the radio microphone—"Westchester tower . . . Cessna 2729 uniform . . . three miles northwest . . . land in one-six on final . . ."—and then, after an easy landing, he climbed quickly out of the cockpit and strode toward his wife's station wagon outside the terminal.

But along the way a small man smoking a cigar turned toward Patterson, waved at him, and said, "Say, excuse me, but aren't you . . . aren't you . . . Sonny Liston?"

Patterson stopped. He glared at the man, bewildered. He wasn't sure whether it was a joke or an insult, and he really did not know what to do.

"Aren't you Sonny Liston?" the man repeated, quite serious.

"No," Patterson said, quickly passing by the man, "I'm his brother."

When he reached Mrs. Patterson's car, he asked, "How much time till school lets out?"

"About fifteen minutes," she said, starting up the engine. Then she said, "Oh, Floyd, I just should have told Sister, I shouldn't have . . ."

"*You* tell Sister; *I'll* tell the boys."

Mrs. Patterson drove as quickly as she could into Scarsdale, with Patterson shaking his head and telling Ted Hanson in the back, "Really can't understand these schoolkids. This is a religious school, and they want $20,000 for a glass window—and yet, some of them carry these racial prejudices, and it's mostly the Jews who are shoulder-to-shoulder with us, and . . ."

"Oh, Floyd," cried his wife, "Floyd, I have to get along here . . . you're not here, you don't live here, I . . ."

She arrived at the school just as the bell began to ring. It was a modern building at the top of a hill, and on the lawn was the statue of a saint, and behind it a large white cross. "There's Jeannie," said Mrs. Patterson.

"Hurry, call her over here," Patterson said.

"Jeannie! Come over here, honey."

The little girl, wearing a blue school uniform and cap, and clasping books in front of her, came running down the path toward the station wagon.

"Jeannie," Floyd Patterson said, rolling down his window, "point out the boys who lifted your dress."

Jeannie turned and watched as several students came down the path; then she pointed to a tall, thin curly-haired boy walking with four other boys, all about twelve to fourteen years of age.

"Hey," Patterson called to him, "can I see you for a minute?"

All five boys came to the side of the car. They looked Patterson directly in the eye. They seemed not at all intimidated by him.

"You the one that's been lifting up my daughter's dress?" Patterson asked the boy who had been singled out.

"Nope," the boy said, casually.

"Nope?" Patterson said, caught off guard by the reply.

"Wasn't him, Mister," said another boy. "Probably was his little brother."

Patterson looked at Jeannie. But she was speechless, uncertain. The five boys remained there, waiting for Patterson to do something.

"Well, er, where's your little brother?" Patterson asked.

"Hey, kid!" one of the boys yelled. "Come over here."

A boy walked toward them. He resembled his older brother; he had freckles on his small, upturned nose, had blue eyes, dark curly hair, and, as he approached the station wagon, he seemed equally un-intimidated by Patterson.

"You been lifting up my daughter's dress?"

"Nope," the boy said.

"Nope!" Patterson repeated, frustrated.

"Nope, I wasn't lifting it. I was just touching it a little."

The other boys stood around the car looking down at Patterson, and other students crowded behind them, and nearby Patterson saw several white parents standing next to their parked cars; he became self-conscious, began to tap nervously with his fingers against the dashboard. He could not raise his voice without creating an unpleas-ant scene, yet could not retreat gracefully; so his voice went soft, and he said, finally: "Look, boy, I want you to stop it. I won't tell your mother—that might get you in trouble—but don't do it again, okay?"

"Okay."

The boys calmly turned and walked, in a group, up the street.

Sandra Patterson said nothing. Jeannie opened the door, sat in the front seat next to her father, and took out a small blue piece of paper that a nun had given her and handed it across to Mrs. Patterson. But Floyd Patterson snatched it. He read it. Then he paused, put the paper down, and quietly announced, dragging out the words, *"She didn't do her religion . . ."*

Patterson now wanted to get out of Scarsdale. He wanted to return to camp. After stopping at the Patterson home in Scarsdale and pick-ing up Floyd Patterson, Jr., who is three, Mrs. Patterson drove them all back to the airport. Jeannie and Floyd Jr. were seated in the back of the plane, and then Mrs. Patterson drove the station wagon alone up to camp, planning to return to Scarsdale that evening with the children.

It was 4 P.M. when Floyd Patterson got back to the camp, and the shadows were falling on the clubhouse, and on the tennis court routed by weeds, and on the big white house in front of which not a single automobile was parked. All was deserted and quiet; it was a loser's camp.

The children ran to play inside the clubhouse; Patterson walked slowly toward his apartment to dress for the workout.

"What could I do with those schoolboys?" he asked. "What can you do to kids of that age?"

It still seemed to bother him—the effrontery of the boys, the realization that he had somehow failed, the probability that, had those same boys heckled someone in Liston's family, the school yard would have been littered with limbs.

While Patterson and Liston both are products of the slum, and while both began as thieves, Patterson had been tamed in a special school with help from a gentle Negro spinster; later he became a Catholic convert and learned not to hate. Still later he bought a dictionary, adding to his vocabulary such words as *vicissitude* and *enigma*. And when he regained his championship from Johansson, he became the Great Black Hope of the Urban League.

He proved that it is possible not only to rise out of a Negro slum and succeed as a sportsman but also to develop into an intelligent, sensitive, law-abiding citizen. In proving this, however, and in taking pride in it, Patterson seemed to lose part of himself. He lost part of his hunger, his anger—and as he walked up the steps into his apartment, he was saying, "I became the good guy. . . . After Liston won the title, I kept hoping that he would change into a good guy too. That would have relieved me of the responsibility, and maybe I could have been more of the bad guy. But he didn't. . . . It's okay to be the good guy when you're winning. But when you're losing, it is no good being the good guy."

Patterson took off his shirt and trousers and, moving some books on the bureau to one side, put down his watch, his cuff links, and a clip of bills.

"Do you do much reading?" he was asked

"No," he said. "In fact, you know I've never finished reading a book in my whole life? I don't know why. I just feel that no writer today has anything for me; I mean, none of them has felt any more deeply than I have, and I have nothing to learn from them. Although Baldwin to me seems different from the rest. What's Baldwin doing these days?"

"He's writing a play. Anthony Quinn is supposed to have a part in it."

"Quinn?" Patterson asked.

"Yes."

"Quinn doesn't like me."

"Why?"

"I read or heard it somewhere; Quinn had been quoted as saying that my fight was disgraceful against Liston, and Quinn said something to the effect that he could have done better. People often say that—*they* could have done better! Well I think that if *they* had to fight, *they* couldn't even go through the experience of waiting for the fight to begin. They'd be up the whole night before, and would be drinking, or taking drugs. They'd probably get a heart attack. I'm sure that, if I was in the ring with Anthony Quinn, I could wear him out without even touching him. I would do nothing but pressure him; I'd stalk him; I'd stand close to him. I wouldn't touch him, but I'd wear him out and he'd collapse. But Anthony Quinn's an old man, isn't he?"

"In his forties."

"Well, anyway," Patterson said, "getting back to Baldwin, he seems like a wonderful guy. I've seen him on television, and, before the Liston

fight in Chicago, he came by my camp. You meet Baldwin on the street
and you say, 'Who's this poor slob?'—he seems just like another guy;
and this is the same impression *I* give people when they don't know me.
But I think Baldwin and me, we have much in common, and someday I'd
just like to sit somewhere for a long time and talk to him."

Patterson, his trunks and sweatpants on, bent over to tie his
shoelaces, and then, from a bureau drawer, took out a T-shirt across
which was printed *Deauville.* He has several T-shirts bearing the same
name. He takes good care of them. They are souvenirs from the high
point of his life. They are from the Deauville Hotel in Miami Beach,
which is where he trained for the third Ingemar Johansson match in
March of 1961.

Never was Floyd Patterson more popular, more admired than during that winter. He had visited President Kennedy; he had been given
a $35,000 jeweled crown by his manager; his greatness was conceded
by sportswriters—and nobody had any idea that Patterson, secretly,
was in possession of a false mustache and dark glasses that he intended to wear out of Miami Beach should he lose the third fight to Johansson.

It was after being knocked out by Johansson in their first fight that
Patterson, deep in depression, hiding in humiliation for months in a
remote Connecticut lodge, decided he could not face the public again
if he lost. So he bought false whiskers and a mustache and planned to
wear them out of his dressing room after a defeat. He had also planned,
in leaving his dressing room, to linger momentarily within the crowd
and perhaps complain out loud about the fight. Then he would slip
undiscovered through the night and into a waiting automobile.

Although there proved to be no need for bringing disguise into the
second or third Johansson fights, or into a subsequent bout in
Toronto against an obscure heavyweight named Tom McNeeley, Patterson brought it anyway; and, after the first Liston fight, he not only

wore it during his thirty-hour automobile ride from Chicago to New York, but also wore it while in an airliner bound for Spain.

"As I got onto this plane, you'd never have recognized me," he said. "I had on this beard, mustache, glasses, and hat—and I also limped, to make myself look older. I was alone. I didn't care what plane I boarded; I just looked up and saw this sign at the terminal reading 'Madrid,' and so I got on that flight after buying a ticket.

"When I got to Madrid, I registered at a hotel under the name 'Aaron Watson.' I stayed in Madrid about four or five days. In the day-time I wandered around to the poorer sections of the city, limping, looking at the people, and the people stared back at me and must have thought I was crazy because I was moving so slow and looked the way I did. I ate food in my hotel room. Although once I went to a restaurant and ordered soup. I hate soup. But I thought it was what old people would order. So I ate it. And after a week of this, I began to actually think I was somebody else. I began to believe it. And it is nice, every once in a while, being somebody else."

Patterson would not elaborate on how he managed to register under a name that did not correspond to his passport; he merely ex-plained, "With money, you can do anything."

Now, walking slowly around the room, his black silk robe over his sweat clothes, Patterson said, "You must wonder what makes a man do things like this. Well, I wonder too. And the answer is, I don't know . . . but I think that within me, within every human being, there is a cer-tain weakness. It is a weakness that exposes itself more when you're alone. And I have figured out that part of the reason I do the things I do, and cannot seem to conquer that one word—*myself*—is because . . . is because . . . I am a coward."

He stopped. He stood very still in the middle of the room, thinking about what he had just said, probably wondering whether he should have said it.

"I am a coward," he then repeated, softly. "My fighting has little to do with that fact, though. I mean you can be a fighter—and a *winning* fighter—and still be a coward. I was probably a coward on the night I won the championship back from Ingemar. And I remember another night, long ago, back when I was in the amateurs, fighting this big, tremendous man named Julius Griffin. I was only 153 pounds. I was petrified. It was all I could do to cross the ring. And then he came at me and moved close to me . . . and from then on I don't know anything. I have no idea what happened. Only thing I know is, I saw him on the floor. And later somebody said, 'Man, I never saw anything like it. You just jumped up in the air and threw thirty different punches.'"

"When did you first think you were a coward?" he was asked.

"It was after the first Ingemar fight."

"How does one see this cowardice you speak of?"

"You see it when a fighter loses. Ingemar, for instance, is not a coward. When he lost the third fight in Miami, he was at a party later at the Fountainebleau. Had I lost, I couldn't have gone to that party. And I don't see how he did."

"Could Liston be a coward?"

"That remains to be seen," Patterson said. "We'll find out what he's like after somebody beats him, how he takes it. It's easy to do anything in victory. It's in defeat that a man reveals himself. In defeat I can't face people. I haven't the strength to say to people, 'I did my best, I'm sorry, and whatnot.'"

"Have you no hate left?"

"I have hated only one fighter," Patterson said. "And that was Ingemar in the second fight. I had been hating him for a whole year before that—not because he beat me in the first fight, but because of what he did after. It was all that boasting in public, and his showing off his right-hand punch on television, his thundering right, his 'toonder and lightning.' And I'd be home watching him on television and *hat-*

ing him. It is a miserable feeling, hate. When a man hates, he can't have any peace of mind. And for one solid year I hated him because, after he took everything away from me, deprived me of everything I was, he *rubbed it in.* On the night of the second fight, in the dressing room, I couldn't wait until I got into the ring. When he was a little late getting into the ring, I thought, 'He's holding me up; he's trying to unsettle me—well, I'll get him!' "

"Why couldn't you hate Liston in the second match?"

Patterson thought for a moment, then said, "Look, if Sonny Liston walked into this room now and slapped me in the face, then you'd see a fight. You'd see the fight of your life because, then, a principle would be involved. I'd forget he was a human being. I'd forget I was a human being. And I'd fight accordingly."

"Could it be, Floyd, that you made a mistake in becoming a prize-fighter?"

"What do you mean?"

"Well, you say you're a coward; you say you have little capacity for hate; and you seemed to lose your nerve against those schoolboys in Scarsdale this afternoon. Don't you think you might have been better suited for some other kind of work? Perhaps a social worker or . . ."

"Are you asking why I continue to fight?"

"Yes."

"Well," he said, not irritated by the question, "first of all, I love boxing. Boxing has been good to me. And I might just as well ask you the question, 'Why do you write?' Or, 'Do you retire from writing everytime you write a bad story?' And as to whether I should have become a fighter in the first place, well, let's see how I can explain it. . . . Look, let's say you're a man who has been in an empty room for days and days without food . . . and then they take you out of that room and put you into another room where there's food hanging all over the place . . . and the first thing you reach for, you eat. When you're hungry, you're not choosy, and so I chose the thing that was closest to me. That was boxing. One day I just wandered into a gymnasium and boxed a boy. And I beat him. Then I boxed another boy. I beat him too. Then I kept boxing. And winning. And I said, 'Here, finally, is something I can do!'

"Now I wasn't a sadist," he quickly added. "But I liked beating people because it was the only thing I could do. And whether boxing was a sport or not, I wanted to make it a sport because it was a thing I could succeed at. And what were the requirements? Sacrifice. That's all. To anybody who comes from the Bedford-Stuyvesant section of Brooklyn, sacrifice comes easy. And so I kept fighting, and one day I became heavyweight champion, and I got to know people like you. And you wonder how I can sacrifice, how I can deprive myself so much. You just don't realize where I've come from. You don't understand where I was when it began for me.

"In those days, when I was about eight years old, everything I got— I stole. I stole to survive, and I did survive, but I seemed to hate myself. My mother told me I used to point to a photograph of myself hanging in the bedroom and say, 'I don't like that boy!' One day my mother found three large Xs scratched with a nail or something over that photograph of me. I don't remember doing it. But I do remember feeling like a parasite at home. I remember how awful I used to feel at night when my father, a longshoreman, would come home so tired that, as my mother fixed food before him, he would fall asleep at the table because he was that tired. I would always take his shoes off and clean his feet. That was my job. And I felt so bad because here I was, not going to school, doing nothing, just watching my father come home; and on Friday nights it was even worse. He would come home with his pay, and he'd put every nickel of it on the table so my mother could buy food for all the children. I never wanted to be around to see that. I'd run and hide. And then I decided to leave home and start stealing—and I did. And I would never come home unless I brought something that I had stolen. Once I remember I broke into a dress store and stole a whole mound of dresses, at 2 A.M., and here I was, this little kid, carrying all those dresses over the wall, thinking they were all the same size, my mother's size, and thinking the cops would never notice me walking down the street with all those dresses piled over my head. They did, of course. . . . I went to the Youth House."

Floyd Patterson's children, who had been playing outside all this time around the country club, now became restless and began to call him, and Jeannie started to pound on his door. So Patterson picked up his leather bag, which contained his gloves, his mouthpiece, and adhesive tape, and walked with the children across the path toward the clubhouse.

He flicked on the light switches behind the stage near the piano. Beams of amber streaked through the dimly lit room and flashed onto the ring. Then he walked to one side of the room, outside the ring. He took off his robe, shuffled his feet in the rosin, skipped rope, and then began to shadowbox in front of the spit-stained mirror, throwing out quick combinations of lefts, rights, lefts, rights, each jab followed by a *"hegh-hegh-hegh-hegh."* Then, his gloves on, he moved to the punching bag in the far corner, and soon the room reverberated to his rhythmic beat against the bobbling bag—rat-tat-tat-*tetteta*, rat-tat-tat-*tetteta*, rat-tat-tat-*tetteta*, rat-tat-tat-*tetteta!*

The children, sitting on pink leather chairs moved from the bar to the fringe of the ring, watched him in awe, sometimes flinching at the force of his pounding against the leather bag.

And this is how they would probably remember him years from now: a dark, solitary, glistening figure punching in the corner of a forlorn spot at the bottom of a mountain where people once came to have fun—until the clubhouse became unfashionable, the paint began to peel, and Negroes were allowed in.

As Floyd Patterson continued to bang away with lefts and rights, his gloves a brown blur against the bag, his daughter slipped quietly off her chair and wandered past the ring into the other room. There, on the other side of the bar and beyond a dozen round tables, was the stage. She climbed onto the stage and stood behind a microphone, long dead, and cried out, imitating a ring announcer, "Ladieeees and gentlemen . . . tonight we present . . ."

She looked around, puzzled. Then, seeing that her little brother had followed her, she waved him up to the stage and began again: "Ladieeees and gentlemen . . . tonight we present . . . *Floydie Patterson.*"

Suddenly, the pounding against the bag in the other room stopped. There was silence for a moment. Then Jeannie, still behind the microphone and looking down at her brother, said, "Floydie, come up here!"

"No," he said.

"Oh, come up here!"

"No," he cried.

Then Floyd Patterson's voice, from the other room, called: "Cut it out. . . . I'll take you both for a walk in a minute."

He resumed punching—rat-tat-tat-*tetteta*—and they returned to his side. But Jeannie interrupted, asking, "Daddy, how come you sweating?"

"Water fell on me," he said, still pounding.

"Daddy," asked Floyd Jr., "how come you spit water on the floor before?"

"To get it out of my mouth."

He was about to move over to the heavier punching bag when the sound of Mrs. Patterson's station wagon could be heard moving up the road.

Soon she was in Patterson's apartment cleaning up a bit, patting the pillows, washing the teacups that had been left in the sink. One hour later the family was having dinner together. They were together for two more hours; then, at 10 P.M., Mrs. Patterson washed and dried all of the dishes and put the garbage out in the can—where it would re-main until the raccoons and skunks got to it.

And then, after helping the children with their coats and walking out to the station wagon and kissing her husband good-bye, Mrs. Patterson began the drive down the dirt road toward the highway. Patterson waved once and stood for a moment watching the taillights go, and then he turned and walked slowly back toward the house.

The Silent Season of a Hero

"I would like to take the great DiMaggio fishing," the old man said. "They say his father was a fisherman. Maybe he was as poor as we are and would understand."

—Ernest Hemingway, *The Old Man and the Sea*

It was not quite spring, the silent season before the search for salmon, and the old fishermen of San Francisco were either painting their boats or repairing their nets along the pier or sitting in the sun talking quietly among themselves, watching the tourists come and go, and smiling, now, as a pretty girl paused to take their picture. She was about twenty-five, healthy and blue-eyed, and wearing a red turtleneck sweater, and she had long, flowing blonde hair that she brushed back a few times before clicking her camera. The fishermen, looking at her, made admiring comments, but she did not understand because they spoke a Sicilian dialect; nor did she notice the tall gray-haired man in a dark suit who stood watching her from behind a big bay window on the second floor of DiMaggio's Restaurant, which overlooks the pier.

He watched until she left, lost in the crowd of newly arrived tourists that had just come down the hill by cable car. Then he sat down again at the table in the restaurant, finishing his tea and lighting another cigarette, his fifth in the last half hour. It was 11:30 A.M. None of the other tables was occupied, and the only sounds came from the bar where a liquor salesman was laughing at something the headwaiter had said. But then the salesman, his briefcase under his arm, headed for the door, stopping briefly to peek into the dining room and call out, "See you later, Joe." Joe DiMaggio turned and waved at the salesman. Then the room was quiet again.

At fifty-one, DiMaggio was a most distinguished-looking man, aging as gracefully as he had played on the ball field, impeccable in his tailoring, his nails manicured, his six-foot two-inch body seeming as lean and capable as when he posed for the portrait that hangs in the restaurant and shows him in Yankee Stadium swinging from the heels at a pitch thrown twenty years ago. His gray hair was thinning at the crown, but just barely, and his face was lined in the right places, and his expression, once as sad and haunted as a matador's, was more in repose these days, though, as now, tension had returned and he chain-smoked and occasionally paced the floor and looked out the window at the people below. In the crowd was a man he did not wish to see.

The man had met DiMaggio in New York. This week he had come to San Francisco and had telephoned several times, but none of the calls had been returned because DiMaggio suspected that the man, who had said he was doing research on some vague sociological project, really wanted to delve into DiMaggio's private life and that of DiMaggio's former wife, Marilyn Monroe. DiMaggio would never tolerate this. The memory of her death is still very painful to him, and yet, because he keeps it to himself, some people are not sensitive to it. One night in a supper club a woman who had been drinking approached his table, and when he did not ask her to join him, she snapped, "All right, I guess I'm *not* Marilyn Monroe."

He ignored her remark, but when she repeated it, he replied, barely controlling his anger, "No—I wish you were, but you're not."

The tone of his voice softened her, and she asked, "Am I saying something wrong?"

"You already have," he said. "Now will you please leave me alone?"

His friends on the wharf, understanding him as they do, are very careful when discussing him with strangers, knowing that should they inadvertently betray a confidence he will not denounce them but rather will never speak to them again; this comes from a sense of propriety not inconsistent in the man who also, after Marilyn Monroe's death, directed that fresh flowers be placed on her grave "forever."

Some of the older fishermen who have known DiMaggio all his life remember him as a small boy who helped clean his father's boat, and as a young man who sneaked away and used a broken oar as a bat on the sandlots nearby. His father, a small mustachioed man known as Zio Pepe, would become infuriated and call him *lagnuso*, lazy, *meschino*, good-for-nothing, but in 1936 Zio Pepe was among those who cheered when Joe DiMaggio returned to San Francisco after his first season with the New York Yankees and was carried along the wharf on the shoulders of the fishermen.

The fishermen also remember how, after his retirement in 1951, DiMaggio brought his second wife, Marilyn, to live near the wharf, and sometimes they would be seen early in the morning fishing off DiMaggio's boat, the *Yankee Clipper*, now docked quietly in the marina, and in the evening they would be sitting and talking on the pier. They had arguments, too, the fishermen knew, and one night Marilyn was seen running hysterically, crying as she ran, along the road away from the pier, with Joe following. But the fishermen pretended they did not see this; it was none of their affair. They knew that Joe wanted her to stay in San Francisco and avoid the sharks in Hollywood, but she was confused and torn then—"She was a child," they said—and even today DiMaggio loathes Los Angeles and many of the people in it. He no longer speaks to his onetime friend Frank Sinatra, who had befriended Marilyn in her final years, and he also is cool to Dean Martin and Peter Lawford and Lawford's former wife, Pat, who once gave a party at which she introduced Marilyn Monroe to Robert Kennedy, and the two of them danced often that night, Joe heard, and he did not take it well. He was very possessive of her that year, his close friends say, because Marilyn and he had planned to remarry; but before they could she was dead, and DiMaggio banned the Lawfords and Sinatra and many Hollywood people from her funeral. When Marilyn Monroe's attorney complained that DiMaggio was keeping her friends away, DiMaggio answered coldly, "If it weren't for those friends persuading her to stay in Hollywood, she would still be alive."

Joe DiMaggio now spends most of the year in San Francisco, and each day tourists, noticing the name on the restaurant, ask the men on the wharf if they ever see him. Oh yes, the men say, they see him nearly every day; they have not seen him yet this morning, they add, but he should be arriving shortly. So the tourists continue to walk along the piers; past the crab vendors, under the circling seagulls, past the fish 'n' chip stands, sometimes stopping to watch a large vessel steaming toward the Golden Gate Bridge, which, to their dismay, is painted red. Then they visit the Wax Museum, where there is a life-size figure of DiMaggio in uniform, and walk across the street and spend a quarter to peer through the silver telescopes focused on the island of Alcatraz, which is no longer a federal prison. Then they return to ask the men if DiMaggio has been seen. Not yet, the men say, although they notice his blue Impala parked in the lot next to the restaurant. Sometimes tourists will walk into the restaurant and have lunch and will see him sitting calmly in a corner signing autographs and being extremely gracious with everyone. At other times, as on this particular morning when the man from New York chose to visit, DiMaggio was tense and suspicious.

When the man entered the restaurant from the side steps leading to the dining room, he saw DiMaggio standing near the window talking with an elderly maître d' named Charles Friscia. Not wanting to walk in and risk intrusion, the man asked one of DiMaggio's nephews to inform

Joe of his presence. When DiMaggio got the message, he quickly turned and left Friscia and disappeared through an exit leading down to the kitchen.

Astonished and confused, the visitor stood in the hall. A moment later Friscia appeared, and the man asked, "Did Joe leave?"

"Joe who?" Friscia replied.

"Joe DiMaggio!"

"Haven't seen him," Friscia said.

"You haven't *seen* him! He was standing right next to you a second ago!"

"It wasn't me," Friscia said.

"You were standing next to him. I saw you. In the dining room."

"You must be mistaken," Friscia said, softly, seriously. "It wasn't me."

"You *must* be kidding," the man said, angrily, turning and leaving the restaurant. Before he could get to his car, however, DiMaggio's nephew came running after him and said, "Joe wants to see you."

He returned, expecting to see DiMaggio waiting for him. Instead he was handed a telephone. The voice was powerful and deep and so tense that the quick sentences ran together: *You are invading my rights; I did not ask you to come; I assume you have a lawyer; you must have a lawyer; get your lawyer!*"

"I came as a friend," the man interrupted.

"That's beside the point," DiMaggio said. "I have my privacy; I do not want it violated; you'd better get a lawyer." Then, pausing, DiMaggio asked, "Is my nephew there?"

He was not.

"Then wait where you are."

A moment later DiMaggio appeared, tall and red-faced, erect and beautifully dressed in his dark suit and white shirt with the gray silk tie and the gleaming silver cuff links. He moved with big steps toward the man and handed him an air-mail envelope, unopened, that the man had written from New York.

"Here," DiMaggio said. "This is yours."

Then DiMaggio sat down at a small table. He said nothing, just lit a cigarette and waited, legs crossed, his head held high and back so as to reveal the intricate construction of his nose, a fine sharp tip above the big nostrils and tiny bones built out from the bridge, a great nose.

"Look," DiMaggio said, more calmly. "I do not interfere with other people's lives. And I do not expect them to interfere with mine. There are things about my life, personal things, that I refuse to talk about. And even if you asked my brothers, they would be unable to tell you about them because they do not know. There are things about me, so many things, that they simply do not know."

"I don't want to cause trouble," the man said. "I think you're a great man, and—"

"I'm not great," DiMaggio cut in. "I'm not great," he repeated, softly. "I'm just a man trying to get along."

Then DiMaggio, as if realizing that he was intruding upon his own privacy, abruptly stood up. He looked at his watch.

"I'm late," he said, very formal again. "I'm ten minutes late. *You're* making me late."

The man left the restaurant. He crossed the street and wandered over to the pier, briefly watching the fishermen hauling their nets and talking in the sun, seeming very calm and contented. Then, after he had turned and was headed back toward the parking lot, a blue Impala stopped in front of him, and Joe DiMaggio leaned out the window and asked, "Do you have a car?" His voice was very gentle.

"Yes," the man said.

"Oh," DiMaggio said. "I would have given you a ride."

Joe DiMaggio was not born in San Francisco but in Martinez, a small fishing village twenty-five miles northeast of the Golden Gate. Zio Pepe had settled there after leaving Isola delle Femmine, an islet off Palermo where the DiMaggios had been fishermen for generations. But in 1915, hearing of the luckier waters off San Francisco's wharf, Zio Pepe left Martinez, packing his boat with furniture and family, including Joe, who was one year old.

San Francisco was placid and picturesque when the DiMaggios arrived, but there was a competitive undercurrent and struggle for power along the pier. At dawn the boats would sail out to where the bay meets the ocean and the sea is rough, and later the men would race back with their hauls, hoping to beat their fellow fishermen to shore and sell it while they could. Twenty or thirty boats would sometimes be trying to gain the channel shoreward at the same time, and a fisherman had to know every rock in the water, and later know every bargaining trick along the shore, because the dealers and restaurateurs would play one fisherman off against the other, keeping the prices down. Later the fishermen became wiser and organized, predetermining the maximum amount each fisherman would catch, but there were always some men who, like the fish, never learned, and so heads would sometimes be broken, nets slashed, gasoline poured onto their fish, flowers of warning placed outside their doors.

But these days were ending when Zio Pepe arrived, and he expected his five sons to succeed him as fishermen, and the first two, Tom and Michael, did; but a third, Vincent, wanted to sing. He sang with such magnificent power as a young man that he came to the attention of the great banker A. P. Giannini, and there were plans to send him to Italy for tutoring and the opera. But there was hesitation around the DiMaggio household, and Vince never went; instead he played ball with the San Francisco Seals, and sportswriters misspelled his name.

It was DeMaggio until Joe, at Vince's recommendation, joined the team and became a sensation, being followed later by the youngest brother, Dominic, who was also outstanding. All three later played in the big leagues, and some writers like to say that Joe was the best hitter, Dom the best fielder, Vince the best singer, and Casey Stengel once said: "Vince is the only player I ever saw who could strike out three times in one game and not be embarrassed. He'd walk into the clubhouse whistling. Everybody would be feeling sorry for him, but Vince always thought he was doing good."

After he retired from baseball, Vince became a bartender, then a milkman, now a carpenter. He lives forty miles north of San Francisco in a house he partly built, has been happily married for thirty-four years, has four grandchildren, has in the closet one of Joe's tailor-made suits that he has never had altered to fit, and when people ask if he envies Joe, he always says, "No, maybe Joe would like to have what I have. He won't admit it, but he just might like to have what I have." The brother Vince most admired was Michael, "a big earthy man, a dreamer, a fisherman who wanted things but didn't want to take from Joe, or to work in the restaurant. He wanted a bigger boat but wanted to earn it on his own. He never got it." In 1953, at the age of forty-four, Michael fell from his boat and drowned.

Since Zio Pepe's death at seventy-seven in 1949, Tom, at sixty-two the oldest brother—two of his four sisters are older—has become nominal head of the family and manages the restaurant that was opened in 1937 as Joe DiMaggio's Grotto. Later Joe sold out his share, and now Tom is the co-owner of it with Dominic. Of all the brothers, Dominic, who was known as the "Little Professor" when he played with the Boston Red Sox, is the most successful in business. He lives in a fashionable Boston suburb with his wife and three children and is president of a firm that manufactures fiber-cushion materials and grossed more than $3.5 million last year.

Joe DiMaggio lives with his widowed sister, Marie, in a tan stone house on a quiet residential street not far from Fisherman's Wharf. He bought the house almost thirty years ago for his parents, and after their death he lived there with Marilyn Monroe; now it is cared for by Marie, a slim and handsome dark-eyed woman who has an apartment on the second floor, Joe on the third. There are some baseball trophies and plaques in the small room off DiMaggio's bedroom, and on his dresser are photographs of Marilyn Monroe, and in the living room downstairs is a small painting of her that DiMaggio likes very much: It reveals only her face and shoulders, and she is wearing a very wide-brimmed sun hat, and there is a soft sweet smile on her lips, an innocent curiosity about her that is the way he saw her and the way he wanted her to be seen by others—a simple girl, "a warm bighearted girl," he once described her, "that everybody took advantage of."

The publicity photographs emphasizing her sex appeal often offended him, and a memorable moment for Billy Wilder, who directed her in *The Seven Year Itch,* occurred when he spotted DiMaggio in a large crowd of people gathered on Lexington Avenue in New York to watch a scene in which Marilyn, standing over a subway grating to cool herself, had her skirt blown high by a sudden wind below. "What the hell is going on here?" DiMaggio was overheard to have said in the crowd, and Wilder recalled, "I shall never forget the look of death on Joe's face."

He was then thirty-nine; she was twenty-seven. They had been married in January of that year, 1954, despite disharmony in temperament and time: He was tired of publicity; she was thriving on it. He was intolerant of tardiness; she was always late. During their honeymoon in Tokyo an American general had introduced himself and asked if, as a patriotic gesture, she would visit the troops in Korea. She looked at Joe. "It's your honeymoon," he said, shrugging, "go ahead if you want to."

She appeared on ten occasions before 100,000 servicemen, and when she returned she said, "It was so wonderful, Joe. You never heard such cheering."

"Yes I have," he said.

Across from her portrait in the living room, on a coffee table in front of a sofa, is a sterling-silver humidor that was presented to him, by his Yankee teammates at a time when he was the most talked-about man in America, and when Les Brown's band had recorded a hit that was heard day and night on the radio:

> *From Coast to Coast, that's all you hear*
> *Of Joe the One-Man Show*
> *He's glorified the horsehide sphere,*
> *Jolting Joe DiMaggio . . .*
> *Joe . . . Joe . . . DiMaggio . . . we*
> *want you on our side.*

The year was 1941, and it began for DiMaggio in the middle of May after the Yankees had lost four games in a row, seven of their last nine, and were in fourth place, five-and-a-half games behind the leading Cleveland Indians. On May 15, DiMaggio hit only a first-inning single in a game that New York lost to Chicago, 13–1; he was barely hitting .300 and had greatly disappointed the crowds that had seen him finish with a .352 average the year before and .381 in 1939.

He got a hit in the next game, and the next, and the next. On May 24, with the Yankees losing 6–5 to Boston, DiMaggio came up with runners on second and third and singled them home, winning the game, extending his streak to ten games. But it went largely unnoticed. Even DiMaggio was not conscious of it until it had reached twenty-nine games in mid-June. Then the newspapers began to dramatize it, the public became aroused, they sent him good-luck charms of every description, and DiMaggio kept hitting, and radio announcers would interrupt programs to announce the news, and then the song again: *"Joe . . . Joe . . . DiMaggio . . . we want you on our side."*

Sometimes DiMaggio would be hitless his first three times up, the tension would build, it would appear that the game would end without his getting another chance—but he always would, and then he would hit the ball against the left-field wall, or through the pitcher's legs, or between two leaping infielders. In the forty-first game, the first of a doubleheader in Washington, DiMaggio tied an American League record that George Sisler had set in 1922. But before the second game began, a spectator sneaked onto the field and into the Yankees' dugout and stole DiMaggio's favorite bat. In the second game, using another of his bats, DiMaggio lined out twice and flied out. But in the seventh inning, borrowing one of his old bats that a teammate was using, he singled and broke Sisler's record, and he was only three games away from surpassing the major-league record of forty-four set in 1897 by Willie Keeler while playing for Baltimore when it was a National League franchise.

An appeal for the missing bat was made through the newspapers. A man from Newark admitted the crime and returned it with regrets. And on July 2, at Yankee Stadium, DiMaggio hit a home run into the left-field stands. The record was broken.

He also got hits in the next eleven games, but on July 17 . . . in Cleveland, at a night game attended by 67,468, he failed against two pitchers, Al Smith and Jim Bagby, Jr., although Cleveland's hero was really its third baseman, Ken Keltner, who in the first inning lunged to his right to make a spectacular backhanded stop of a drive and, from the foul line behind third base, he threw DiMaggio out. DiMaggio received a walk in the fourth inning. But in the seventh he again hit a hard shot at Keltner, who again stopped it and threw him out. DiMaggio hit sharply toward the shortstop in the eighth inning, the ball taking a bad hop, but Lou Boudreau speared it off his shoulder and threw to the second baseman to start a double play and DiMaggio's streak was stopped at fifty-six games. But the New York Yankees were on their way to winning the pennant by seventeen games, and the World Series too, and so in August, in a hotel suite in Washington, the players threw a surprise party for DiMaggio and toasted him with champagne and presented him with this Tiffany silver humidor that is now in San Francisco in his living room.

Marie was in the kitchen making toast and tea when DiMaggio came down for breakfast; his gray hair was uncombed, but, since he wears it short, it was not untidy. He said good morning to Marie, sat down, and yawned. He lit a cigarette. He wore a blue wool bathrobe over his pajamas. It was 8 A.M. He had many things to do today, and he seemed cheerful. He had a conference with the president of Continental Television, Inc., a large retail chain in California of which he is a partner and vice president; later he had a golf date, and then a big banquet to attend, and, if that did not go on too long and he were not too tired afterward, he might have a date.

Picking up the morning paper, not rushing to the sports page, DiMaggio read the front-page news, the people-problems of '66: Kwame Nkrumah was overthrown in Ghana; students were burning their draft cards (DiMaggio shook his head); the flu epidemic was spreading through the whole state of California. Then he flipped inside through the gossip columns, thankful they did not have him in there today—they had printed an item about his dating "an electrifying airline hostess" not long ago, and they also spotted him at dinner with Dori Lane, "the frantic frugger" in Whiskey à Go Go's glass cage—

and then he turned to the sports page and read a story about how the injured Mickey Mantle might never regain his form.

It had all happened so quickly, the passing of Mantle, or so it seemed; he had succeeded DiMaggio as DiMaggio had succeeded Ruth, but now there was no great young power hitter coming up and the Yankee management, almost desperate, had talked Mantle out of retirement; and on September 18, 1965, they gave him a "day" in New York during which he received several thousand dollars' worth of gifts—an automobile, two quarter horses, free vacation trips to Rome, Nassau, Puerto Rico—and DiMaggio had flown to New York to make the introduction before 50,000. It had been a dramatic day, an almost holy day for the believers who had jammed the grandstands early to witness the canonization of a new stadium saint. Cardinal Spellman was on the committee, President Johnson sent a telegram, the day was officially proclaimed by the mayor of New York, an orchestra assembled in center field in front of the trinity of monuments to Ruth, Gehrig, Huggins; and high in the grandstands, billowing in the breeze of early autumn, were white banners that read: "Don't Quit Mick," "We Love the Mick."

The banners had been held by hundreds of young boys whose dreams had been fulfilled so often by Mantle, but also seated in the grandstands were older men, paunchy and balding, in whose middle-aged minds DiMaggio was still vivid and invincible, and some of them remembered how one month before, during a pregame exhibition at Old-timers' Day in Yankee Stadium, DiMaggio had hit a pitch into the left-field seats, and suddenly thousands of people had jumped wildly to their feet, joyously screaming—the great DiMaggio had returned; they were young again; it was yesterday.

But on this sunny September day at the stadium, the feast day of Mickey mantle, DiMaggio was not wearing No. 5 on his back nor a black cap to cover his graying hair; he was wearing a black suit and white shirt and blue tie, and he stood in one corner of the Yankees' dugout waiting to be introduced by Red Barber, who was standing near home plate behind a silver microphone. In the outfield Guy Lombardo's Royal Canadians were playing soothing soft music; and moving slowly back and forth over the sprawling green grass between the left-field bullpen and the infield were two carts driven by groundskeepers and containing dozens and dozens of large gifts for Mantle: a six-foot, 100-pound Hebrew National salami, a Winchester rifle, a mink coat for Mrs. Mantle, a set of Wilson golf clubs, a Mercury 95-horsepower outboard motor, a Necchi portable, a year's supply of Chunky Candy. DiMaggio smoked a cigarette but cupped it in his hands as if not wanting to be caught in the act by teenage boys near enough to peek down into the dugout. Then, edging forward a step, DiMaggio poked his head out and looked up. He could see nothing above except the packed towering green grandstands that seemed a mile high and moving, and he could see no clouds or blue sky, only a sky of faces. Then the announcer called out his name—*"Joe DiMaggio!"*—and suddenly there was a blast of cheering that grew louder and louder, echoing and reechoing within the big steel canyon, and DiMaggio stomped out his cigarette and climbed up the dugout steps and onto the soft green grass, the noise resounding in his ears; he could almost feel the breeze, the breath of 50,000 lungs upon him, 100,000 eyes watching his every move, and for the briefest instant as he walked he closed his eyes.

Then in his path he saw Mickey Mantle's mother, a smiling elderly woman wearing an orchid, and he gently reached out for her elbow, holding it as he led her toward the microphone next to the other dignitaries lined up on the infield. Then he stood, very erect and without expression, as the cheers softened and the stadium settled down.

Mantle was still in the dugout, in uniform, standing with one leg on the top step, and lined on both sides of him were the other Yankees, who, when the ceremony was over, would play the Detroit Tigers. Then into the dugout, smiling, came Senator Robert Kennedy, accompanied by two tall curly-haired young assistants with blue eyes, Fordham freckles. Jim Farley was the first on the field to notice the senator, and Farley muttered, loud enough for others to hear, "Who the hell invited *him?*"

Toots Shor and some of the other committeemen standing near Farley looked into the dugout, and so did DiMaggio, his glance seeming cold, but he remaining silent. Kennedy walked up and down within the dugout shaking hands with the Yankees, but he did not walk onto the field.

"Senator," said the Yankees' manager, Johnny Keane, "why don't you sit down?" Kennedy quickly shook his head, smiled. He remained standing, and then one Yankee came over and asked about getting relatives out of Cuba, and Kennedy called over one of his aides to take down the details in a notebook.

On the infield the ceremony went on, Mantle's gifts continued to pile up—a Mobilette motorbike, a Sooner Schooner wagon barbecue, a year's supply of Chock Full O'Nuts coffee, a year's supply of Topps Chewing Gum—and the Yankee players watched, and Maris seemed glum.

"Hey, Rog," yelled a man with a tape recorder, Murray Olderman, "I want to do a thirty-second tape with you."

Maris swore angrily, shook his head.

"It'll only take a second," Olderman said.

"Why don't you ask Richardson? He's a better talker than me."

"Yes, but the fact that it comes from you . . ."

Maris swore again. But finally he went over and said in an interview that Mantle was the finest player of his era, a great competitor, a great hitter.

Fifteen minutes later, standing behind the microphone at home plate, DiMaggio was telling the crowd, "I'm proud to introduce the man who succeeded me in center field in 1951," and from every corner of the stadium the cheering, whistling, clapping came down. Mantle stepped forward. He stood with his wife and children, posed for the photographers kneeling in front. Then he thanked the crowd in a short speech and, turning, shook hands with the dignitaries standing nearby. Among them now was Senator Kennedy, who had been spotted in the dugout five minutes before by Red Barber and been called out and introduced. Kennedy posed with Mantle for a photographer, then shook hands with the Mantle children, and with Toots Shor and James Farley and others. DiMaggio saw him coming down the line, and at the last second he backed away, casually, hardly anybody noticing it, and Kennedy seemed not to notice it either, just swept past shaking more hands.

Finishing his tea, putting aside the newspaper, DiMaggio went upstairs to dress, and soon he was waving good-bye to Marie and driving toward his business appointment in downtown San Francisco with his partners in the retail television business. DiMaggio, while not a millionaire, has invested wisely and has always had, since his retirement from baseball, executive positions with big companies that have paid him well. He also was among the organizers of the Fisherman's National Bank of San Francisco last year, and, though it never came about, he demonstrated an acuteness that impressed those businessmen who had thought of him only in terms of baseball. He has had offers to manage big-league baseball teams but always has rejected them, saying, "I have enough trouble taking care of my own problems without taking on the responsibilities of twenty-five ballplayers."

So his only contact with baseball these days, excluding public appearances, is his unsalaried job as a batting coach each spring in Florida with the New York Yankees, a trip he would make once again on the following Sunday, three days away, if he could accomplish what for him is always the dreaded responsibility of packing, a task made no easier by the fact that he lately has fallen into the habit of keeping his clothes in two places—some hang in his closet at home, some hang in the back room of a saloon called Reno's.

Reno's is a dimly lit bar in the center of San Francisco. A portrait of DiMaggio swinging a bat hangs on the wall, in addition to portraits of other star athletes, and the clientele consists mainly of the sporting crowd and newspapermen, people who know DiMaggio quite well and around whom he speaks freely on a number of subjects and relaxes as he can in few other places. The owner of the bar is Reno Barsocchini, a broad-shouldered and handsome man of fifty-one with graying wavy hair who began as a fiddler in Dago Mary's tavern thirty-five years ago. He later became a bartender there and elsewhere, including DiMaggio's Restaurant, and now he is probably DiMaggio's closest friend. He was the best man at the DiMaggio-Monroe wedding in 1954, and when they separated nine months later in Los Angeles, Reno rushed down to help DiMaggio with the packing and drive him back to San Francisco. Reno will never forget the day.

Hundreds of people were gathered around the Beverly Hills home that DiMaggio and Marilyn had rented, and photographers were perched in the trees watching the windows, and others stood on the lawn and behind the rosebushes waiting to snap pictures of anybody who walked out of the house. The newspapers that day played all the puns—"Joe Fanned on Jealousy"; "Marilyn and Joe—Out at Home"— and the Hollywood columnists, to whom DiMaggio was never an idol, never a gracious host, recounted instances of incompatibility, and Oscar Levant said it all proved that no man could be a success in two national pastimes. When Reno Barsocchini arrived, he had to push his way through the mob, then bang on the door for several minutes before being admitted. Marilyn Monroe was upstairs in bed; Joe DiMaggio was downstairs with his suitcases, tense and pale, his eyes bloodshot.

Reno took the suitcases and golf clubs out to DiMaggio's car, and then DiMaggio came out of the house, the reporters moving toward him, the lights flashing.

"Where are you going?" they yelled.

"I'm driving to San Francisco," he said, walking quickly.

"Is that going to be your home?"

"That *is* my home and always has been."

"Are you coming back?"

DiMaggio turned for a moment, looking up at the house.

"No," he said, "I'll never be back."

Reno Barsocchini, except for a brief falling out over something he will not discuss, has been DiMaggio's trusted companion ever since, joining him whenever he can on the golf course or on the town, otherwise waiting for him in the bar with other middle-aged men. They may wait for hours sometimes, waiting and knowing that when he arrives he may wish to be alone. But it does not seem to matter, they are endlessly awed by him, moved by the mystique; he is a kind of male Garbo. They know that he can be warm and loyal if they are sensitive to his wishes, but they must never be late for an appointment to meet him. One man, unable to find a parking place, arrived a half hour late once, and DiMaggio did not talk to him again for three months. They know, too, when dining at night with DiMaggio, that he generally prefers male companions and occasionally one or two young women, but never wives; wives gossip, wives complain, wives are trouble, and men wishing to remain close to DiMaggio must keep their wives at home.

When DiMaggio strolls into Reno's bar, the men wave and call out his name, and Reno Barsocchini smiles and announces, "Here's the Clipper!"—the "Yankee Clipper" being a nickname from his baseball days.

"Hey, Clipper, Clipper," Reno had said two nights before, "where you been, Clipper? . . . Clipper, how 'bout a belt?"

DiMaggio refused the offer of a drink, ordering instead a pot of tea, which he prefers to all other beverages except before a date, when he will switch to vodka.

"Hey, Joe," a sportswriter asked, a man researching a magazine piece on golf, "why is it that a golfer, when he starts getting older, loses his putting touch first? Like Snead and Hogan, they can still hit a ball well off the tee, but on the greens they lose the strokes."

"It's the pressure of age," DiMaggio said, turning around on his bar stool. "With age you get jittery. It's true of golfers; it's true of any man when he gets into his fifties. He doesn't take chances like he used to. The younger golfer, on the greens, he'll stroke his putts better. The older man, he becomes hesitant. A little uncertain. Shaky. When it comes to taking chances, the younger man, even when driving a car, will take chances that the older man won't."

"Speaking of chances," another man said, one of the group that had gathered around DiMaggio, "did you see that guy on crutches in here last night?"

"Yeah, had his leg in a cast," a third said. "Skiing."

"I would never ski," DiMaggio said. "Men who ski must be doing it to impress a broad. You see these men, some of them forty, fifty, getting onto skis. And later you see them all bandaged up, broken legs . . ."

"But skiing's a very sexy sport, Joe, All the clothes, the tight pants, the fireplace in the ski lodge, the bear rug—Christ, nobody goes to ski. They just go out there to get it cold so they can warm it up."

"Maybe you're right," DiMaggio said. "I might be persuaded."

"Want a belt, Clipper?" Reno asked.

DiMaggio thought for a second, then said, "All right—first belt tonight."

Now it was noon, a warm sunny day. DiMaggio's business meeting with the television retailers had gone well; he had made a strong appeal to

George Shahood, president of Continental Television, Inc., which has eight retail outlets in northern California, to cut prices on color television sets and increase the sales volume, and Shahood had conceded it was worth a try. Then DiMaggio called Reno's bar to see if there were any messages, and now he was in Lefty O'Doul's car being driven along Fisherman's Wharf toward the Golden Gate Bridge en route to a golf course thirty miles upstate. Lefty O'Doul was one of the great hitters in the National League in the early thirties, and later he managed the San Francisco Seals when DiMaggio was the shining star. Though O'Doul is now sixty-nine, eighteen years older than DiMaggio, he nevertheless possesses great energy and spirit, is a hard-drinking, boisterous man with a big belly and roving eye; and when DiMaggio, as they drove along the highway toward the golf club, noticed a lovely blonde at the wheel of a car nearby and exclaimed, "Look at *that* tomato!" O'Doul's head suddenly spun around, he took his eyes off the road, and yelled, "Where, *where?*" O'Doul's golf game is less than what it was—he used to have a two-handicap—but he still shoots in the 80s, as does DiMaggio.

DiMaggio's drives range between 250 and 280 yards when he doesn't sky them, and his putting is good, but he is distracted by a bad back that both pains him and hinders the fullness of his swing. On the first hole, waiting to tee off, DiMaggio sat back watching a foursome of college boys ahead swinging with such freedom. "Oh," he said with a sigh, "to have *their* backs."

DiMaggio and O'Doul were accompanied around the golf course by Ernie Nevers, the former football star, and two brothers who are in the hotel and movie-distribution business. They moved quickly up and down the green hills in electric golf carts, and DiMaggio's game was exceptionally good for the first nine holes. But then he seemed distracted, perhaps tired, perhaps even reacting to a conversation of a few minutes before. One of the movie men was praising the film *Boeing, Boeing,* star-

ring Tony Curtis and Jerry Lewis, and the man asked DiMaggio if he had
seen it.

"No," DiMaggio said. Then he added, swiftly, "I haven't seen a film
in eight years."

DiMaggio hooked a few shots, was in the woods. He took a No. 9
iron and tried to chip out. But O'Doul interrupted DiMaggio's con-
centration to remind him to keep the face of the club closed. DiMaggio hit the ball. It caromed off the side of his club, went skipping like
a rabbit through the high grass down toward a pond. DiMaggio rarely
displays any emotion on a golf course, but now, without saying a word,
he took his No. 9 iron and flung it into the air. The club landed in a
tree and stayed up there.

"Well," O'Doul said, casually, "there goes *that* set of clubs."

DiMaggio walked to the tree. Fortunately, the club had slipped to
the lower branch, and DiMaggio could stretch up on the cart and get
it back.

"Every time I get advice," DiMaggio muttered to himself, shaking
his head slowly and walking toward the pond, "I shank it."

Later, showered and dressed, DiMaggio and the others drove to a
banquet about ten miles from the golf course. Somebody had said it
was going to be an elegant dinner, but when they arrived they could
see it was more like a county fair; farmers were gathered outside a big
barnlike building, a candidate for sheriff was distributing leaflets at
the front door, and a chorus of homely ladies was inside singing "You
Are My Sunshine."

"How did we get sucked into this?" DiMaggio asked, talking out of
the side of his mouth, as they approached the building.

"O'Doul," one of the men said. "It's his fault. Damned O'Doul
can't turn *anything* down."

"Go to hell," O'Doul said.

Soon DiMaggio and O'Doul and Ernie Nevers were surrounded by the crowd, and the woman who had been leading the chorus came rushing over and said, "Oh, Mr. DiMaggio, it certainly is a pleasure having you."

"It's a pleasure being here, ma'am," he said, forcing a smile.

"It's too bad you didn't arrive a moment sooner; you'd have heard our singing."

"Oh, I heard it," he said, "and I enjoyed it very much."

"Good, good," she said. "And how are your brothers Dom and Vic?"

"Fine. Dom lives near Boston. Vince is in Pittsburgh."

"Why, *hello* there, Joe," interrupted a man with wine on his breath, patting DiMaggio on the back, feeling his arm. "Who's gonna take it this year, Joe?"

"Well, I have no idea," DiMaggio said.

"What about the Giants?"

"Your guess is as good as mine."

"Well, you can't count the Dodgers out," the man said.

"You sure can't," DiMaggio said.

"Not with all that pitching."

"Pitching is certainly important," DiMaggio said.

Everywhere he goes the questions seem the same, as if he has some special vision into the future of new heroes, and everywhere he goes, too, older men grab his hand and feel his arm and predict that he could still go out there and hit one, and the smile on DiMaggio's face is genuine. He tries hard to remain as he was—he diets, he takes steam baths, he is careful; and flabby men in the locker rooms of golf clubs sometimes steal peeks at him when he steps out of the shower, observing the tight muscles across his chest, the flat stomach, the long sinewy legs. He has a young man's body, very pale and little hair; his face is dark and lined, however, parched by the sun of several seasons. Still he is always an impressive figure at banquets such as this—an *immortal*, sportswriters called him, and that is how they have written

about him and others like him, rarely suggesting that such heroes
might ever be prone to the ills of mortal men, carousing, drinking,
scheming; to suggest this would destroy the myth, would disillusion
small boys, would infuriate rich men who own ball clubs and to whom
baseball is a business dedicated to profit and in pursuit of which they
trade mediocre players' flesh as casually as boys trade players' pictures on bubble-gum cards. And so the baseball hero must always act
the part, must preserve the myth, and none does it better than
DiMaggio; none is more patient when drunken old men grab an arm
and ask, "Who's gonna take it this year, Joe?"

Two hours later, dinner and the speeches over, DiMaggio is
slumped in O'Doul's car headed back to San Francisco. He edged
himself up, however, when O'Doul pulled into a gas station in which a
pretty red-haired girl sat on a stool, legs crossed, filing her fingernails. She was about twenty-two, wore a tight black skirt and tighter
white blouse.

"Look at *that*," DiMaggio said.

"Yeah," O'Doul said.

O'Doul turned away when a young man approached, opened the
gas tank, began wiping the windshield. The young man wore a greasy
white uniform on the front of which was printed the name "Burt."
DiMaggio kept looking at the girl, but she was not distracted from her
fingernails. Then he looked at Burt, who did not recognize him. When
the tank was full, O'Doul paid and drove off. Burt returned to his girl;
DiMaggio slumped down in the front seat and did not open his eyes
again until they had arrived in San Francisco.

"Let's go see Reno," DiMaggio said.

"No, I gotta go see my old lady," O'Doul said. So he dropped
DiMaggio off in front of the bar, and a moment later Reno's voice was
announcing in the smoky room, "Hey, here's the Clipper!" The men
waved and offered to buy him a drink. DiMaggio ordered a vodka and

sat for an hour at the bar talking to a half dozen men around him. Then a blonde girl who had been with friends at the other end of the bar came over, and somebody introduced her to DiMaggio. He bought her a drink, offered her a cigarette. Then he struck a match and held it. His hand was unsteady.

"Is that me that's shaking?" he asked.

"It must be," said the blonde. "I'm calm."

Two nights later, having collected his clothes out of Reno's back room, DiMaggio boarded a jet; he slept crossways on three seats, then came down the steps as the sun began to rise in Miami. He claimed his luggage and golf clubs, put them into the trunk of a waiting automobile, and less than an hour later he was being driven into Fort Lauderdale, past palm-lined streets, toward the Yankee Clipper Hotel.

"All my life it seems I've been on the road traveling," he said, squinting through the windshield into the sun. "I never get a sense of being in any one place."

Arriving at the Yankee Clipper Hotel, DiMaggio checked into the largest suite. People rushed through the lobby to shake hands with him, to ask for his autograph, to say, "Joe, you look great." And early the next morning, and for the next thirty mornings, DiMaggio arrived punctually at the baseball park and wore his uniform with the famous No. 5, and the tourists seated in the sunny grandstands clapped when he first appeared on the field each time, and then they watched with nostalgia as he picked up a bat and played "pepper" with the younger Yankees, some of whom were not even born when, twenty-five years ago this summer, he hit in fifty-six straight games and became the most cherished man in America.

But the younger spectators in the Fort Lauderdale park, and the sportswriters, too, were more interested in Mantle and Maris, and nearly every day there were news dispatches reporting how Mantle and Maris felt, what they did, what they said, even though they said and did very little except walk around the field frowning when photographers asked for another picture and when sportswriters asked how they felt.

After seven days of this, the big day arrived—Mantle and Maris would swing a bat—and a dozen sportswriters were gathered around the big batting cage that was situated beyond the left-field fence; it was completely enclosed in wire, meaning that no baseball could travel more than thirty or forty feet before being trapped in rope; still Mantle and Maris would be swinging, and this, in spring, makes news.

Mantle stepped in first. He wore black gloves to help prevent blisters, He hit right-handed against the pitching of a coach named Vern Benson, and soon Mantle was swinging hard, smashing line drives against the nets, going *ahhh ahhh* as he followed through with his mouth open.

Then Mantle, not wanting to overdo it on his first day, dropped his bat in the dirt and walked out of the batting cage. Roger Maris stepped in. He picked up Mantle's bat.

"This damn thing must be thirty-eight ounces," Maris said. He threw the bat down into the dirt, left the cage, and walked toward the dugout on the other side of the field to get a lighter bat.

DiMaggio stood among the sportswriters behind the cage, then turned when Vern Benson, inside the cage, yelled, "Joe, wanna hit some?"

"No chance," DiMaggio said.

"Com'on, Joe," Benson said.

The reporters waited silently Then DiMaggio walked slowly into the cage and picked up Mantle's bat. He took his position at the plate, but obviously it was not the classic DiMaggio stance; he was holding the bat about two inches from the knob, his feet were not so far apart, and, when DiMaggio took a cut at Benson's first pitch, fouling it, there was none of that ferocious follow through, the blurred bat did not come whipping all the way around, the No. 5 was not stretched full across his broad back.

DiMaggio fouled Benson's second pitch, then he connected solidly with the third, the fourth, the fifth. He was just meeting the ball easily, however, not smashing it, and Benson called out, "I didn't know you were a choke hitter, Joe."

"I am now," DiMaggio said, getting ready for another pitch.

He hit three more squarely enough, and then he swung again and there was a hollow sound.

"Ohhh," DiMaggio yelled, dropping his bat, his fingers stung, "I was waiting for that one." He left the batting cage rubbing his hands together. The reporters watched him. Nobody said anything. Then DiMaggio said to one of them, not in anger nor in sadness, but merely as a simply stated fact, "There was a time when you couldn't get me out of there."

Peter O'Toole on the Ould Sod

All the children in the classroom had their pencils out and were drawing horses, as the nun had instructed—all, that is, except one little boy who, having finished, was sitting idly behind his desk.

"Well," the nun said, looking down at his horse, "why not draw something else—a saddle, or something?"

A few minutes later she returned to see what he had drawn. Suddenly, her face was scarlet. The horse now had a penis and was urinating in the pasture.

Wildly, with both hands, the nun began to flail the boy. Then other nuns rushed in, and they, too, flailed him, knocking him to the floor, and not listening as he sobbed, bewilderedly, "But, but . . . I was only drawing what I saw . . . only what I saw!"

"OH, THOSE BITCHES!" SAID PETER O'Toole, now thirty-one, still feeling the sting after all these years. "Those destitute, old unmarried birds with those withered, sexless hands! God, how I hated those nuns!"

He threw his head back, finished his Scotch, then asked the stewardess for another. Peter O'Toole was sitting in an airplane that one hour before had left London, where he has long lived in exile, and was flying to Ireland, his birthplace. The plane was filled with businessmen and rosy-cheeked Irishwomen, and also a scattering of priests, one of whom held a cigarette in what seemed to be a long, thin pair of wire tweezers—presumably so he would not touch tobacco with fingers that would later hold the Sacrament.

114

O'Toole, unaware of the priest, smiled as the stewardess brought his drink. She was a floridly robust little blonde in a tight green tweed uniform.

"Oh, look at that ass," O'Toole said softly, shaking his head, raising his eyes with approval. "That ass is covered with tweed made in Connemara, where I was born. . . . Nicest asses in the world, Ireland. Irishwomen still are carrying water on their heads and carrying their husbands home from pubs, and such things are the greatest posture builders in the world."

He sipped his Scotch and looked out the window. The plane was now descending, and through the clouds he could see the soft, verdant fields, the white farmhouses, the gentle hills of outer Dublin, and he said he felt, as returning Irishmen often do, both some sadness and some joy. They are sad at seeing again what it was that forced them to leave, and feel some guilt, too, for having left, though they know they could never have fulfilled their dreams amid all this poverty and strangling strictness; yet they are happy because Ireland's beauty seems imperishable, unchanged from the time of their childhood, and thus each trip back home to Ireland is a blissful reunion with youth.

Though Peter O'Toole remains an uprooted Irishman by choice, he leaves London and returns to Ireland every now and then to do some drinking, to play the horses at the Punchestown racetrack outside Dublin, and to spend some solitary hours thinking. He had had very little time for private thinking recently; there had been those grueling two years in the desert with *Lawrence of Arabia*, and then starring on the London stage in Bertold Brecht's *Baal*, and then costarring with Richard Burton in the film *Becket*, and then he would star in *Lord Jim*, with other films to follow.

Big money was rolling in now, for the first time in his life. He had just bought a nineteen-room house in London and finally was able to afford paintings by Jack B. Yeats. Yet O'Toole was no more contented or secure now than he had been as an underfed drama student living on a barge, a barge that sank one night after too many people had come to a party.

He could still be wild and self-destructive, and the psychiatrists had been no help. All he knew was that within him, simmering in the smithy of his soul, were confusion and conflict, and they were probably responsible for his talent, his rebellion, his exile, his guilt. They were all linked somehow with Ireland and the Church, with his smashing up so many cars that his license had to be taken away, and with marching in Ban-the-Bomb parades, with becoming obsessed with Lawrence of Arabia, with detesting cops, barbed wire, and girls who shave under their arms; with being an aesthete, a horseplayer, a former altar boy, a drinker who now wanders through the streets at night buying the same book ("My life is littered with copies of *Moby Dick*") and reading the same sermon in that book ("and if we obey God, we must disobey ourselves"); with being gentle, generous, sensitive, yet suspicious ("You're talking to an Irish bookie's son; you can't con me!"); with devotion to his wife, loyalty to old friends, great concern over the uncertain eyesight of his three-year-old daughter, now wearing very thick glasses ("Daddy, Daddy! I broke my eyes!" "Don't cry, Kate, don't cry—we'll get you a new pair"); with theatrical genius that is equally moving whether performing pantomime or Hamlet; with an anger that can be sudden ("Why should I tell *you* the truth? Who are you, Bertrand Russell?") and with anger that quickly subsides ("Look, I'd tell you if I knew why, but I don't know, just don't know . . ."); and with the as yet unrealized contradictions in the Peter O'Toole who, at this very moment, was about to land in Ireland . . . where he was born thirty-one years ago . . . where he would have his next drink.

Two bumps, and the plane was safely down, racing across the concrete, then spinning around and rolling toward the Dublin air termi-

nal. When the door was opened, a crowd of photographers and reporters moved in, flashbulbs fixed, and soon they were popping away
as Peter O'Toole, a thin, lanky man of six feet three inches, wearing a
green corduroy jacket, a green bow tie, and green socks (he wears
nothing *but* green socks, even with tuxedos), came down the steps,
smiling and waving in the sun. He posed for pictures, gave a radio interview, bought everybody a drink. He laughed and backslapped; he
was charming and suave; he was his public self, his airport self.

Then he got into a limousine that would take him into the city, and
soon he was riding through the narrow, winding roads past the farmhouses, past the goats and cows and green, very green land stretching
for miles in the distance.

"A lovely land," O'Toole said, with a sigh. "God, you can love it! But
you can't live in it. It's a frightening thing. My father, who lives in
England, won't put a foot in Ireland anymore. And yet, you mention
one word against Ireland, and he goes stark raving mad.

"Oh, Ireland," O'Toole went on, "it's the sow that ate its own farrow. Tell me one Irish artist that ever produced here, just one! God,
Jack Yeats couldn't sell a painting in this country, and *all the talent* . . .
oh, daddy. . . . You know what Ireland's biggest export is? It's men.
Men . . . Shaw, Joyce, Synge, they couldn't stay here. O'Casey couldn't
stay. Why? Because O'Casey preaches the Doctrine of Joy, daddy,
that's why. . . . Oh, the Irish know despair, *by God they do!* They are
Dostoyevskian about it. But Joy, dear love, in *this* land! . . . Oh, dear
Father," O'Toole went on, pounding his breast, "forgive me, Father,
for I have fucked Mrs. Rafferty. . . . Ten Hail Marys, son, five Our Fathers. . . . But Father, Father, I didn't enjoy fucking Mrs. Rafferty. . . .
Good, son, *good* . . .

"Ireland," O'Toole repeated, "you can love it . . . can't *live* in it."

Now he was at the hotel. It was near the Liffey River not far from
the tower described by Joyce in *Ulysses*. O'Toole had a drink at the bar.

He seemed very quiet and somber, so different from the way he had been at the airport.

"The Celts are, at rock bottom, deep pessimists," Peter O'Toole said, tossing down his Scotch. Part of his own pessimism, he added, springs from his birthplace, Connemara, "the wildest part of Ireland, famine country, a land without horizons"—a land that Jack Yeats paints so well into his Irish faces, faces that remind O'Toole so much of his seventy-five-year-old father, Patrick O'Toole, a former book-maker, a dashing gentleman, tall and very slim, like Peter; who nearly always drank too much and fought with the police, like Peter; and who was not very lucky at the racetrack, like Peter; and people in the neighborhood back in Connemara used to shake their heads for Patty O'Toole's wife, Constance ("a saint"), and would say, "Oh, what would Patty O'Toole ever do without Connie?"

"When my father would come home from the track after a good day," said Peter O'Toole, leaning against the bar, "the whole room would light up; it was fairyland. But when he lost, it was black. In our house, it was always either a wake . . . or a wedding."

Later in his boyhood, Peter O'Toole was taken out of Ireland; his father, wishing to be closer to the racetracks clustered in northern England's industrial district, moved the family to Leeds, a slum of one-down, two-up houses.

"My first memory of Leeds as a child was being lost," said Peter O'Toole, tossing down another drink. "I remember wandering around the city . . . remember seeing a man painting a telephone pole *green*. . . . And I remember him going away and leaving his paintbrushes and things behind. . . . And I remember finishing the pole for him. . . . And I remember being brought to the police station. . . . And remember looking up at the desk, all white tile, white as a nun's hand, and then I remember seeing a big, fucking nasty looking down at me."

At thirteen, Peter O'Toole had quit school and had gone to work briefly in a warehouse and learned to break string without scissors, a talent he has never lost, and after that he worked as a copyboy and photographer's assistant at the *Yorkshire Evening News*, a job he liked very much until it occurred to him that newspapermen remain primarily along the sidelines of life recording the deeds of famous men, and rarely become famous themselves, and he very much wanted to become famous, he said. At eighteen years of age, he had copied in his notebook the lines that would be his credo, and now, in this bar in Dublin, tilting back on his barstool, he recited them aloud:

> *I do not choose to be a common man . . . it is my right to be uncommon—if I can. . . . I seek opportunity—not security. . . . I want to take the calculated risk; to dream and to build, to fail and to succeed . . . to refuse to barter incentive for a dole. . . . I prefer the challenges of life to the guaranteed existence, the thrill of fulfillment to the stale calm of utopia.* *

After he finished, two drunken men at the far end of the bar clapped their hands, and O'Toole bought them, and himself, another drink.

His career as an actor, he said, began after his tour in the navy and a year of study at the Royal Academy of Dramatic Art. One of his first acting jobs was with the Bristol Old Vic Company impersonating a Georgian peasant in a Chekhov play.

"I was supposed to lumber onto the stage and say, 'Dr. Ostroff, the horses have arrived,' and then walk off," O'Toole said. "But not *me*. I decided this Georgian peasant was really *Stalin!* And so I played it with a slight limp, like Stalin's, and fixed my makeup like Stalin . . . and

[*from American statesman Dean Alfange]

when I came on the stage, smoldering with resentment for the aris-
tocracy, I could hear a hush come over the audience. Then I glared at
Dr. Ostroff . . . and said, 'Dr. Horsey, the Ostroffs have arrived'"

In the next three years at the Bristol Old Vic, he played seventy-
three roles, including Hamlet, but, until he got the movie role in
Lawrence of Arabia, nobody had heard of Peter O'Toole, said Peter
O'Toole, his voice hard.

"*Lawrence!*" O'Toole spat out, swallowing his Scotch. "I became
obsessed by that man, and it was bad. A true artist should be able to
jump into a bucket of shit and come out smelling of violets, but I spent
two years and three months making that picture, and it was two years,
three months of thinking about nothing *but* Lawrence, and you were
him, and that's how it was day after day, day after day, and it became
bad for me, personally, and it killed my acting later.

"After Lawrence, as you know, I did *Baal*, and a close friend of
mine, after my dress rehearsal, came back and said, 'What's the matter, Peter, what *is* it?' I asked what the hell he meant, and he said,
'There's no *give!*' . . . Christ, his words struck terror in me. Oh, it was
bad acting! I was looking at the floor . . . couldn't get my voice going
again. . . . I was flabby, diffuse. . . . Later I said, 'You're in trouble,
daddy,' and I felt it in my fucking toes. I was emotionally bankrupt
after that picture.

"On a BBC show, on Harry Craig's show—that mother dug too
deep!—I said that after *Lawrence* I was afraid of being mutilated. That
filming for that length of time, two years, three months, and having all
the responsibility for the performance but none of the control . . .
Christ, in one scene of the film I saw a close-up of my face when I was
twenty-seven years old, and then, eight seconds later, there was another close-up of me when I was twenty-nine years old! Eight god-
damn seconds, and two years of my life had gone from me!

"Oh, it's painful seeing it all there on the screen, solidified, embalmed," he said, staring straight ahead toward the rows of bottles. "Once a thing is solidified, it stops being a living thing. That's why I love the theater. It's the Art of the Moment. I'm in love with ephemera, and I hate permanence. Acting is making words into flesh, and I love classical acting because . . . because you need the vocal range of an opera singer . . . the movement of a ballet dancer . . . you have to be able to *act* . . . it's turning your whole body into a musical instrument on which you yourself play. . . . It's more than behaviorism, which is what you get in the movies. . . . Chrissake, what *are* movies anyway? Just fucking moving photographs, that's all. But the theater! Ah, there you have the *impermanence* that I love. It's a reflection of life somehow. It's . . . it's . . . like building a statue of snow."

Peter O'Toole looked at his watch. Then he paid the barman and waved good-bye to the drunks in the corner. It was 1:15 P.M.—time to be getting to the track.

The chauffeur, a fat and quiet man who had been dozing in the hotel lobby all this time, woke up when he heard O'Toole singing and sauntering out of the bar, and he quickly hopped up when O'Toole announced cheerfully, bowing slightly, "To the races, m'good man."

In the car on the way to Punchestown, O'Toole, who was in good spirits but not drunk by any means, recalled the joy he'd had as a boy when his father would take him to the racetrack. Sometimes, O'Toole said, his father would miscalculate the odds at his bookie stand, or would lose so heavily on one of his own bets that he would not have enough cash to pay off his winning customers; so, immediately after the race was over, but before the customers could charge toward the O'Toole bookie booth, Patrick O'Toole would grab Peter's hand and say, "C'm'on, son, let's be off!"—and the two of them would slip through the shrubbery and disappear quickly from the track, and could not return again for a long time.

Punchestown's grandstand was jammed with people when O'Toole's chauffeur drove toward the clubhouse. There were long lines of people waiting to buy tickets, too, well-dressed people in tweed suits and tweed caps, or Tyrolean hats with feathers sticking up. Beyond the people was the paddock, a paddock of soft, very green grass on which the horses pounded back and forth, circling and turning, nostrils flaring. And behind the paddock, making lots of noise, were rows and rows of bookies, all of them elderly men wearing caps and standing behind their brightly painted wooden stands, all of them echoing the odds and waving little pieces of paper in the breeze.

Peter O'Toole watched them for a moment, silently. Then, suddenly, a woman's voice could be heard calling, "PEE-*tah*, Pee-*tah*, Pee-*tah* O'Toole, well, how *ah* you?"

O'Toole recognized the woman as one of Dublin society, a well-built woman of about forty whose husband owned racehorses and lots of stock in Guinness.

O'Toole smiled and held her hand for a few moments, and she said, "Oh, you look better every day, Pee-tah, even better than you did on those bloody Arab camels. Come to our trailer behind the clubhouse and have drinks with us, dear, won't you?"

O'Toole said he would but first wanted to place a bet.

He placed a five-pound bet on a horse in the first race, but, before the horse could clear the final hedge, the rider was thrown. O'Toole lost the next five races, too, and the liquor was also getting to him. Between races he had stopped in at the Guinness trailer, a big white van filled with rich men and champagne and elegant Irishwomen who brushed up very close to him, called him "Pee-tah," and said he should come back to Ireland more often, and, as he smiled and put his long arms around them, he sometimes found that he was leaning on them for support.

Just before the final race, O'Toole wandered out into the fresh air and sun and placed a ten-pound bet on a horse about which he knew nothing; then, instead of going back into the Guinness van, he leaned against the rail near the track, his bloodshot blue eyes gazing at the row of horses lined up at the gate. The bell sounded, and O'Toole's horse, a big chestnut gelding, pulled out ahead, and, swinging around the turn, kicking divots of grass into the air, it maintained the lead, leaped over a hedge, pounded onward, leaped over another hedge, still ahead by two lengths. Now Peter O'Toole began to wake up, and seconds later he was waving his fist in the air, cheering and jumping, as the horse moved across the finish line—and galloped past, the jockey leaning up on the saddle, an easy victor.

"Pee-tah, Pee-tah, you've won!" came the cries from the van.

"Pee-tah, darling, let's have a drink!"

But Peter O'Toole was not interested in a drink. He rushed immediately to the ticket window before the bookie could get away. O'Toole got his money.

After the races, with the late afternoon sun going down and the air suddenly chilly, O'Toole decided he would avoid the parties in Dublin; instead he asked the chauffeur to take him to Glendalough, a quiet, beautiful, almost deserted spot along a lake between two small mountains in outer Dublin, not far from where the earliest O'Tooles were buried, and where he, as a boy, used to take long walks.

By 5:30 P.M. the driver was edging the big car around the narrow dirt roads at the base of the mountain, then he stopped, there being no more road. O'Toole got out, lifted the collar of his green corduroy jacket, and began to walk up the mountain, a bit uneasily, because he was still slightly dazed by all the drinking.

"Oh, Christ, what color!" he shouted, his voice echoing through the valley. "Just look at those trees, those young trees—they're *running*, for chrissake, they're not planted there—and they're so luscious, like pubic hair, and that *lake*, no fish in *that* lake! And no birds sing; it's so quiet, no birds singing in Glendalough on account of there being no fish . . . for them to sing for."

Then he slumped down on the side of the mountain, tossed his head back against the grass. Then he held his hands in the air and said, "See that? See that right hand?" He turned his right hand back and forth, saying, "Look at those scars, daddy," and there were about thirty or forty little scars inside his right hand as well as on his knuckles, and his little finger was deformed.

"I don't know if there's any significance to it, daddy, but . . . but *I am a left-hander who was made to be right-handed.* . . . Oh, they would wack me over the knuckles when I used my left, those nuns, and maybe, just maybe, that is why I hated school so much."

All his life, he said, his right hand has been a kind of violent weapon. He has smashed it through glass, into concrete, against other people.

"But look at my *left* hand," he said, holding it high. "Not a single scar on it. Long and smooth as a lily."

He paused, then said, "You know, I can write absolutely backward, mirror writing. . . . Look." He pulled out his airplane ticket and, with a ballpoint pen, wrote out his name.

ɘlooꞱ'O ɿɘƚɘꟼ

He laughed. Then, standing and brushing the dirt from his green jacket and trousers, he staggered down the mountain toward the car and began to leave behind the eerie quiet of the lake, the running trees, and the island of those wizened white nuns.

*Vogue*land

EACH WEEKDAY MORNING A GROUP of suave and wrinkle-proof women, who call one another "dear" and "dahling," and can speak in italics and curse in French, move into Manhattan's Graybar Building, elevate to the nineteenth floor, and then slip behind their desks at *Vogue*—a magazine that has long been the supreme symbol of sophistication for every American female who ever dreamed of being frocked by Balenciaga, shod by Roger Vivier, coiffed by Kenneth, or set free to swing from the Arc de Triomphe in maiden-form mink.

Not since Sappho has anybody worked up such a lather over women as have the editors of *Vogue*. With almost every issue they present stunning goddesses who seemingly become more perfect, more devastating with the flip of each page. Sometimes the *Vogue* model is leaping across the page in mocha-colored silk, or piloting a teak-tipped ketch through the Lesser Antilles, or standing, Dior-length, in front of the Eiffel Tower as racy Renaults buzz by—but never hit her—as she poses in the middle of the street, one leg kicking, mouth open, teeth agleam, two gendarmes winking in the background, all Paris in love with her and her dinner dress of mousseline de soie.

At other times the *Vogue* model is wearing "never-out-of-season black" on the Queensboro Bridge with a white cat crawling up her back, a cat she presumably leaves home when she later jets down to Puerto Rico to lunch with Casals while being watched from the hills by native women holding naked children—women who smile at her, admire her silk tussah skirt ("Nantucket nipped"), love her as she spikes up the nine-hole course inside the fortress of old El Morro.

While these fashion models in *Vogue* are merely stupendous, the socialites photographed for that magazine are rich, beautiful, indefatigable, vivid, vital, brilliant, witty, serve on more committees than congressmen, know more about airplanes than Wolfgang Langewiesche, thrive on country air and yet are equally at home in the smart poker parlors of Cannes; they never age, fade, or get dandruff, and are also (in the words of *Vogue*'s battery of sycophantic caption writes) "amusable," "exquisite," "delicate," "fun," and "smashing."

In one *Vogue* issue, for instance, Mrs. Loel Guinness, photographed before she sashayed from Lausanne to Palm Beach, was described as "vivid, vital, amusing." And, in another issue, Mrs. Columbus O'Donnel possessed a "quick, amused sparkle," Queen Sirikit of Thailand was "amusable, exquisite," and the Countess of Dalkeith was "ravishing" and as effulgent as Lady Caroline Somerset—herself a "delicate moonbeam beauty." Mrs. Murray Vanderbilt, last year a "slender brunette with direct, heartbreaker eyes, and a soft, open laugh," this year is a "beauty with a strong sense of purpose"—her purpose being to fly to Paris to have her portrait painted by "jaunty, rakish" Kees Van Dongen on a Tuesday, and then fly back to New York the same night, "investing," as *Vogue* said, "only 23 hours, 45 minutes."

Should there be that extraordinary case when a celebrated woman in *Vogue* is not a "rare beauty"—as, for instance, when she is almost homely—she is then described as "wise" or "filled with wisdom" or reminiscent of heroines in exquisite, vital novels. Madame Helene Rochas "looks rather like the heroine of a novel by Stendhal." And, should *Vogue* make mention of a non-*Vogue* type, such as Ingrid Bergman, who spends little money in the cosmetic industry, she is credited with having a nose which is "rather generous."

The noses of *Vogue* heroines are usually long and thin, as are the noses of many *Vogue* editors—noses they can look down upon their generally shorter, younger, and less-sophisticated Condé Nast relatives at *Glamour* magazine, also located on the nineteenth floor of the Graybar Building. But it is usually quite simple to tell the two staffs apart because the *jeunes filles* at *Glamour*, in addition to possessing a high quota of noses that *Vogue* might dismiss as "eager, retroussé," are also given to wearing shirtdresses, college-girl circle pins, smiling in the elevator, and saying, "Hi." A *Vogue* lady once described the *Glamour* staff as "those peppy, Hi people."

One day a few years ago a wide-eyed, newly hired *Vogue* secretary went bouncing into an editor's office with a package, and said, "Hi"—at which the editor is supposed to have cringed, and finally snapped, "We don't say *that* around *here!*"

"Everyone at *Glamour* of course hopes to work her way up to the *Vogue* staff of grim vigilantes," says the writer Eve Marriam, once a fashion copy editor at *Glamour*. "But it rarely happens. *Vogue* has to be careful. The upcomer might use the word *cute* instead of *panche;* she might talk about giving a *party* instead of a *dinner;* or describe a suede coat 'for weekending with the station-wagon set' rather than 'for your country home.' Or talk of going to a jewelry store instead of a *bijouterie.* Most maladroit of all, she might talk in terms of a *best buy* rather than an *investment,* or a *coup.* Or refer to a *ballgown* as—one shudders to think of it—a *formal.*"

One has only to leave the elevator and enter the nineteenth floor to experience a sudden sensation of being *in Vogue.* The floors are black and star-studded, and the spacious outer room is tastefully furnished with a "delicate, amusable" receptionist with a British accent—perchance in keeping with the magazine's policy of spelling many words the British way: *colour, honour, jewellery,* and *marvellous* (pronounced *MAA*-vellous!).

To the rear of the receptionist is a curved corridor leading to *Vogue*'s editorial offices. The first office, that of the Beauty Editor, smells of pomades and powders, rejuvenators and other fountains of youth. Beyond this point, and around a second curve, are a half-dozen offices of other editors, and dividing them is the large, noisy Fashion Room. From nine till five the Fashion Room and the offices around it throb with the shrill, exuberant voices of fifty women, the incessant ring of telephones, the blurred image of leggy silhouettes shooting past, their heels clacking with *élan*. In one corner, the Fabrics Editor picks at silk swatches; in another corner, near a window, the Shoe Editor ponders what's next in "smashing" footwear; in still another corner, the Model Procurer flips through a filing cabinet that contains such highly classified data on models as which will pose for corset ads, which have the best legs, which have clawlike fingers (ideal for modeling gloves), and which have small, pretty hands (ideal for making small, expensive perfume bottles seem larger).

From the nearby offices of an editor named Carol Phillips ("delicate, amusable, pure-profiled beauty") can be heard the well-bred titters and talk of other *Vogue* tastemakers who stand, arms akimbo, toes pointed out, in front of Mrs. Phillips's desk. Inevitably their chatter blends with the dialogue that ricochets through the corridor, making it at times most difficult for the Baron De Gunzburg, a senior fashion editor, to concentrate fully on the *London Times* crossword puzzle that a messenger fetches for him each morning from the out-of-town newsstand in Times Square. The Baron, who is called "Nickkee" by *Vogue* ladies, and who makes his 7s in the European-style 7, is a former dancer with a Russian ballet and a onetime actor in a German film called *The Vampire*. (In the film he played a poet who spent two weeks in a casket before getting a chance to murder the vampire; nowadays the Baron is rarely without a black tie, and it is said that once, while entering a Seventh Avenue elevator without specifying his choice of floors, he was immediately whisked up to the floor of a tailor who made uniforms for undertakers.)

Upstairs from the Baron, in one of the few offices occupied by *Vogue* on the twentieth floor, Feature Editor Allene Talmey, whom editorial director Frank Crowninshield once described as a "Soufflé of Crowbars," bats out her famous column "People Are Talking About"—a collection of items that she and other *Vogue* ladies are talking about, and think *everybody* should be talking about. She writes:

> PEOPLE ARE TALKING ABOUT . . . *the present need for the Greek word,* bottologia, *meaning much speaking, or vain repetitions, as used by St. Matthew (6:7)* . . .
>
> PEOPLE ARE TALKING ABOUT . . . *the christening presents given to the daughter of the great Austrian conductor, Herbert von Karajan* . . .
>
> PEOPLE ARE TALKING ABOUT . . . *Takraw, a game beautiful to watch* . . .
>
> PEOPLE ARE TALKING ABOUT . . . *hummingbirds* . . .
>
> PEOPLE ARE TALKING ABOUT . . . *the Eastern half of the world.*

While some of *Vogue*'s critics contend that the magazine's literary policy can be summed up with "When in Doubt, Reprint Colette," it must be said in *Vogue*'s behalf that it has printed work by some excellent writers, among them Marianne Moore, Jacques Barzun, Rebecca West, and Allene Talmey. And yet one of *Vogue*'s former art directors, the inimitable Dr. Mehemet Femy Agha, once said, "Although Allene is wonderful, I've often told her she's like a piano player in a whorehouse. She may be a very good piano player, but nobody goes there to hear music. Nobody buys *Vogue* to read good literature; they buy it to see the clothes."

Among the first to see the clothes is the Baron De Gunzburg, who, having finished the *London Times* crossword puzzle, is now in the Garment Center on Seventh Avenue reclining in a posh divan in the showroom of the clothier Herbert Sondheim, who is giving *Vogue* magazine a private preview of Sondheim's spring frocks. Sitting next to the Baron is another *Vogue* editor, Mildred Morton ("pure-profiled blonde with slightly bored, raised eyebrow").

"You are the first persons in the entire world to be seeing these," says Mr. Sondheim, a short, rather stout, gravel-voiced man who rubs his hands, smiles from ear to ear.

A moment later a blonde model appears from behind the curtain, prances toward the Baron and Mrs. Morton, and coos, "Number 628."

The Baron writes down the style number in his Hermes leather notebook and watches her twirl around and then walk back through the curtain.

"That's pomecia," says Mr. Sondheim.

"Expensive?" asks Mrs. Morton.

"Pomecia cotton is about $2.50 a yard," Mr. Sondheim says.

"Number 648," says a second model, a brunette, who slithers past Mr. Sondheim, dips, then twirls around in front of the Baron De Gunzburg.

"Awfully smart," says the Baron, letting his fingers give the model's pomecia evening dress a professional pinch. "I just *love* the slashed coat."

Mrs. Morton raises her right eyebrow.

"Are you getting away this winter?" the Baron asks Mr. Sondheim.

"Probably," he says. "Palm Beach."

The Baron seems unimpressed.

"Number 624," announces the brunette model, appearing again with a flourish of frock, a dip, a spin.

"Wonderful texture, pomecia," Mr. Sondheim says, quickly getting businesslike again. "Furthermore, it doesn't crease."

"Like the other two better, don't you, Nick-*kee?*" asks Mrs. Morton.

The Baron is silent. The model twirls in front of him again, then stands with her back to him.

"What is your number?" the Baron asks, in a clipped British tone. "*Numba* 639," she shoots back over her shoulder. The Baron writes it down and then watches the model disappear behind the curtain to the clatter of plastic hangers.

Five minutes later, Mr. Sondheim's collection has been shown, and the Baron gives him the style numbers of the dresses *Vogue* wishes to have photographed and shown exclusively. Mr. Sondheim is delighted to comply, for having clothes appear firs in *Vogue*'s editorial pages almost guarantees their successful sale.

It all started back on December 17, 1892, when "quiet, clubby" Arthur Baldwin Turnure (Princeton '76), husband of one of America's first lady golf bugs, founded *Vogue* magazine. By 1895 he had created a sensation by displaying in his magazine the dresses and underwear to be worn by Miss Consuelo Vanderbilt on the occasion of her marriage to the Duke of Marlborough.

In 1909 *Vogue* was purchased by Condé Nast, under whom it flourished as never before, and no other magazine in the fashion field has ever been able to challenge it. *Harper's Bazaar*, which has always been less conservative—"It goes one rhinestone too *far*," a *Vogue* lady explains—does not provide its readers with quite so much of what Mary McCarthy calls "Democratic snobbery."

Some years ago Miss McCarthy, who did a rather extensive study of women's fashion magazines for the *Reporter*, concluded that as one descended through the less chichi magazines—such as *Charm, Glamour, Mademoiselle*—one found more genuine solicitude for the reader and her problems—"the pain of being a B.G. (Business Girl), the envy of superiors, self-consciousness, awkwardness, loneliness, sexual fears, timid friendliness to the Boss, endless evenings with the mirror and the tweezers, desperate Saturday social strivings ('Give a party and ask *everyone* you know'), the struggle to achieve any identity in the dead cubbyhole of office life."

And in another study of female magazines, this one done in *Social Forces* by two sociologists, Bernard Barber of Barnard College and Lyle S. Lobel, then of Harvard, it was stated that while the symbols of prestige in *Vogue* were "sophistication and chic," these same symbols were scorned by the respectable, PTA-types on the *Ladies Home Journal*, where there "is a distaste for 'high style,' for what is 'daring' or 'unusual.'"

But above *Vogue*'s ultrachic level, according to the sociologists, there looms an even more-envied class of women: the unfashionable "old money" rich.

"At this top-most level, where there is little need to compete for status through consumption," wrote Barber and Lobel, "women may even maintain a certain independence of current changeful 'fashion.' Their quality clothes can remain roughly the same for several years. . . . Even eccentric, like the old ladies on Beacon Street in Boston."

Describing the *Vogue* level, they continued: "In the social class just below the 'old money' families we find most of the 'high fashion,' Paris-conscious style leaders. Since they are aware of the class above, perhaps trying to gain entrance into it, these women seek to combine opulence with 'quiet elegance.' 'Fashion copy' for this group stresses the *pose* of assured distinction, effortless superiority, and inbred elegance."

Before *Vogue* magazine can display its pose of assured distinction and elegance, of course, it must summon its high-fashion models and have them photographed by fashion photographers, and on this particular afternoon *Vogue*'s colour photography sitting was being held in the penthouse studio of the noted photographer Horst Horst, a marvellous spot overlooking the East River. In the studio, while Horst Horst adjusts his German, Japanese, and Swedish cameras, his Chinese houseboy tacks enormous sheets of balmy sky-blue cardboard to the wall, creating a summery background. In the middle of the floor, in front of a box of flowers, is a plush stool of warm, Hazelmu brown on which the model will sit. In the adjoining dressing room, *Vogue*'s Mrs. Simpson, while awaiting the arrival of the model, Dorothea Mc-Gowan, does needlepoint from a Matisse pattern.

"I'd go mad, *mad* without this," Mrs. Simpson says of her needlepoint.

In another corner of the dressing room, *Vogue*'s wardrobe mistresses press a half-dozen Galanos chiffon gowns that the model will wear. Finally, ten minutes later, Dorothea McGowan, a tall, pale girl, lunges in with her hair in curlers. Immediately she removes her coat, unhinges her hair, dashes for the mirror, and quickly begins to stroke her canvaslike facial skin with a Japanese paintbrush.

"Which shoes, Mrs. Simpson?" she asks.

"Try the red ones, dear," Mrs. Simpson says, looking up from Matisse.

"Let's go," calls Horst from the other room.

Within a few minutes, after expert facial painting, Dorothea transforms herself from the pale, gangling Brooklyn girl she had been upon entering the studio into a sophisticated ageless woman about to pose for her seventh *Vogue* cover. She walks confidently into the studio, stands fifteen feet in front of Horst, stretches her calf muscles, spreads her legs slightly, places hands on hips, and prepares for her love affair with the camera.

Horst Horst, hands caressing his tripod, crouches and is about to shoot when Mrs. Simpson, standing on the sidelines like a duenna, shouts, "Wait." And the trance is momentarily broken as Mrs. Simpson says, "Her nails look terrible."

"Do they?" asks Dorothea, no longer the confident woman but now again the girl from Brooklyn.

"Yes, do you have your nails with you?"

The model goes into the dressing room to put on her false nails and then returns in front of the camera. Mrs. Simpson, satisfied now, returns to her needlepoint in the next room, and the Chinese boy places a fan in front of Dorothea, blowing her chiffon dress into her thin, lean body.

Dorothea throws her head back.

"Oh, such a rich feeling when the fan blows," she titters.

"Do something with your leg," Horst says.

She bends it backward, opens her mouth. And Horst's camera goes *click*. Then she leans down against the stool, lips puckered. Horst goes *click*.

"Oh, that's good," Horst says. "Do it again" (click).

Dorothea smiles (click); opens her mouth (click); wider, a big *O* (click).

"Hat's coming off." She giggles.

"Just smile, don't grin," he says (click). "Make a long neck."

She stretches (click).

"That's my girl," he says (click).

"Yesss," he repeats slowly (click).

And now, without any directions from him, she automatically strikes different poses, each one punctuated with a click; her face now bitchy, now primed for love, now blazy-eyed, now as demure as a Vassar virgin's. And Horst all the while is saying, excitedly behind the camera, "Yesss" (click), "Yesss" (click), "Yesss" (click).

"What are these little flowers?" Dorothea asks finally, breaking out of the mood.

"Azaleas," Horst says, lighting a cigarette. Dorothea pulls off a large rhinestone ring from her right hand, places it on her left, and then says, "You know, if you take a ring off one finger and put it on another finger, it still feels like you have it on the first finger."

Horst Horst looks at her in mild wonderment. Then Dorothea goes to change her dress. And the Chinese boy, built like a speed swimmer, turns off the fan and quickly changes the background from blue cardboard to pink. When Dorothea returns, Mrs. Simpson is back for another look.

"Dorothea," Mrs. Simpson says, "you have little hairs sticking out in the back of your neck."

"Oh?" Dorothea says, touching her neck.

Dorothea, turning toward the dressing room, notices the pink background, and her face becomes alive with anticipation.

"Oh," she exclaims, "I have pink . . . pink, PINK!"

Looking for Hemingway

*I remember very well the impression I had of Hemingway that first after-
noon. He was an extraordinarily good-looking young man, twenty-three
years old. It was not long after that that everybody was twenty-six. It became the period of being twenty-six. During the next two or three years all
the young men were twenty-six years old. It was the right age apparently
for that time and place.*

—Gertrude Stein

EARLY IN THE FIFTIES ANOTHER young generation of American expa-
triates in Paris became twenty-six years old, but they were not Sad
Young Men, nor were they Lost; they were the witty, irreverent sons of
a conquering nation, and, though they came mostly from wealthy parents and had been graduated from Harvard or Yale, they seemed endlessly delighted in posing as paupers and dodging the bill collectors,
possibly because it seemed challenging and distinguished them from
American tourists, whom they despised, and also because it was another way of having fun with the French, who despised *them*. Nevertheless, they lived in happy squalor on the Left Bank for two or three
years amid the whores, jazz musicians, and pederast poets, and became involved with people both tragic and mad, including a passionate Spanish painter who one day cut open a vein in his leg and finished
his final portrait with his own blood.

In July they drove down to Pamplona to run from the bulls, and
when they returned they played tennis with Irwin Shaw at Saint-Cloud

on a magnificent court overlooking Paris—and, when they tossed up the ball to serve, *there,* sprawled before them, was the whole city: the Eiffel Tower, Sacré-Coeur, the Opéra, the spires of Notre Dame in the distance. Irwin Shaw was amused by them. He called them "The Tall Young Men."

The tallest of them, at six feet four inches, was George Ames Plimpton, a quick, graceful tennis player with long, skinny limbs, a small head, bright blue eyes, and a delicate, fine-tipped nose. He had come to Paris in 1952, at the age of twenty-six, because several other tall, young Americans—and some short, wild ones—were publishing a literary quarterly to be called the *Paris Review,* over the protest of one of their staff members, a poet, who wanted it to be called *Druids' Home Companion* and to be printed on birch bark. George Plimpton was made editor in chief, and soon he could be seen strolling through the streets of Paris with a long, woolen scarf flung around his neck, or sometimes with a black evening cape billowing from his shoulders, cutting a figure reminiscent of Toulouse-Lautrec's famous lithograph of Aristide Bruant, that dashing litterateur of the nineteenth century.

Though much of the editing of the *Paris Review* was done at side-walk cafés by editors awaiting their turns on the pinball machine, the magazine nevertheless became very successful because the editors had talent, money, and taste, and they avoided using such typical little-magazine words as *zeitgeist* and *dichotomous,* and published no crusty critiques about Melville or Kafka, but instead printed the poetry and fiction of gifted young writers not yet popular. They also started a superb series of interviews with famous authors—who took them to lunch, introduced them to actresses, playwrights, and producers, and everybody invited everybody else to parties, and the parties have not stopped, even though ten years have passed; Paris is no longer the scene, and the Tall Young Men have become thirty-six years old.

They now live in New York. And most of the parties are held at
George Plimpton's large bachelor apartment on Seventy-second Street
overlooking the East River, an apartment that is also the headquarters
for what Elaine Dundy calls "the Quality Lit Set," or what Candida
Donadio, the agent, calls "The East Side Gang," or what everybody else
just calls "the *Paris Review* Crowd." The Plimpton apartment today is
the liveliest literary salon in New York—the only place where, standing
in a single room on almost any night of the week, one may find James
Jones; William Styron; Irwin Shaw; a few call girls for decoration;
Norman Mailer; Philip Roth; Lillian Hellman; a bongo player; a junkie
or two; Harold L. Humes; Jack Gelber; Sadruddin Aga Khan; Terry
Southern; Blair Fuller; the cast from *Beyond the Fringe*; Tom Keogh;
William Pène du Bois; Bee Whistler Dabney (an artist who descends
from Whistler's mother); Robert Silvers; and an angry veteran of the
Bay of Pigs invasion; and a retired bunny from the Playboy Club; John
P. C. Train; Joe Fox; John Phillips Marquand; and Robert W. Dowling's
secretary; Peter Duchin; Gene Andrewski; Jean vanden Heuvel; and
Ernest Hemingway's former boxing coach; Frederick Seidel; Thomas
H. Guinzburg; David Amram; and a bartender from down the street;
Barbara Epstein; Jill Fox; and a local distributor of pot; Piedy Gimbel;
Dwight Macdonald; Bill Cole; Jules Feiffer; *and* into such a scene one
wintry night earlier this year walked another old friend of George
Plimpton's—Jacqueline Kennedy.

"Jackie!" George called out, opening the door to greet the First
Lady and also her sister and brother-in-law, the Radziwills. Mrs.
Kennedy, smiling broadly between gleaming earrings, extended her
hand to George, whom she has known since her dancing-school days,
and they chatted for a few seconds in the hallway while George helped
her with her coat. Then, peeking into the bedroom and noticing a
mound of overcoats piled higher than a Volkswagen, Mrs. Kennedy
said, in a soft, hushed, sympathetic voice, "Oh, *George*—your *b e d!*"

George shrugged and then escorted them through the hall down three steps into the smoky scene.

"Look," said one hipster in the corner, "there's Lee Radziwill's sister!"

George first introduced Mrs. Kennedy to Ved Mehta, the Indian writer, and then slipped her skillfully past Norman Mailer toward William Styron.

"Why, hel*LO*, Bill," she said, shaking hands, "nice to see you."

For the next few moments, talking with Styron and Cass Canfield, Jr., Mrs. Kennedy stood with her back to Sandra Hochman, a Greenwich Village poetess, a streaked blonde in a thick woolly sweater and partially unzipped ski pants.

"I think," Miss Hochman whispered to a friend, tossing a backward nod at Mrs. Kennedy's beautiful white brocade suit, "that I am a bit *déshabillée.*"

"Nonsense," said her friend, flicking cigarette ashes on the rug. And, in truth, it must be said that none of the seventy other people in that room felt that Sandra Hochman's outfit contrasted unpleasantly with the First Lady's; in fact, some did not even notice the First Lady, and there was one who noticed her but failed to recognize her.

"My," he said, squinting through the smoke toward the elaborately teased coiffure of Mrs. Kennedy, "that *really* is the look this year, isn't it? And that chick has almost made it."

While Mrs. Kennedy conversed in the corner, Princess Radziwill talked with Bee Whistler Dabney a few feet away, and Prince Radziwill stood alone next to the baby grand piano humming to himself. He often hums to himself at parties. In Washington he is known as a great hummer.

Fifteen minutes later Mrs. Kennedy, expected soon at a dinner given by Adlai Stevenson, said good-bye to Styron and Canfield and, escorted by George Plimpton, headed for the steps toward the hall.

Norman Mailer, who had meanwhile drunk three glasses of water, was standing by the steps. He looked hard at her as she passed. She did not return his glance.

Three quick steps, and she was gone—down the hall, her coat on, her long white gloves on, down two flights of steps to the sidewalk, the Radziwills and George Plimpton behind her.

"Look," squealed a blonde, Sally Belfrage, gazing down from the kitchen window at the figures below climbing into the limousine, "there's *George!* And *look* at that car!"

"What's so unusual about that car?" somebody asked. "It's only a Cadillac."

"Yes, but it's *black*, and so-o-o *un*chromed."

Sally Belfrage watched as the big car, pointed in the direction of another world, moved quietly away, but in the living room the party went on louder than before, with nearly everyone oblivious to the fact that the host had disappeared. But there was liquor to be consumed, and, besides, by just casting an eye over the photographs on the walls throughout the apartment, one could easily feel the presence of George Plimpton. One photograph shows him fighting small bulls in Spain with Hemingway; another catches him drinking beer with other Tall Young Men at a Paris café; others show him as a lieutenant marching a platoon of troops through Rome, as a tennis player for King's College, as an amateur prizefighter sparring with Archie Moore in Stillman's Gymnasium, an occasion during which the rancid smell of the gym was temporarily replaced by the musk of El Morocco and the cheers of Plimpton's friends when he scored with a solid jab—but it quickly changed to *"Ohhhhhhh"* when Archie Moore retaliated with a punch that broke part of the cartilage in Plimpton's nose, causing it to bleed and causing Miles Davis to ask afterward, "Archie, is that black blood or white blood on your gloves?" to which one of Plimpton's friends replied, "Sir, *that* is blue blood."

Also on the wall is Plimpton's rebab, a one-stringed instrument of goatskin that Bedouin tribesmen gave him prior to his doing a walk-on in *Lawrence of Arabia* during a dust storm. And above his baby grand piano—he plays it well enough to have won a tie-for-third prize on Amateur Night at the Apollo theater a couple of years ago in Harlem—is a coconut sent him by a lady swimmer he knows in Palm Beach, and also a photograph of another girl, Vali, the orange-haired Existentialist known to all Left Bank concierges as *la bête*, and also a major-league baseball that Plimpton occasionally hurls full distance across the living room into a short, chunky, stuffed chair, using the same windup as when he pitched batting practice against Willie Mays while researching his book *Out of My League*, which concerns how it feels to be an amateur among pros—and which, incidentally, is a key not only to George Ames Plimpton but to many others on the *Paris Review* as well.

They are obsessed, so many of them, by the wish to know how the other half lives. And so they befriend the more interesting of the odd, avoid the downtown dullards on Wall Street, and dip into the world of the junkie, the pederast, the prizefighter, and the adventurer in pursuit of kicks and literature, being influenced perhaps by that glorious generation of ambulance drivers that preceded them to Paris at the age of twenty-six.

In Paris in the early fifties, their great white hope was Irwin Shaw because, in the words of Thomas Guinzburg, a Yale man then managing editor of the *Paris Review*, "Shaw was a tough, tennis-playing, hard-drinking writer with a good-looking wife—the closest thing we had to Hemingway." Of course, the editor in chief, George Plimpton, then as now, kept the magazine going, kept the group together, and set a style of romanticism that was—and is—infectious.

Arriving in Paris in the Spring of 1952 with a wardrobe that included the tails his grandfather had worn in the twenties, and which George himself had worn in 1951 while attending a ball in London as an escort to the future queen of England, he moved immediately into a tool shed behind a house owned by Gertrude Stein's nephew. Since the door of the shed was jammed, Plimpton, to enter it, had to hoist himself, his books, and his grandfather's tails through the window. His bed was a long, thin cot flanked by a lawn mower and garden hose, and was covered by an electric blanket that Plimpton could never remember to turn off—so that, when he returned to the shed at night and plopped into the cot, he was usually greeted by the angry howls of several stray cats reluctant to leave the warmth that his forgetfulness had provided.

One lonely night, before returning home, Plimpton took the walk through Montparnasse down the same streets and past the same cafés that Jake Barnes took after leaving Lady Brett in *The Sun Also Rises*. Plimpton wanted to see what Hemingway had seen, to feel what Hemingway had felt. Then, the walk over, Plimpton went into the nearest bar and ordered a drink.

In 1952 the *Paris Review*'s headquarters was a one-room office at 8 Rue Garancière. It was furnished with a desk, four chairs, a bottle of brandy, and several lively, long-legged Smith and Radcliffe girls who were anxious to get onto the masthead so that they might convince their parents back home of their innocence abroad. But so many young women came and went that Plimpton's business manager, a small, sharp-tongued Harvard wit named John P. C. Train, decided it was ridiculous to try to remember all their names, whereupon he declared that they should henceforth all be called by one name—"Apetecker." And the Apetecker alumnae came to include, at one time or another, Jane Fonda, Joan Dillon Moseley (daughter of Treasury Secretary Dillon), Gail Jones (daughter of Lena Horne), and Louisa Noble (daughter of the Groton football coach), a very industrious but forgetful girl who was endlessly losing manuscripts, letters, dictionaries. One day, after John P. C. Train received a letter from a librarian complaining that Miss Noble was a year overdue on a book, he wrote back:

> *Dear Sir:*
>
> *I take the liberty of writing to you in my own hand because Miss L. Noble took with her the last time she left this office the typewriter on which I was accustomed to compose these messages. Perhaps when she comes into your library you will ask if we might not have this machine.*
>
> *Subscription blank enclosed.*
>
> *Yours faithfully,*
> *J. P. C. Train*

Since the *Paris Review*'s one-room office obviously was too small to fulfill the staff's need for mixing business with pleasure, and since there was also a limit to the number of hours they could spend at cafés, everybody would usually gather at 5 P.M. at the apartment of Peter and Patsy Matthiessen on 14 Rue Perceval, where by that time a party was sure to be in progress.

Peter Matthiessen, then fiction editor of the *Paris Review*, was a tall, thin Yale graduate who as a youngster had attended St. Bernard's School in New York with George Plimpton, and who now was working on his first novel, *Race Rock*. Patsy was a small, lovely, vivacious blonde with pale blue eyes and a marvelous figure, and all the boys of twenty-six were in love with her. She was the daughter of the late Richard Southgate, onetime chief of protocol for the State Department, and Patsy had gone to lawn parties with Kennedy children, had chauffeurs and governesses, and, in her junior year at Smith, in 1948, had come to Paris and met Peter. Three years later, married, they returned to Paris

and acquired for twenty-one dollars a month this apartment in Montparnasse that had been left vacant when Peter's old girlfriend had gone
off to Venezuela.

The apartment had high ceilings, a terrace, and lots of sun. On one
wall was a Foujita painting of a gigantic head of a cat. The other wall
was all glass, and there were large trees against the glass and wild
growth crawling up it, and visitors to this apartment often felt that
they were in a monstrous fishbowl, particularly by 6 P.M., when the
room was floating with Dutch gin and absinthe and the cat's head
seemed bigger, and a few junkies would wander in, nod, and settle
softly, soundlessly in the corner.

This apartment, in the fifties, was as much a meeting place for the
young American literati as was Gertrude Stein's apartment in the
twenties, and it also caught the atmosphere that would, in the sixties,
prevail at George Plimpton's apartment in New York.

William Styron, often at the Matthiessens', describes their apartment in his novel *Set This House on Fire*, and other novelists there were
John Phillips Marquand and Terry Southern, both editors on the *Paris
Review*, and sometimes James Baldwin, and nearly always Harold L.
Humes, a chunky, indefatigable, impulsive young man with a beard,
beret, and a silver-handled umbrella. After being dismissed from
MIT for taking a Radcliffe girl sailing several hours beyond her bedtime, and after spending an unhappy tour with the navy making may-
onnaise in Bainbridge, Maryland, Harold Humes burst onto the Paris
scene in full rebellion.

He became a chess hustler in cafés, earning several hundred
francs a night. It was in the cafés that he met Peter Matthiessen, and
they both talked of starting a little magazine that would be the *Paris
Review*. Before coming to Paris, Humes had never worked on a magazine, but had grown fond of a little magazine called *Zero*, edited by a
small Greek named Themistocles Hoetes, whom everybody called

"Them." Impressed by what Them had done with *Zero*, Humes purchased for $600 a magazine called the *Paris News Post*, which John Ciardi later called the "best fourth-rate imitation of the *New Yorker* I have ever seen," and to which Matthiessen felt condescendingly superior, and so Humes sold it for $600 to a very nervous English girl, under whom it collapsed one issue later. Then Humes and Matthiessen and others began a long series of talks on what policy, if any, they would follow should the *Paris Review* ever get beyond the talking and drinking stages.

When the magazine was finally organized, and when George Plimpton was selected as its editor instead of Humes, Humes was disappointed. He refused to leave the cafés to sell advertising or negotiate with French printers. And in the summer of 1952 he did not hesitate to leave Paris with William Styron, accepting an invitation from a French actress, Mme. Nénot, to go down to Cap Myrt, near Saint-Tropez, and visit her fifty-room villa that had been designed by her father, a leading architect. The villa had been occupied by the Germans early in the war. And so when Styron and Humes arrived they found holes in its walls, through which they could look out to the sea, and the grass was so high and the trees so thick with grapes that Humes's little Volkswagen became tangled in the grass. So they went on foot toward the villa, but suddenly stopped when they saw, rushing past them, a young, half-naked girl, very brown from the sun, wearing only handkerchiefs tied bikini-style, her mouth spilling with grapes. Screaming behind her was a lecherous-looking old French farmer whose grape arbor she obviously had raided.

"Styron!" Humes cried, gleefully, *"we have arrived!"*

"Yes," he said, "we are *here!*"

More nymphets came out of the trees in bikinis later, carrying grapes and also half cantaloupes the size of cartwheels, and they offered some to Styron and Humes. The next day they all went swimming and fishing, and, in the evening, they sat in the bombed-out villa, a breathtaking site of beauty and destruction, drinking wine with the young girls who seemed to belong only to the beach. It was an electric summer, with the nymphets batting around like moths against the screen. Styron remembers it as a scene out of Ovid, Humes as the high point of his career as an epicurean and scholar.

George Plimpton remembers that summer not romantically but as it was—a long, hot summer of frustration with French printers and advertisers; and the other *Review* staff members, particularly John P. C. Train, were so annoyed at Humes's departure that they decided they would drop his name from the top of the masthead, where he belonged as one of the founders, down to near the bottom under "advertising and circulation."

When the first issue of the *Paris Review* came out, in the spring of 1953, Humes was in the United States. But he had heard what they had done to him, and, infuriated, he now planned his revenge. When the ship arrived at the Hudson River pier with the thousands of *Paris Reviews* that would be distributed throughout the United States, Harold Humes, wearing his beret and swearing, *"Le Paris Review c'est moi!"* was at the dock waiting for them; soon he had ripped the cartons open, and, with a rubber stamp bearing his name in letters larger than any on the masthead, he began to pound his name in red over the masthead of each issue, a feat that took several hours to accomplish and which left him, in the end, totally exhausted.

"But . . . but . . . how *c-o-u-l-d* you have *done* such a thing?" George Plimpton asked when he next saw Humes.

Humes was now sad, almost tearful; but, with a final flash of vengeance, he said, "I am damned well not going to get shoved around!"

Rages of this sort were to become quite common at the *Paris Review*. Terry Southern was incensed when a phrase in one of his short stories was changed from "don't get your crap hot" to "don't get hot." Two poets wished to dissect John P. C. Train when, after a French printer had accidentally spilled the type from one poem into another, and the two poems appeared as one in the magazine, Train *casually* remarked that the printer's carelessness had actually improved the work of both poets.

Another cause for chaos was the Paris police force, which seemed ever in pursuit of John Train's nocturnal squad of flying poster plasterers, a union of Yale men and Arab youths who ran through Paris at night sticking large *Paris Review* advertising posters on every lamppost, bus, and *pissoir* they could. The ace of the squadron, a tall Yale graduate named Frank Musinsky, was so impressive that John Train decided to name all the other young men "Musinsky"—just as he had previously named the girls "Apeteker"—which Musinsky considered quite an honor, even though his real name was not Musinsky. Musinsky acquired the name because his grandfather, whose surname was Supovitch (sic), had switched names in Russia many years ago with a countryman named Musinsky who, for a price, agreed to take Frank's grandfather's place in the Russian army.

Nobody knows what became of him in the Russian army, but Frank's grandfather came to the United States, where his son later prospered in the retail shoe business, and his grandson, Frank, after Yale and his tour with Train's flying squad, got a job in 1954 with the *New York Times*—and soon lost it.

He had been hired as a copyboy in the *Times* sports department and, as such, was expected to devote himself to running galley proofs and filling pastepots, and was not expected to be sitting behind a desk, feet propped up, reading Yeats and Pound and refusing to move.

One night an editor shouted, "Musinsky, without doubt you're the worst copyboy in the history of the *Times*," to which Musinsky, rising haughtily, snapped, "Sir, to quote e. e. cummings, whom I'm sure you have heard of, 'There is some shit I shall not eat.'" Frank Musinsky turned and left the *Times*, never to return.

Meanwhile, Frank's place in the Paris flying squad was taken by several other Musinskys—Colin Wilson was one—and they all helped to preserve the *Review*'s traditional irreverence for the bourgeoisie, the Establishment, and even for the late Aga Khan, who, after offering to give a $1,000 prize for fiction, then submitted his own manuscript. The editor quickly snapped up his money, but just as quickly returned the manuscript, making it clear that his prose style was not what they were seeking, even though the Aga's own son, Sadruddin Khan, a Harvard friend of Plimpton's, had just become publisher of the *Paris Review*, an offer that George proposed and Sadruddin accepted rather impulsively one day when they both were running from the bulls at Pamplona—a moment during which George suspected, correctly, that Sadruddin might agree to just about anything.

As improbable as it may seem, what with all the Musinskys and Apeteckers flying this way and that, the *Paris Review* did very well, publishing fine stories by such younger writers as Philip Roth, Mac Hyman, Pati Hill, Evan Connell, Jr., and Hughes Rudd, and, of course, distinguishing itself most of all by its "Art of Fiction" interviews with famous authors, particularly the one with William Faulkner by Jean Stein vanden Heuvel and the one with Ernest Hemingway by Plimpton, which began in a Madrid café with Hemingway asking Plimpton, "You go to the races?"

"Yes, occasionally."

"Then you read *The Racing Form*," Hemingway said. "There you have the true Art of Fiction."

But as much as anything else, the *Paris Review* survived because it had money. And its staff members had fun because they knew that, should they ever land in jail, their friends or families would always bail them out. They would never have to share with James Baldwin the experience of spending eight days and nights in a dirty French cell on the erroneous charge of having stolen a bedsheet from a hotelkeeper, all of which led Baldwin to conclude that while the wretched round of hotel rooms, bad food, humiliating concierges, and unpaid bills may have been the "Great Adventure" for the Tall Young Men, it was not for him because, he said, "there was a real question in my mind as to which would end soonest, the Great Adventure or me."

The comparative opulence of the *Paris Review*, of course, made it the envy of the other little magazines, particularly the staff members of a quarterly called *Merlin*, some of whose editors charged the *Review* people with dilettantism, resented their pranks, resented that the *Review* would continue to be published while *Merlin*, which had also discovered and printed new talent, would soon fold.

In those days *Merlin*'s editor was Alexander Trocchi, born in Glasgow of a Scotch mother and Italian father, a very exciting, tall, and conspicuous literary figure with a craggy, satanic face, faun's ears, a talent for writing, and a powerful presence that enabled him to walk into any room and take charge. He would soon become a friend of George Plimpton, John Phillips Marquand, and the other *Review* people, and years later he would come to New York to live on a barge, and still later in the back room of the *Paris Review*'s Manhattan office, but eventually he would be arrested on narcotics charges, would jump bail, and would leave the United States with two of George Plimpton's Brooks Brothers suits. But he would leave behind a good novel about drug addiction, *Cain's Book*, with its memorable line: "Heroin is habit-forming . . . habit-forming . . . rabbit-forming . . . Babbitt-forming."

Alexander Trocchi's staff at *Merlin* in those days was made up largely of humorless young men in true rebellion, which the *Paris Review* staff was not; the *Merlin* crowd also read the leftist monthly *Les Temps Modernes* and were concerned with the importance of being *en-*

gagé. Their editors included Richard Seaver, who was reared in the Pennsylvania coal-mine district and in whose dark, humid Paris garage *Merlin* held its staff meetings, and also Austryn Wainhouse, a disenchanted Exeter-Harvard man who wrote a strong, esoteric novel, *Hedyphagetica,* and who, after several years in France, is now living in Martha's Vineyard building furniture according to the methods of the eighteenth century.

While the entire *Merlin* staff was poor, none was so poor as the poet Christopher Logue, about whom it was said that once, when playing a pinball machine in a café, he noticed a ragged old peasant lady staring at a five-franc piece lying on the floor near the machine, but before she could pick it up Logue's foot quickly reached out and stomped on it. He kept his foot there while the old lady screamed and while he continued, rather jerkily, to hold both hands to the machine trying to keep the ball bouncing—and *did,* until the owner of the café grabbed him and escorted him out.

Sometime later, when Logue's girlfriend left him, he came under the influence of a wild Svengali character then living in Paris, a pale, waxen-faced South African painter who was a disciple of Nietzsche and his dictum "Die at the right time," and who, looking for kicks, actually encouraged Logue to commit suicide—which Logue, in his depressed state, said he would do.

Austryn Wainhouse, who had suspected that suicide was very much on Logue's mind, had spent the following week sitting outside of Logue's hotel each night watching his window, but one afternoon when Logue was late for a luncheon date with Wainhouse, the latter rushed to the poet's hotel and there, on the bed, was the South African painter.

"Where's Chris?" Wainhouse demanded.

"I am not going to tell you," the painter said. "You can beat me if you wish; you're bigger and stronger than I, and . . ."

"I *don't* want to beat you," Wainhouse shouted. It then occurred to him how ridiculous was the South African's remark since he (Wainhouse) was actually much smaller and hardly stronger than the painter. "Look," he said finally, "don't you leave here," and then he ran quickly to a café where he knew he would find Trocchi.

Trocchi got the South African to talk and admit that Christopher Logue had left that morning for Perpignan, near the Spanish border twelve hours south of Paris, where he planned to commit suicide in much the same way as the character in the Samuel Beckett story in *Merlin*, entitled "The End"—he would hire a boat and row out to sea, further and further, and then pull up the plugs and slowly sink.

Trocchi, borrowing 30,000 francs from Wainhouse, hopped on the next train for Perpignan, five hours behind Logue. It was dark when he arrived, but early the next morning he began his search.

Logue, meanwhile, had tried to rent a boat, but did not have enough money. He also carried with him, along with some letters from his former girlfriend, a tin of poison, but he did not have an opener, nor were there rocks on the beach, and so he wandered about, frustrated and frantic, until he finally came upon a refreshment stand where he hoped to borrow an opener.

It was then that the tall figure of Trocchi spotted him and placed a hand on Logue's shoulder. Logue looked up.

"Alex," Logue said, casually handing him the tin of poison, "will you open this for me?"

Trocchi put the tin in his pocket.

"*Alex,*" Logue then said, "what are *you* doing here?"

"Oh," Trocchi said lightly, "I've come down to embarrass you."

Logue broke down in tears, and Trocchi helped him off the beach, and then they rode, almost in total silence, back to Paris on the train.

Immediately George Plimpton and several others on the *Paris Review* who were very fond of Logue, and proud of Trocchi, raised enough money to put Christopher Logue on a kind of monthly allowance. Later Logue returned to London and published books of poetry, and his plays, *Antigone* and *The Lily-White Boys* were performed at the Royal Court Theatre in London. Still later he began to write songs for the Establishment, London's satirical nightclub act.

After the Logue episode, which, according to George Plimpton, sent at least a half-dozen young novelists to their typewriters trying to build a book around it, life in Paris at the *Review* was once more happy and ribald—but, a year later with the *Review* still doing well, Paris slowly seemed to pall.

John P. C. Train, then managing editor, put a sign on his in-basket reading, "Please Do Not Put Anything In The Managing Editor's Box," and one day when a pleasant, blue-eyed Oklahoman named Gene Andrewski wandered in with a manuscript and mentioned that he had once helped produce his college humor magazine, John Train quickly handed him a beer and said, "How would you like to run this magazine?" Andrewski said he would think it over. He thought it over for a few seconds, looked around at everybody else drinking beer, and agreed to become a kind of Assistant Managing Editor in Charge of Doing Train's Job. "The main reason I took the job," Andrewski later explained, "was I wanted the freedom."

In 1956 Peter Duchin moved to Paris and lived on a barge on the Seine, and many *Paris Review* people made this their new headquarters. There was no water on the barge, and in the morning everybody had to shave with Perrier. But the attempt at merriment on the barge seemed futile because, by this time, most of the old crowd had left. Paris was, as Gertrude Stein suggested, the right place for twenty-six, but now most of them were thirty years old. And so they returned to New York—but not in the melancholy mood of Malcolm Cowley's exiles of the twenties, who were forced home during the early currents of the crash, but rather with the attitude that the party would now shift to the other side of the Atlantic. Soon New York was aware of their presence, particularly the presence of Harold L. Humes.

After taking over a large apartment on upper Broadway with his wife, his daughters, and his unclipped wirehair terrier, and installing seven telephones and a large paper cutter that had the cracking eighteenth-century sound of a guillotine, Humes lashed out with a series of ideas and tall deeds: He hit on a theory of cosmology that would jolt Descartes, finished a second novel, played piano in a Harlem jazz club, began to shoot a movie called *Don Peyote*, a kind of Greenwich Village version of *Don Quixote* starring an unknown from Kansas City named Ojo de Vidrio, whose girlfriend eventually grabbed the film and ran off with it. Humes also invented a paper house, an *actual paper house* that is waterproof, fireproof, and large enough for people to live in; he set up a full-sized model on the Long Island estate of George Plimpton's family, and Humes's corporation, which included some backers from the *Paris Review* crowd, insured Humes's brain for $1 million.

During the Democratic National Convention in 1960, Humes led a phalanx of screaming Stevensonians onto the scene after employing the gate-crashing techniques of the ancient armies of Athens. When back in New York he called for an investigation of the New York police force, whereupon the police commissioner called for an investigation of *Humes*—and discovered fourteen unpaid traffic tickets. Humes went to jail just long enough to be discovered by the commissioner of corrections, Anna Kross, who upon recognizing him behind bars said, "Why, Mr. Humes, what are *you* doing in *there?*" to which he responded with Thoreau's line to Emerson, "Why, Miss Kross, what are *you* doing out *there?*"

When released on bail that was produced by Robert Silvers, another *Paris Review* editor, Harold Humes was asked by newspaper reporters how he liked the cell, and he replied, once more after Thoreau, "In a time of injustice, the place for an honest man is in jail."

Robert Silvers, one of the few quiet editors on the *Review*, a man with no apparent vices except smoking in bed, had no place to stay when he returned from Paris, and so he temporarily occupied the guest room in George Plimpton's apartment on East Seventy-second Street, where he proceeded to burn many holes in the mattress. He then plugged up the holes with peach pits. George Plimpton did not object. Robert Silvers was an old friend, and, besides, the mattress did not belong to Plimpton. It belonged to a fashion model who had once occupied the apartment, and who surprised both Plimpton and Silvers one day with a letter asking if they would please send the mattress to her home in France. They did, pits and all, and, having heard no complaints, they both nurture some delight in the thought that somewhere in Paris, somewhere in the very chic apartment of a high-fashion model, there is a mattress stuffed with peach pits.

Fortunately for Plimpton, he did not have to buy a new mattress for his guest room because, at about that time, the *Paris Review*, which had an office in a tenement on Eighty-second Street, had been evicted; and so Plimpton took home the small bed that had been in the back room of the *Paris Review*'s office—a room that had been the locale of several parties that had reduced the premise to a collage of broken bottles, bent spoons, rats, and chewed manuscripts.

After the eviction from the tenement, the *Paris Review*'s New York office shifted to the unlikely and quiet borough of Queens, where, in a large home between Grand Central Parkway and a cemetery, Lillian von Nickern Pashaian, when she is not tending to her three children, canaries, and turtles, accepts manuscripts that are addressed to the *Paris Review* and forwards them for a reading to either Jill Fox in Bedford Village, New York, or to Rose Styron in Roxbury, Connecticut. If *they* like what they have read, they forward the manuscript to George Plimpton's apartment on Seventy-second Street, where, between all his other activities, he gives a final reading and decides whether or not it will be accepted. If it is accepted, the author usually becomes the recipient of a small check and all he can drink at the next Plimpton party.

A Plimpton party is often planned only a few hours before it begins. George will pick up the phone and call a few people. They, in turn, will call others. Soon there is the thunder of feet ascending the Plimpton staircase. The inspiration for the party may have been that Plimpton won a court-tennis match earlier that day at the Racquet and Tennis Club, or that one member of the *Paris Review* crowd has a book coming out (in which case the publisher is invited to share the expenses), or that a member has just returned to Manhattan from a trip—a trip that might have carried John P. C. Train, a financial speculator, to Africa, or Peter Matthiessen to New Guinea to live with Stone Age tribesmen, or Harold Humes to the Bronx to fight in court over a parking ticket.

And in giving so many parties, in giving out keys to his apartment, in keeping the names of old friends on the *Paris Review* masthead long after they have ceased to work for it, George Ames Plimpton has managed to keep the crowd together all these years, and has also created around himself a rather romantic world, a free, frolicsome world within which he, and they, may briefly escape the inevitability of being thirty-six.

It exudes charm, talent, beauty, adventure. It is the envy of the uninvited, particularly of some child-bearing Apeteckers in the suburbs who often ask, "When is that group going to settle down?" Some in the group have remained bachelors. Others have married women who like parties—or have been divorced. Still others have an understanding that, if the wife is too tired for a party, the husband goes alone. It is largely a man's world, all of them bound by their memories of Paris and the Great Adventure they shared, and it has very few exiles, although it has had some—one being the beautiful blonde who was very much on everyone's mind in Paris ten years ago, Patsy Matthiessen.

Patsy and Peter are divorced. She is now married to Michael Gold-berg, an abstract painter, lives on West Eleventh Street, and moves in the little world of downtown intellectuals and painters. Recently she spent several days in a hospital after being bitten by the dog of the widow of Jackson Pollock. In her apartment she has a cardboard box full of snapshots of the *Paris Review* crowd of the fifties. But she re-members those days with some bitterness.

"The whole life seemed after a while to be utterly meaningless," she said. "And there was something very *manqué* about them—this going to West Africa, and getting thrown in jail, and getting in the ring with Archie Moore. . . . And *I* was a Stepin Fetchit in that crowd, get-ting them tea at four, and sandwiches at ten."

A few blocks away, in a small, dark apartment, another exile, James Baldwin, said, "It didn't take long before I really was no longer a part of them. They were more interested in kicks and hashish cigarettes than I was. I had already done that in the Village when I was eighteen or sev-enteen. It was a little boring by then.

"They also used to go to Montparnasse, where all the painters and writers went, and where I hardly went. And they used to go there and hang around at the cafés for hours and hours looking for Hemingway. They didn't seem to realize," he said, "that Hemingway was long gone."

Joe Louis: The King as a Middle-Aged Man

"HI, SWEETHEART!" JOE LOUIS CALLED to his wife, spotting her waiting for him at the Los Angeles airport.

She smiled, walked toward him, and was about to stretch up on her toes and kiss him—but suddenly stopped.

"Joe," she said, "where's your tie?"

"Aw, sweetie," he said, shrugging, "I stayed out all night in New York and didn't have time—"

"All *night!*" she cut in. "When you're out here all you do is sleep, sleep, sleep."

"Sweetie," Joe Louis said, with a tired grin, "I'm an ole man."

"Yes," she agreed, "but when you go to New York, you try to be young again."

They walked slowly through the airport lobby toward their car, being followed by a redcap with Joe's luggage. Mrs. Louis, the third wife of the forty-eight-year-old former fighter, always meets him at the airport when he is returning from a business trip to New York, where he is vice president of a Negro public-relations firm. She is an alert, pleasingly plump woman in her forties who is a very successful trial lawyer in California. She had never known a prizefighter before she met Joe. Previously, she had been married to a fellow lawyer, a Phi Beta Kappa—a man she once described as being "exposed to books, not to life." After her divorce, she vowed she wanted a man "exposed to life, not to books."

She met Joe in 1957 through an introduction from a West Coast lady friend, and, two years later, to the surprise of her courtroom associates in Los Angeles, she married him. "How in the hell did *you* meet Joe Louis?" they kept asking, and she usually replied, "How in the hell did Joe Louis meet me?"

Arriving at the car, Joe Louis tipped the redcap and opened the door for his wife. Then he drove past palm trees and quiet neighborhoods for a few miles, and finally turned into a long driveway that flanks an impressive, ten-room, Spanish-style house that is worth $75,000. Mrs. Louis bought it a few years ago and filled it with Louis XV furniture—and eight television sets. Joe Louis was a television addict, she explained to her friends, adding that he even has a set in his bathroom above the tub; the set is placed at such an angle that Joe, when taking a shower across the room, can peek over the shower curtain and see a reflection of the TV screen through a strategically placed mirror.

"Television and golf," Mrs. Louis said, helping to carry her husband's things into the house, "that's Joe Louis today." She said this unruefully, and, later kissing her husband on the cheek, she suddenly seemed a lot less formal than she had at the airport. After hanging his coat in the closet, she quickly put on a kettle for tea.

"Cookies, honey?" she asked.

"Nah," he said, sitting slope-shouldered at the breakfast table, his eyelids drooping from lack of sleep. Soon she was upstairs, turning down the covers of their gigantic bed, and five minutes later Joe Louis had plunged upon it and was fast asleep. When Mrs. Louis returned to the kitchen, she was smiling.

"In court, I'm a lawyer," she said, "but when I'm home, I'm *all* woman." Her voice was husky, suggestive. "I treat a man *right*, I treat a man like a *king*—if he treats *me* right," she added, pouring herself a glass of milk.

"Each morning I bring Joe breakfast in bed," she said. "Then I turn on Channel 4 so he can watch the *Today* show. Then I go down and get him the *Los Angeles Times*. Then I leave the house for court.

"By 11 A.M.," she continued, "it's time for him to tee off at the Hill-crest Country Club, and, if he plays eighteen holes, he should be fin-ished by three o'clock, and will probably drive over to the Fox Hills Country Club for eighteen more. But if he isn't hitting the ball right, he'll stop after eighteen and go buy a bucket of balls and hit 'em for hours. He don't buy *regular* balls—no, not Joe Louis!—he buys the Se-lect balls, the best, which cost $1.25 a bucket. And he'll hit—if he's real mad—two, three, or four buckets full, $5 worth.

"Some nights he comes home, all excited, and says, 'Well, sweet-heart, I *finally* got it today! After all these years playing golf, I just re-alized what I been doing wrong.'

"But," she said, "a day later he may come home, all mad from throw-ing clubs, and say, 'I'm never gonna play again!' I'll say, 'But, honey, you told me yesterday you *had* it!' He'll say, 'I *had* it, but I didn't *keep* it!'

"The next morning it might be raining, and I'll say, 'Sweetheart, you gonna play golf today? It's raining.' And he'll say, 'It rains on the course, but it don't rain on the players.' And off to the golf course he goes."

Joe Louis's present wife, Martha, is as different from his first two wives as he is from Martha's Phi Beta Kappa husband.

Joe's first wife, Marva, a sleek Chicago steonographer whom he married in 1935 and remarried in 1946, belonged to his lush years, to the years when he blew most of his $5-million boxing fortune on trin-kets, jewels, furs, trips abroad, gambling on the golf course, poor in-vestments, lavish tips, and clothes. In 1939, a year in which he had already purchased twenty suits, thirty-six shirts, and two tuxedos, he also hired tailors to create clothing styles of his own invention, such as two-tone floppy green trousers, suit coats without lapels, and camel's-hair jackets with leather piping. When he was not training or fighting—he won the title by knocking out James J. Braddock in 1937—Joe Louis was doing the town with Marva ("I could make her laugh") or was gambling as much as $1,000 a hole at golf, a game that two sportswriters, Hype Igoe and Walter Stewart, introduced to him in 1936. "One guy built a house in California with the money he took Joe for," an old friend of Louis's said.

Joe's second wife, Rose Morgan, the cosmetics and beauty expert to whom he was married from 1955 to 1958, is a stunning, curvesome woman dedicated to her prosperous business, and she refused to stay up all night with Joe. "I tried to make him settle down," she said. "I told him he couldn't sleep all day and stay out all night anymore. Once he asked me why not, and I told him I'd worry and wouldn't be able to sleep. So he said he'd wait till I fell asleep before going out. Well, I stayed up till 4 A.M.—and then *he* fell asleep." Rose was also disenchanted with him in 1956 when, in an effort to make some money toward the $1 million he owed the government in back taxes, he began touring as a wrestler. "To me, Joe Louis was like the president of the United States," Rose said. "How would you like to see the president of the United States washing dishes? That's how I felt about Joe wrestling."

Joe's third wife, while having none of the obvious sex appeal of his first two, has succeeded where they had failed because she is wiser than they, and because Joe was ripe for taming when he fell in love with Martha. She seems to be many things to him: a combination lawyer, cook, mistress, press agent, tax consultant, valet de chambre, and everything but caddie. And she was obviously pleased recently when her friend, the singer Mahalia Jackson, noticed the closets bulging with Joe's belongings and remarked, "Well, Martha, I guess he's finally ready to settle down; this is the first time in his life he's got all his clothes under one roof."

It does not seem to matter to Martha that she got Joe Louis in his declining years—at a time when he weighs 240 pounds, is going bald, is somewhat less than prosperous, and no longer possesses the quick reflexes either to hit or pick up checks. "There's a soul about this man, and a quietness that I love," she said, adding that her love has been returned. Joe even goes to church with her on Sundays, she said, and often appears in court to watch her handle cases. Though he neither smokes nor drinks, Joe still goes to nightclubs occasionally to hear some of the many musicians and singers he lists among his friends, she says, and she is aware of the number of women who still find Joe Louis sexually appealing and would consider a night with him time well spent. "If those sort of women like living on the side streets of a man's life," Martha said, "I wish them well. But I am his wife, and when I come on the scene they got to get the hell out."

Martha is aware, too, that Joe Louis still is friendly with his former wives—who, after getting divorced from him, went to polar extremes in choosing their future husbands. Marva, after leaving Joe, married a doctor in Chicago. Rose followed her divorce from Joe with a marriage to a lawyer. When Joe is in Chicago, he often calls Marva (the mother of his two children) and sometimes goes over for dinner. When in New York, he does the same thing with Rose. "Joe Louis never really cuts off a woman," Martha observed, more amused than piqued. "He just adds another to his list." Actually, Joe has been responsible for his three wives getting acquainted with each other, and he is delighted that they get along. He introduced his first wife to his present wife at the Patterson-Johansson title fight in New York, and on another occasion he arranged to have his present wife's hair done by his second wife—free.

Joe Louis had told me all about this earlier in the day on the plane during our flight to Los Angeles from New York (where I had spent some time following him around Manhattan and watching him function as a public-relations executive). "I called Rose on the phone," Joe had said, "and told her, 'Now Rose Morgan, don't you charge my wife,' She said, 'No, Joe, I won't.' That Rose Morgan is a wonderful woman," Joe mused, shaking his head.

"You know, I been married to three of the finest women in the world. My only mistake in life was getting divorced."

"Why did you then?" I asked.

"Oh," he said, "in those days I wanted to be free, and sometimes I just wanted to be alone. I was crazy. I'd go out of the house and stay weeks without coming home. Or maybe I'd stay home in bed for days watching television."

Just as he blames himself for the failure of his first two marriages, so does he accept the blame for all of his other difficulties, such as his inability to hold on to his money, and his negligence in paying taxes. During his last visit to New York, some old boxing friends were saying, "Joe, if only you were fighting today, you'd be making twice what you did in the old days, with the money fighters now get from closed-circuit TV and all." But Joe Louis shook his head and said, "I ain't sorry I fought when I did. In my time, I made $5 million, wound up broke, and owe the government $1 million in taxes. If I was fighting today, I'd earn $10 million, would still wind up broke, and would owe the government $2 million in taxes."

Such remarks, simple yet mixed with an almost absurd sense of humor, were delivered often by Joe Louis during the hours I followed him in New York—much to my surprise.

Rightly or wrongly, I had imagined that this middle-aged hero would merely be a flabby version of the rather dim-witted champion that Don Dunphy used to interview over the radio after the knockout of another Great White Hope—and I had assumed that Joe Louis, at forty-eight, would still hold his title as perhaps the most quiet athlete since Dummy Taylor, the Giant pitcher, who was a mute.

Of course, I was aware of those few, famous Joe Louis remarks—like the one about Billy Conn: "Maybe he kin run, but he can't hide"; and Pvt. Joe Louis's answer in World War II when somebody asked how he felt about fighting for nothing: "I ain't fighting for nothing, I'm fighting for my country." But I had read, too, that Joe Louis was incredibly naïve—so naïve that in 1960 he agreed to do public-relations work for Fidel Castro. I had also seen recent news photos of Joe posing outside courtrooms with Hulan E. Jack, the ex—Manhattan borough president who tried to conceal gratuities concerning the remodeling of his apartment. And once Senator John L. McClellan hinted that Louis had received $2,500 for sitting for two hours at the bribery trial of James R. Hoffa; although there were denials all around, the undeniable image of Joe Louis then was that while he was a "credit to his race—the human race," he was now probably a debt to everybody else.

And so it was with some unexpected elation that I found Joe Louis to be an astute businessman in New York, a shrewd bargainer, and a man with a sense of humor often quite subtle. For instance, as we were boarding the plane at Idlewild Airport for Los Angeles and I had to exchange my tourist-class ticket for first class so I could sit next to Joe, I casually asked him how the airlines could justify the forty-five dollar difference in price. "First-class seats are up in front of the plane," Louis said, "and they get you to L.A. faster."

The day before, I had seen Joe Louis argue some extra money out of New York television executives who are doing a television show on his life.

"Hey," Joe said, carefully reading every word of the contract before signing it, "this says you'll pay my plane ticket from L.A. to New York and back, and my hotel bill, but what about my living expenses when I'm here?"

"But, Mr. Louis," one executive said, nervously, "we never discussed that."

"Who's gonna pay? How ma gonna eat?" Louis asked, his voice rising with irritation.

"But, but . . ."

Louis stood up, put the pen down, and would not have signed at all had not the president of the television company finally said, "Okay, Joe, I'm sure something can be worked out."

Assured that it would, Louis then signed, shook hands with every-one, and left the office.

"Well," he said, on the sidewalk, "I won that round."

Then he added, "I know what I'm worth, and I don't want less." He said the movie producers of *Requiem for a Heavyweight* wanted him to appear as a referee but only offered him a fee of $500 plus $50-a-day living expenses. Though the whole part would have kept Louis on the screen only forty-five seconds, Louis said it was worth a fee of $1,000. The producers said that was too much. But a few days later, Louis said, they called him back. He got his $1,000.

Though his tax difficulties have eradicated all his assets—including two trust funds he had set up for his children—Joe Louis is still a man of great pride. He refused the money that hundreds of citizens sent him to help with his government debt, although he still owes the government thousands and could have used the cash. Last year Joe Louis earned less than $10,000, most of it from refereeing wrestling matches (he earns between $750 and $1,000 a night), and from en-dorsements or appearances. The last big money he made was the $100,000-a-year guarantee he got in 1956 for wrestling. He won all his matches—except those in which he was disqualified for using his fists—but his career ended not long afterward when the 300-pound cowboy Rocky Lee accidentally stepped on Louis's chest one night, cracked one of his ribs, and damaged some of his heart muscles.

Today Joe Louis is a matchmaker with a group of California boxing promoters he formed (United World Boxing Enterprises), and still has his name used by a Chicago milk company; but the only financial in-terests he has are with the Manhattan public-relations firm of Louis-Rowe Enterprises, Inc., a swinging outfit on West Fifty-seventh Street that handles Louis Armstrong and the new singer Dean Barlow, among other Negro entertainers, and would have had a profitable thing going in Cuba had there not been such an uproar over Joe Louis representing Castro and saying, as he did in 1960, "There is no place in the world except Cuba where the Negro can go in the wintertime with absolutely no discrimination."

Without being a racist, Joe Louis today is very much concerned with the Negro's fight for equality and, possibly for the first time in his life, is quite outspoken on the subject. Frankly, Joe Louis saw nothing wrong in endorsing Cuba in 1960 as a vacationland for American Negroes and is also quick to point out that he canceled his firm's $287,000-a-year contract with Cuba's National Institute of Tourism *before* the United States severed diplomatic relations with the Castro regime. Even now, Louis feels Castro is far, far better for the Cuban people than the United Fruit Company.

When Joe Louis reads newspapers, I noticed that it was not the sports page that got his first attention but rather such stories as the announcement that Lieut. Commander Samuel Gravely, Jr., had become the first Negro in U.S. naval history to command a warship. "Things are getting better," Louis said. I noticed, too, that one afternoon, as he was switching the television dial in search of a golf match, he happened upon a panel show on which a delegate from Ghana was speaking; Louis listened until the African finished before switching to the golf tournament.

While the second Max Schmeling fight was billed by American newspapers as a grudge match in which Louis sought revenge against the "Super Race" that regarded Negroes as an inferior breed, Joe Louis said this was strictly a publicity stunt to build up the gate. Louis said he never really felt hostility toward Schmeling, although he did not like one of Schmeling's friends who strode about the fight camp wearing a Nazi armband. Louis said that he is far more bitter toward Eastern Air Lines than he ever was at the Schmeling camp, having never forgiven Eastern for refusing him limousine service in 1946 from a New Orleans hotel to the airport after Louis had fought an exhibition. Louis, who would have missed his plane had he not gotten there on his own, wrote a letter of protest to Eastern's Eddie Rickenbacker. "He never answered," Louis said.

As a result, Louis said he has never flown Eastern since, even when it would have been much more convenient; he also said he has told many of his friends to avoid the airline and believes this has cost Eastern considerable revenue in the past sixteen years.

It is one of the aims of Joe Louis, and his public-relations partner, Billy Rowe, to convince big business executives that the Negro market, if discouraged or ignored, can be hazardous to sales figures; but if properly encouraged, it can be very profitable. The Louis-Rowe agency claims that each year American Negroes pour $22 billion into big business, spend more than 18 percent of America's travel dollar, and that Negroes in Harlem alone spend $200,000 a day gambling on sports events and the numbers game.

Negroes would spend much more, Louis and Rowe argue, if big business would increase its advertising budget for the Negro market and would make its advertising campaigns more specialized—i.e., would show more Negro models in Negro newspapers selling certain brands of soap, beer, and so forth. This is the message that Rowe delivers when he, accompanied by Louis, visits Madison Avenue ad agencies, insurance companies, stockbrokerages, and racetracks; Rowe, a fast-talking, endlessly articulate man who dresses like a Broadway dude and resembles Nat King Cole (but is handsomer), dominates most conversations, although Louis gets in a good line now and then.

Billy Rowe, who is forty-seven and was once a deputy police commissioner in New York—he still carries a pistol everywhere he goes—occupies a larger, fancier office than Joe at their agency. While Joe has only one of his plaques hanging on the wall—the "State of Michigan

Hall of Fame" plaque—Billy Rowe has covered a wall with eighteen of *his* plaques and scrolls, including commendations for youth work from the Minisink Men's Guidance Council, letters from the governor, and two gold trophies that do not even belong to him. Modesty is not his primary virtue.

Mr. Rowe, who lives in a fourteen-room house (with four television sets) in the suburbs of New Rochelle, arrives at the office a full hour ahead of Louis and has the day's—and some of the week's—appointments all lined up by the time Louis strolls in, usually around 11 A.M., with a big wink for the girl at the switchboard.

"Hey, Dad," Rowe greets Louis, "we got an appointment with the mayor on the thirteenth. We'd had it before, but he's fighting with the governor."

Louis nodded, then yawned, then suddenly became wide-eyed when he noticed walking toward him a voluptuous Harlem nightclub singer named Ann Weldon. Without saying a word, Miss Weldon swished right up to Louis and wiggled close to him.

"You get any closer," Louis said, "I gonna have to marry you."

She swooned and slithered away.

"Hey, Dad," Rowe said, "you gonna eat lunch at Lindy's?"

"Yeah."

"Who's picking up the check?"

"Yonkers Raceway."

"In that case," Rowe said, "I'll join you."

An hour later, headed for Lindy's, Rowe and Louis left the office and jammed into the crowded elevator, where nearly everyone grinned or winced as they recognized Joe Louis.

"Hi, champ," they said. "Hello, Joe."

"Sure wouldn't want to start a fight in this car," the elevator man said.

"No," Joe said, "not enough room for me to run."

"Joe," a man said, shaking Louis's hand, "you sure look in good shape."

"Only in shape for a steak," Louis said.

"Joe," another man said, "seems like only yesterday I seen you fight Billy Conn. Time sure flies."

"Yeah," said Louis. "It do, don't it?"

And on and on it went, as Louis walked down Broadway: cabdrivers waved at him, bus drivers honked at him, and dozens of men stopped him and recalled how they had once traveled 130 miles to get to one of his fights, and how they'd put their heads down to light a cigarette in the first round, then before they could look up, Louis had flattened his opponent and they had missed everything: or how they'd had guests at the house that night to hear the fight, and while they were struggling in the kitchen to get the ice out, somebody came in from the living room and said, "It's all over! Louis knocked 'im out with the first punch."

It was astonishing, most of all to Louis, that they had remembered him so—especially since he has not had a fight since his unwise comeback in 1951, when Rocky Marciano knocked him out. Two years before that Louis had retired undefeated, having defended his title twenty-five times, more than any other champion.

In Lindy's, the waiters, fussing over Louis, led him and Rowe to a table occupied by an official from Yonkers Raceway. Before the lunch was half over, Louis was making a pitch for the track's account, saying that a good public-relations campaign by Louis-Rowe would get more Negroes to the track than ever before. The official said he would present their proposal to the board of directors and would let Louis and Rowe know the result.

"Joe, we better get moving," Rowe said, looking at his watch. "We gotta see Joe Glaser. That Glaser's got so much money that the bank charges him storage." Rowe laughed at his joke and said, "Joe, tell that to Glaser when you see him."

Five minutes later, Louis and Rowe were escorted by Glaser's assistants into the new, plush quarters of Mr. Glaser, the talent-booking man, who pounded Joe on the back and said, loud enough for his assistants in the other offices to hear, "Joe Louis is one of the finest men in the world!"

And Billy Rowe said, because he could not resist, "Joe Glaser's got so much money that the bank charges him storage."

Everybody laughed, except Joe Louis, who glanced sideways at Rowe.

After leaving Glaser's, Louis and Rowe had appointments at the Investors Planning Corporation of America, where they submitted proposals for selling more mutual funds to Negroes; then visited the Cobleigh and Gordon, Inc. agency, where they discussed a Negro newsletter that Rowe and Louis wish to produce; then dropped into Toots Shor's; and finally went to dinner at La Fonda del Sol, where Rowe had arranged for a couple of Harlem nightclub starlets to join them.

"Oh, Joe," one of the girls said, as a Spanish guitar strummed behind her, "when you used to fight, I was a young girl, and in our house we all gathered around the radio—and I wasn't allowed to talk."

Joe winked.

"Joe," another said, "while I'm sitting so close, how's about autographing this menu—for my son."

Louis grinned and playfully pulled from a pocket his hotel key, dangled it, then slid it across the table at her.

"You don't want to let your son down, do you?" he asked.

Everybody laughed, but she did not know whether or not Joe was kidding.

"If I do," she said primly, "I'm sure he'll understand—when he gets older." She slid the key back. Joe howled and signed the menu.

After dinner, Louis and the rest planned to go nightclubbing in Harlem, but I had an appointment to see Louis's second wife, Rose Morgan. Rose now lives in the large, magnificent uptown apartment that overlooks the Polo Grounds and once was occupied by Joe and his first wife, Marva.

Opening the door, Rose Morgan was chic, impeccably groomed, almost exotic in a Japanese loll suit. She led the way across a sprawling, thick rug to a boomerang-shaped white sofa; there, sitting cross-legged and arms akimbo, she said, "Oh, I don't know what it was about Joe. He just got under your skin."

But being married to Joe was not as exciting as being courted by Joe, Rose observed, shaking her head. "When I'd come home from work, 6:30 or 7 P.M., Joe'd be there watching television and eating apples. But," she continued, after a pause, "we're now very good friends. In fact, I just wrote him a letter the other day telling him I found some things of his around and want to know if he wants them."

"Like what?"

"I have the robe he wore when he started boxing," she said, "and his road shoes, and also a film of the first Billy Conn fight. Would you like to watch it?"

Just then, Rose's husband, the lawyer, walked in, followed by some friends from Philadelphia. Rose's husband is a short, portly, manicured man who, after introducing everyone, suggested a round of drinks.

"I'm just showing Joe's fight film," Rose said.

"Hate to put you through all the trouble," I told her.

"Oh, it's *no* trouble," Rose said. "I haven't seen it in years, and I'd love to see it again."

"Is it all right with you if we watch it?" I asked Rose's husband.

"Yes, yes, it's all right with me," he said, quietly. It was obvious that he was just being polite and would rather not have to sit through it; yet there was no way of stopping Rose, for she quickly had the projector out of the closet and soon the lights were off and the fight was on.

"Joe Louis was definitely the greatest of all time," one of the men from Philadelphia said, clinking the ice in his glass. "There was a time when nothing was more important to colored people than God and Joe Louis."

The menacing, solemn image of Joe Louis, then twenty years younger than he is today, moved across the screen toward Conn; when he clouted Conn, Billy's bones seemed to shake.

"Joe didn't waste no punches," somebody said from the sofa.

Rose seemed excited at seeing Joe at his top form, and every time a Louis punch would jolt Conn, she'd go, "Mummmm" (sock). "Mummmm" (sock). "Mummmm."

Billy Conn was impressive through the middle rounds, but as the screen flashed Round 13, somebody said, "Here's where Conn's gonna make his mistake; he's gonna try to slug it out with Joe Louis." Rose's husband remained silent, sipping his Scotch.

When the Louis combinations began to land, Rose went, "Mummmm, mummmm," and then the pale body of Conn began to collapse against the canvas.

Billy Conn slowly began to rise. The referee counted over him. Conn had one leg up, then two, then was standing—but the referee forced him back. It was too late.

But Rose's husband in the back of the room disagreed.

"I thought Conn got up in time," he said, "but that referee wouldn't let him go on."

Rose Morgan said nothing—just swallowed the rest of her drink.

Mr. Bad News

Let's talk of graves, of worms and epitaphs,
Make dust our paper and with rainy eyes
Write sorrow on the bosom of the earth.
Let's choose executors and talk of wills.
　　　　　　　—Shakespeare, *Richard II*

WINSTON CHURCHILL GAVE YOU YOUR heart attack," the wife of the obituary writer said, but the obituary writer, a short and rather shy man wearing horn-rimmed glasses and smoking a pipe, shook his head and replied, very softly, "No, it was not Winston Churchill."

"Then T. S. Eliot gave you your heart attack," she quickly added, lightly, for they were at a small dinner party in New York and the others seemed amused.

"No," the obituary writer said, again softly, "it was not T. S. Eliot."

If he was at all irritated by his wife's line of questioning, her assertion that writing lengthy obituaries for the *New York Times* under deadline pressure might be speeding him to his own grave, he did not show it, did not raise his voice; but then he rarely does. Only once has Alden Whitman raised his voice at Joan, his present wife, a youthful brunette, and on that occasion he *screamed*. Alden Whitman does not recall precisely why he screamed. Vaguely he remembers accusing Joan of misplacing something around the house, but he suspects that in the end *he* was the guilty one. Though this incident occurred more than two years ago, lasting only a few seconds, the memory of it still haunts him—a rare occasion when he truly lost control; but since then he has remained a quiet man, a predictable man who early each morning, while Joan is asleep, slips out of bed and begins to make breakfast: a pot of coffee for her, one of tea for himself. Then he sits for an hour or so in his study smoking a pipe, sipping his tea, scanning the newspapers, his eyebrows raising slightly whenever he reads that a dictator is missing, a statesman is ill.

By midmorning he will dress in one of the two or three suits he owns and, looking briefly into a mirror, will tighten his bow tie. He is not a handsome man. He has a plain, somewhat round face that is almost always serious, if not dour, and it is topped by a full head of brown hair which, though he is fifty-two, is without a trace of gray. Behind his horn-rimmed glasses are small, very small, blue eyes that he douses with drops of pilocarpine every three hours for his case of controlled glaucoma, and he has a thick, reddish mustache beneath which protrudes, most of the day, a pipe held tightly between a full bridge of false teeth.

His real teeth, all thirty-two of them, were knocked out or loosened by three strong-arm men in an alley one night in 1936 in Alden Whitman's hometown, Bridgeport, Connecticut. He was twenty-three years old then, a year out of Harvard and full of verve, and his assailants apparently opposed opinions supported by Whitman. He bears no ill will toward those who attacked him, conceding they had their point of view, nor is he at all sentimental about his missing teeth. They were full of cavities, he says, a blessing to be rid of them.

After he is finished dressing, Whitman says good-bye to his wife, but not for long. She too works for the *Times*, and it was there, one spring day in 1958, that he spotted her walking through the large, noisy City Room on the third floor dressed in paisley and carrying an inky page proof down from the women's department on the ninth floor, where she works. After learning her name, he proceeded to

send anonymous notes in brown envelopes up to her through the
house mail, the first of which read, "You look ravishing in paisley,"
and was signed, "The American Paisley Association." Later he identified himself, and they dined on the night of May 13 at the Teheran
Restaurant, on West Forty-fourth Street, and talked until the maître d'
asked them to leave.

Joan was fascinated by Whitman, especially by his marvelous,
magpie mind cluttered with all sorts of useless information: He could
recite the list of popes backward and forward; knew the names of
every king's mistress and his date of reign; knew that the Treaty of
Westphalia was signed in 1648, that Niagara Falls is 167 feet high,
that snakes do not blink; that cats attach themselves to places, not
people, and dogs to people, not places; he was a regular subscriber to
the *New Statesman, Le Nouvel Observateur,* to nearly every journal in
the Out-of-Town Newsstand in Times Square, he read two books a
day, he had seen Bogart in *Casablanca* three-dozen times. Joan knew
she had to see *him* again, even though she was sixteen years his junior and a minister's daughter, and he was an atheist. They were married on November 13, 1960.

After Whitman leaves his apartment, which is on the twelfth floor
of an old brick building on West 116th Street, he walks slowly uphill
toward the subway kiosk on Broadway. At this time of morning the
sidewalk is rushing with youth—pretty Columbia co-eds in tight skirts
clasping books to their breasts and walking quickly to class, young
long-haired men distributing leaflets attacking American policies in
Vietnam and Cuba—and yet this neighborhood near the Hudson River
is also solemn with reminders of mortality: Grant's Tomb, the grave of
St. Claire Pollock, the memorial statues to Louis Kossuth and Governor Tilden and Joan of Arc; the churches, the hospitals, the Fireman's
Monument, the sign on the upper Broadway office building "The
Wages of Sin is Death," the old-ladies' home, the two aging men who

live near Whitman—a recently retired *Times* obituary writer and the *Times* obituary writer who retired before *him.*

Death is on Whitman's mind as he sits in the subway that now races downtown toward Times Square. In the morning paper he has read that Henry Wallace is not well, that Billy Graham has visited the Mayo Clinic. Whitman plans, when he arrives at the *Times* in ten minutes, to go directly to the newspaper's morgue, the room where all news clippings and advance obituaries are filed, and examine the "conditions" of the advance obituaries on Reverend Graham and former vice president Wallace (Wallace died a few months later). There are 2,000 advance obituaries in the *Times*'s morgue, Whitman knows, but many of them, such as the ones on J. Edgar Hoover and Charles Lindbergh and Walter Winchell, were written long ago and now require updating. Recently, when President Johnson was in the hospital for gallbladder surgery, his advance obituary was brought up-to-the-minute; so was Pope Paul's before his trip to New York; so was Joseph P. Kennedy's. For an obituary writer there is nothing worse than to have a world figure die before his obituary is up-to-date; it can be a harrowing experience, Whitman knows, requiring that the writer become an instant historian, assessing in a few hours the dead man's life with lucidity, accuracy, and objectivity.

When Adlai Stevenson died suddenly in London in 1965, Whitman, who was just beginning his new assignment as the *Times*'s mortician and was anxious to make good, learned of it through a telephone call from Joan. Whitman broke into a cool sweat, slipped out of the City Room, went to lunch. He took the elevator up to the cafeteria on the eleventh floor. But soon he felt a soft tap on his shoulder. It was one of the metropolitan editor's assistants asking, "Will you be down soon, Alden?"

Whitman, his lunch finished, returned downstairs and was given a basket full of folders containing data on Adlai Stevenson. Then, carrying them to the back of the room, he opened them and spread them out on a table in the thirteenth row of the City Room, reading, digesting, making notes, his pipe tip tapping against his false teeth, *cluck-cluck.*

Finally, he turned, facing his typewriter. Soon, paragraph by paragraph, the words began to flow: "Adlai Stevenson was a rarity in American public life, a cultivated, urbane, witty, articulate politician whose popularity was untarnished by defeat and whose stature grew in diplomacy. . . ." It ran 4,500 words and would have gone longer had there been time.

Difficult as it was, it was not nearly so demanding as a 3,000-word deadline assignment he was given on Martin Buber, the Jewish philosopher, about whom he knew virtually nothing. Fortunately, Whitman was able to reach by telephone a scholar who was very familiar with Buber's teachings and life, and this, together with the clippings in the *Times*'s morgue, enabled Whitman to complete the job. But he was far from pleased with it, and that night Joan was constantly aware of the sound of his pacing up and down the floor of their apartment, drink in hand, and the words uttered in contempt and self-derision, "fraud . . . superficial . . . fraud." Whitman went to work the following day expecting to be criticized. But instead he was informed that there had been several congratulatory telephone messages from intellectuals around New York, and Whitman's reaction, far from relief, was to immediately suspect all those who had praised him.

The obituaries that leave Whitman untroubled are those that he is able to complete before the individual dies, such as the rather controversial one he did on Albert Schweitzer, which both paid tribute to "Le Grand Docteur" for his humanitarianism yet damned him for his lofty paternalism; and the one on Winston Churchill, a 20,000-word piece in which Whitman and several other *Times* men were involved and which was finished almost two weeks before Sir Winston's death.

Whitman's obituaries on Father Divine, Le Corbusier, and T. S. Eliot *were* produced under deadline pressure but caused him no panic because he was quite familiar with the work and lives of all three, particularly Eliot, who had been the poet-in-residence at Harvard during Whitman's student days there. His obituary on Eliot began: *"This is the way the world ends / This is the way the world ends / This is the way the world ends / Not with a bang but a whimper,"* and it went on to describe Eliot as a most unlikely poetic figure, lacking "flamboyance or oddity in dress or manner, and there was nothing of the romantic about him. He carried no auras, cast no arresting eye and wore his heart, as nearly as could be observed, in its proper anatomical place."

It was while writing the Eliot obituary that a copyboy had dropped onto Whitman's desk a number of statements praising the poet's work, and one of these came from a fellow poet, Louis Untermeyer. When Whitman read Untermeyer's statement, he raised an eyebrow in disbelief. He had thought Louis Untermeyer was dead.

This is part of an occupational astigmatism that afflicts many obituary writers. After they have written or read an advance obituary about someone, they come to think of that person as being dead in advance. Alden Whitman has discovered, since moving from his copyreader's job to his present one, that in his brain have become embalmed several people who are *alive*, or were at last look, but whom he is constantly referring to in the *past* tense. He thinks, for example, of John L. Lewis as being dead and also E. M. Forster and Floyd Dell, Rudolf Hess and Rhode Island's former senator Green, Ruth Etting and Gertrude Ederle, among many others.

Furthermore, he admits that, after having written a fine advance obituary, his pride of authorship is such that he can barely wait for that person to drop dead so that he may see his masterpiece in print. While this revelation may mark him as something less than romantic, it must be said in his defense that he thinks no differently than most obituary writers; they are, even by City Room standards, rather special.

A former obituary writer for the *New York World-Telegram and Sun*, Edward Ellis, who is also the author of a book about suicides, admits that he enjoys seeing, from time to time, his old advance obituaries fulfilling their destiny in the *Telegram*.

At the Associated Press, Mr. Dow Henry Fonda announces with satisfaction that he is all set with up-to-date obituaries on Teddy Kennedy, Mrs. John F. Kennedy, John O'Hara, Grayson Kirk, Lammot du Pont Copeland, Charles Munch, Walter Hallstein, Jean Monnet, Frank Costello, and Kelso. The United Press International, which has a dozen four-drawer filing cabinets of "preparation stories"—including one on five-year-old John F. Kennedy, Jr., and the children of Queen Elizabeth—does not have any full-time death specialist but passes the corpse copy around, some of the best of it going to a veteran reporter named Doc Quigg about whom it has been said, with pride, that he can "smooth 'em out, make 'em sing."

An obituarian's traditional eagerness about breaking into print is not exclusively based on author's pride, according to one antique in the trade, but it is also a holdover perhaps from the days when editors did not pay their obituary writers, whom they often hired on a free-lance basis, until the subject of the obit had died—or, as they sometimes phrased it in those days, "passed away," "departed from this Earth," "gone to his reward." Occasionally, while waiting, those in the City Room would form a so-called ghoul pool in which everybody would put up $5 or $10 and try to select from the list of advance obituaries the name of the person who would go first. Karl Schriftgiesser, the *Times*'s gravedigger about twenty-five years ago, recalls that some ghoul-pool winners in those days collected as much as $300.

There are no such pools in evidence around the *Times* today, but Whitman, for quite different reasons, does keep in his desk a kind of list of the living to whom he is giving *priority*. These individuals are included because he thinks their days are numbered, or because he believes their life's work is finished and sees no reason to delay the inevitable writing task, or because he merely finds the individual "interesting" and wishes to write the obituary in advance for his own enjoyment.

Whitman also has what he calls a "deferred list," which is composed of aging but durable world leaders, *monstres sacrés*, who are still in power or still making news in other ways, and to attempt a "final" obituary on such individuals not only would be difficult but would require continuous alterations or insertions in the future; so even if these "deferred" people may have out-of-date obituaries in the *Times* morgue—people like de Gaulle, Franco—Whitman still chooses to let them wait awhile for a final polishing. Whitman realizes of course that any or all of these "deferred" customers may suddenly tap out, but he also has candidates that he thinks will die sooner or remain out of the news longer, and so he continues to give priority to those *not* on his deferred list, and should he be wrong—well, he has been wrong before.

There are, naturally, some people that Whitman may *think* will soon die, and for whom he has already tucked away a final tribute in the *Times*'s morgue, that may *not* die for years and years; they may diminish in importance or influence in the world, perhaps, but they keep right on living. If this be the case—if the name dies before the man, as A. B. Housman would put it—then Whitman reserves the right to cut the obituary down. Vivisection. He is a precise, unemotional man. While death obsessed Hemingway and diminished John Donne, it provides Alden Whitman with a five-day-a-week job that he likes very much and he would possibly die sooner if they took the job away and put him back on the copydesk where he could no longer write about it.

And so each weekday morning, after riding the subway down to Times Square from his apartment on upper Broadway, Whitman an-

ticipates another day at the *Times*, another session with men who are
dead, men who are dying, or men who, if Whitman's guess is correct,
will soon die. He arrives in the lobby of the Times Building usually at
eleven, his soft rubber-soled shoes hardly making a sound against the
glossy marble floor. In his mouth is his pipe, and in his left hand is a
container of tea that he bought a moment ago across the street at a
small lunch counter run by a large Greek whose face he has known for
years, never his name. Whitman then elevates to the third floor, says
good morning to the receptionist, swings into the City Room, says
good morning to all the other reporters who sit behind their desks,
rows and rows of desks, and they greet him in turn, they know him
well, they are happy it is *he*, not they, who must write for the obituary
page—a page that is read very carefully, they know, maybe *too* carefully
by readers with a morbid curiosity, readers searching for clues to life,
readers searching for vacant apartments.

Occasionally all reporters must do their share of the smaller obituaries, which are bad enough, but the long ones are hard work; they must
be accurate and interesting, they must be infallible in their analysis,
and will be later judged, as will the *Times*, by historians. And yet for the
writer there is no glory, no byline, it being a policy of the newspaper to
eliminate bylines from such stories, but Whitman does not care.
Anonymity superbly suits him. He prefers being everyman, anyman,
nobody—*Times* Employee No. 97353, Library Card No. 663 7662, the
possessor of a Sam Goody Courtesy Card, the borrower of his mother-
in-law's 1963 Buick Compact on sunny weekends, an eminently un-
quotable man, a onetime manager for the Roger Ludlowe High School
football, baseball, and basketball teams who is now keeping toll for the
Times. All day long while his colleagues are running this way and that,
pursuing the here and now, Whitman sits quietly at his desk near the
back, sipping his tea, dwelling in his strange little world of the half-
living, the half-dead in this enormous place called the City Room.

It is a room as large as a football field, maybe twice as large, and it is lined with rows and rows of gray metal desks, all the same shade, each with a telephone held by reporters who are talking to their news sources about the latest rumors, tips, reports, allegations, threats, robberies, rapes, accidents, crises, problems, problems—it is a Problem Room, and from all over the world via cable, telex, telegram, ticker, or telephone the news reports on world problems are rocketed into this *one* room, hour after hour: disaster in the Danube, turmoil in Tanzania, peril in Pakistan, touchy Trieste, rumors in Rio, the Saigon scene, coups d'état, informed sources said, reliable sources said, African problems, Jewish problems, NATO, SEATO, Sukarno, Sihanouk—and Whitman sits, sipping tea, in the back of this room paying little attention to all this; he is concerned with the *final* fact.

He is thinking of the words he will use when these men, these problem makers, finally die. He is leaning forward behind his typewriter now, shoulders forward, thinking of the words that will, bit by bit, build the advance obituaries of Mao Tse-tung, of Harry S Truman, of Picasso. He is also contemplating Garbo and Marlene Dietrich, Steichen and Haile Selassie. On one piece of paper, from a previous hour's work, Whitman has typed: ". . . Mao Tse-tung, the son of an obscure rice farmer, died one of the world's most powerful rulers. . . ." On another piece of paper: ". . . At 7:09 P.M., April 12, 1945, a man few people had ever heard of became president of the United States. . . ." On still another piece: ". . . there was Picasso the painter, Picasso the faithful and faithless lover, Picasso the generous man, even Picasso the playwright. . . ." And, from an earlier day's notes: ". . . As an actress, Mrs. Rudolph Sieber was nondescript, her legs were by no means as beautiful as Mistinguett's, but Mrs. Sieber as Marlene Dietrich was for years an international symbol of sex and glamour. . . ."

Whitman is not satisfied with what he has written, but he goes over the words and phrases with care, and then he pauses and thinks aloud, *Ah, what a wonderful collection of photographs will appear on the* *Time's obituary page when the great Steichen dies.* Then Whitman reminds himself that he must not forget to purchase the issue of the *Saturday Review* with its fine cover story on the white-haired British communications tycoon Baron Roy Thomson, now seventy years old. This story may soon come in handy. Another man of interest, Whitman says, is the noted humorist Frank Sullivan, who lives in Saratoga Springs, New York. A few days ago Whitman telephoned one of Mr. Sullivan's close friends, the playwright Marc Connelly, and almost began with, "You *knew* Mr. Sullivan, didn't you?" But he caught himself and said, instead, that the *Times* was "bringing its files up-to-date"—yes, that is the phrase—on Frank Sullivan and could a lunch be arranged with Mr. Connelly so that Mr. Whitman could learn something of Mr. Sullivan? A lunch was arranged. Next Whitman hopes to go up to Saratoga Springs and discuss the life of Marc Connelly over lunch with Mr. Sullivan.

When Whitman goes to concerts, as he so often does, he cannot resist looking around the hall and observing the distinguished members in the audience about whom he might be particularly curious someday soon. Recently, at Carnegie Hall, he noticed that one of the spectators seated up ahead was Arthur Rubinstein. Quickly, Whitman lifted his opera glasses and brought Mr. Rubinstein's face into sharp focus, noticing the expression around the eyes, the mouth, the soft gray hair, and noticing, too, when Rubinstein stood up at intermission, how surprisingly short he was.

Whitman made notes on such details, knowing that someday they would help bring life to his work, knowing that masterful obituaries, like fine funerals, must be planned well in advance. Churchill himself had arranged his own funeral; and the relatives of Bernard Baruch, before he died, visited the Frank E. Campbell Funeral Chapel to arrange the details; and now Baruch's son, though in apparent good health, has done the same thing—as has a little charwoman who recently purchased a mausoleum for more than $6,000 and had her name put on it, and now every month or so she travels up to the cemetery in Westchester County to get a look at it.

"Death never takes a wise man by surprise," wrote La Fontaine, and Whitman agrees and keeps his "files up-to-date," although he never permits any man to read his own obituary; as the late Elmer Davis said, "A man who has read his own obituary will never be quite the same again."

Several years ago, after a *Times* editor had recovered from a heart attack and returned to the office, the reporter who had done the editor's obituary showed it to him so that any errors or omissions might be corrected. The editor read it. That evening he had another heart attack. Ernest Hemingway, on the other hand, thoroughly enjoyed reading the newspaper accounts of his death during a plane crash in Africa. He had the newspaper clippings pasted up in a thick scrapbook and claimed to begin each day with "a regular morning ritual of a glass of cold champagne and a couple of pages of obituaries." Elmer Davis had twice been erroneously reported as having died in catastrophes, and while he conceded that "to turn up alive after you have been reported dead is an unwarrantable imposition on your friends," he nonetheless denied the rumor and was "more generally believed than is usually the case when people have to contradict something that the papers have said about them."

Some newspapermen, possibly not trusting their colleagues, have written their own advance obituaries and inconspicuously slipped them into the morgue to await the proper moment. One of these advance obituaries, written by a *New York Daily News* reporter named Lowell Limpus, appeared under his own by-line in that newspaper in 1957 and began: "This is the last of the 8,700 or more stories I've written to appear in the *News*. It must be the final one because I died yes-

terday. . . . I wrote this, my own obituary, because I know more about
the subject than anybody else and I'd rather have it honest than flow-
ery. . . ."

While the obituary page might have once been sodden with senti-
mentality, it is rarely so today except in that italicized column of death
notices that usually appears on the right-hand side of the page above
the flowered ads of the undertakers. The relatives of the deceased pay
to have these notices published, and in them every dead man is invariably described as a "loving" father, a "beloved" husband, a "dear"
brother, an "adored" grandfather, or a "revered" uncle. All the names
of the dead are listed in alphabetical order and set in capital letters
and bold type so that the casual reader may scan them quickly, like the
baseball scores, and it is the rare reader that ponders over them. One
such rarity is a seventy-three-year-old gentleman named Simon de
Vaulchier.

Mr. de Vaulchier, a retired research librarian, was for a brief period a kind of professional reader of the obituary pages of New York's
metropolitan dailies. And he compiled for the Jesuit magazine *America* the research for a study in which it was observed, among other
things, that most of the dead in the *New York Post* were Jewish, most of
those in the *New York World-Telegram and Sun* were Protestant, most
of those in the *Journal-American* were Catholic. A rabbi added a foot-
note, after reading the survey, to the effect that they *all* seemed to die
for the *Times*.

If one is to believe only what one reads in the *Times*, however, then
the individuals with the highest fatality rate are chairmen of the board,
Mr. de Vaulchier noted. Admirals usually got longer obits than gener-
als in the *Times*, he continued, architects did better than engineers,
painters did better than other artists and always seemed to die in
Woodstock, New York. Women and Negroes hardly ever seemed to die.

Obituary writers never die. At least Mr. de Vaulchier said he has never read such an obituary in a newspaper, although early last year on the occasion of Whitman's heart attack he came quite close.

After Whitman had been taken to Knickerbocker Hospital in New York, a reporter in the City Room was assigned to "bring the files on him up-to-date." Whitman, since recovering, has never seen this advance obituary, nor does he expect to, but he imagines that it ran seven or eight paragraphs in length and, when it is finally used, will begin something like this:

"Alden Whitman, a member of the *New York Times* staff who wrote obituary articles on many of the world's notable personalities, died suddenly last night at his home, 600 West 116th Street, of a heart attack. He was fifty-two years old. . . ."

It will be very factual and verifiable, he is sure, and will record that he was born on October 27, 1913, in Nova Scotia and was brought to Bridgeport by his parents two years later; that he was twice married, had two children by the first wife, was active in the New York Newspaper Guild, and that in 1956 he, among other newsmen, was questioned by Senator James O. Eastland about his Leftist activities. The obituary will possibly list the schools he attended but will not mention that during his elementary years he skipped *twice* (to his mother's delight; she was a schoolteacher, and this happy event did her reputation with the school board no harm); it will list his places of employment but will not report that in 1936 he got his teeth knocked out, nor that in 1937 he nearly drowned while swimming (an experience he found highly pleasant), nor that in 1940 he came within an inch of being crushed by part of a falling parapet; nor that in 1949 he lost control of his automobile and skidded helplessly to the very edge of a mountain in Colorado; nor that in 1965, after surviving his coronary thrombosis, he repeated what he had been saying most of his life: There is no God; I do not fear death because there is no God; there will be no Judgment Day.

"But what will happen to you then, after you die, Mr. Whitman?"

"I have no soul that is going anywhere," he said. "It is simply a matter of bodily extinction."

"If you had died during your heart attack, what, in your opinion, would have been the first thing your wife would have done?"

"She would first have seen to it that my body was disposed of in the way that I wanted," he said. "To be cremated without fuss or fanfare."

"And then what?"

"Then, after she'd gotten to that, she would have turned her attention to the children."

"And then?"

"Then, I guess, she would have broken down and had a good cry."

"Are you sure?"

Whitman paused.

"Yes, I would assume so," he said finally, puffing on his pipe. "This is the formal outlet for grief under such circumstances."

Ali in Havana

IT IS A WARM, BREEZY, palm-flapping winter evening in Havana, and the leading restaurants are crowded with tourists from Europe, Asia, and South America being serenaded by guitarists relentlessly singing *"Guan-tan-a-mera . . . guajira . . . Guan-tan-a-mera"*; and at the Café Cantante there are clamorous salsa dancers, mambo kings, grunting, bare-chested male performers lifting tables with their teeth, and turbaned women swathed in hip-hugging skirts, blowing whistles while gyrating their glistening bodies into an erotic frenzy. In the café's audience as well as in the restaurants, hotels, and other public places throughout the island, cigarettes and cigars are smoked without restraint or restriction. Two prostitutes are smoking and talking privately on the corner of a dimly lit street bordering the manicured lawns of Havana's five-star Hotel Nacional. They are copper-colored women in their early twenties wearing faded miniskirts and halters, and as they chat, they are watching attentively while two men—one white, the other black—huddle over the raised trunk of a parked red Toyota, arguing about the prices of the boxes of black-market Havana cigars that are stacked within.

The white man is a square-jawed Hungarian in his midthirties, wearing a beige tropical suit and a wide yellow tie, and he is one of Havana's leading entrepreneurs in the thriving illegal business of selling top-quality hand-rolled Cuban cigars below the local and international market price. The black man behind the car is a well-built, baldish, gray-bearded individual in his midfifties from Los Angeles named Howard Bingham; and no matter what price the Hungarian quotes, Bingham shakes his head and says, "No, no—that's too much!"

"You're crazy!" cries the Hungarian in slightly accented English, taking one of the boxes from the trunk and waving it in Howard Bingham's face. "These are Cohiba Esplendidos! The best in the world! You will pay one thousand dollars for a box like this in the States."

"Not me," says Bingham, who wears a Hawaiian shirt with a camera strapped around his neck. He is a professional photographer, and he is staying at the Hotel Nacional with his friend Muhammad Ali. "I wouldn't give you more than fifty dollars."

"You really are crazy," says the Hungarian, slicing through the box's paper seal with his fingernail, opening the lid to reveal a gleaming row of labeled Esplendidos.

"Fifty dollars," says Bingham.

"A hundred dollars," insists the Hungarian. "And hurry! The police could be driving around." The Hungarian straightens up and stares over the car toward the palm-lined lawn and stanchioned lights that glow in the distance along the road leading to the hotel's ornate portico, which is now jammed with people and vehicles; then he turns and flings a glance back toward the nearby public street, where he notices that the prostitutes are now blowing smoke in his direction. He frowns.

"Quick, quick," he says to Bingham, handing him the box. "One hundred dollars."

Howard Bingham does not smoke. He and Muhammad Ali and their traveling companions are leaving Havana tomorrow, after participating in a five-day American humanitarian-aid mission that brought a planeload of medical supplies to hospitals and clinics depleted by the United States's embargo, and Bingham would like to return home with some fine contraband cigars for his friends. But, on the other hand, one hundred is still too much.

"Fifty dollars," says Bingham determinedly, looking at his watch. He begins to walk away.

"Okay, okay," the Hungarian says petulantly. "Fifty."

Bingham reaches into his pocket for the money, and the Hungarian grabs it and gives him the Esplendidos before driving off in the Toyota. One of the prostitutes takes a few steps toward Bingham, but the photographer hurries on to the hotel. Fidel Castro is having a reception tonight for Muhammad Ali, and Bingham has only a half hour to change and be at the portico to catch the chartered bus that will take them to the government's headquarters. He will be bringing one of his photographs to the Cuban leader: an enlarged, framed portrait showing Muhammad Ali and Malcolm X walking together along a Harlem sidewalk in 1963. Malcolm X was thirty-seven at the time, two years away from an assassin's bullet; the twenty-one-year-old Ali was about to win the heavyweight title in a remarkable upset over Sonny Liston in Miami. Bingham's photograph is inscribed, "To President Fidel Castro, from Muhammad Ali." Under his signature, the former champion has sketched a little heart.

Although Muhammad Ali is now fifty-four and has been retired from boxing for more than fifteen years, he is still one of the most famous men in the world, being identifiable throughout five continents; and as he walks through the lobby of the Hotel Nacional toward the bus, wearing a gray sharkskin suit and a white cotton shirt buttoned at the neck without a tie, several guests approach him and request his autograph. It takes him about thirty seconds to write "Muhammad Ali," so shaky are his hands from the effects of Parkinson's syndrome; and though he walks without support, his movements are quite slow, and Howard Bingham and Ali's fourth wife, Yolanda, are following nearby.

Bingham met Ali thirty-five years ago in Los Angeles, shortly after the fighter had turned professional and before he discarded his "slave name" (Cassius Marcellus Clay) and joined the Black Muslims. Bingham subsequently became his closest male friend and has photographed every aspect of Ali's life: his rise and fall three times as the heavyweight champion; his three-year expulsion from boxing, beginning in 1967, for refusing to serve in the U.S. military during the Vietnam War ("I ain't got no quarrel with them Vietcong"); his four marriages; his fatherhood of nine children (one adopted, two out of wedlock); his endless public appearances in all parts of the world—Germany, England, Egypt (sailing on the Nile with a son of Elijah Muhammad's), Sweden, Libya, Pakistan (hugging refugees from Afghanistan), Japan, Indonesia, Ghana (wearing a dashiki and posing with President Kwame Nkrumah), Zaire (beating George Foreman), Manila (beating Joe Frazier) . . . and now, on the final night of his 1996 visit to Cuba, he is en route to a social encounter with an aging contender he has long admired—one who has survived at the top for nearly forty years despite the ill will of nine American presidents, the CIA, the Mafia, and various militant Cuban-Americans.

Bingham waits for Ali near the open door of the charter bus that is blocking the hotel's entrance; but Ali lingers within the crowd in the lobby, and Yolanda steps aside to let some people get closer to her husband.

She is a large and pretty woman of thirty-eight, with a radiant smile and a freckled, fair complexion that reflects her interracial ancestry. A scarf is loosely draped over her head and shoulders, her arms are covered by long sleeves, and her well-designed dress in vivid hues hangs below her knees. She converted to Islam from Catholicism when she married Ali, a man sixteen years her senior but one with whom she shared a familial bond dating back to her girlhood in their native Louisville, where her mother and Ali's mother were sisterly soul mates who traveled together to attend his fights. Yolanda had occasionally joined Ali's entourage, becoming acquainted not only with the boxing element but with Ali's female contemporaries who were his lovers, his wives, the mothers of his children; and she remained in touch with Ali throughout the 1970s, while she majored in psychology at Vanderbilt and later earned her master's degree in business at UCLA. Then—with the end of Ali's boxing career, his third marriage, and his vibrant health—Yolanda intimately entered his life as casually and naturally as she now stands waiting to reclaim her place at his side.

She knows that he is enjoying himself. There is a slight twinkle in his eyes, not much expression on his face, and no words forthcoming from this once most talkative of champions. But the mind behind his Parkinson's mask is functioning normally, and he is characteristically committed to what he is doing: He is spelling out his full name on whatever cards or scraps of paper his admirers are handing him. "Muhammad Ali." He does not settle for a time-saving "Ali" or his mere initials. He has never shortchanged his audience.

And in this audience tonight are people from Latin America, Canada, Africa, Russia, China, Germany, France. There are 200 French travel agents staying at the hotel in conjunction with the Cuban government's campaign to increase its growing tourist trade (which last year saw about 745,000 visitors spending an estimated $1 billion on the island). There is also on hand an Italian movie producer and his lady friend from Rome and a onetime Japanese wrestler, Antonio Inoki, who injured Ali's legs during a 1976 exhibition in Tokyo (but who warmly embraced him two nights ago in the hotel's lounge as they sat listening to Cuban pianist Chucho Valdes playing jazz on a Russian-made Moskva baby grand); and there is also in the crowd, standing taller than the rest, the forty-three-year-old, six-foot five-inch Cuban heavyweight hero Teófilo Stevenson, who was a three-time Olympic gold medalist, in 1972, 1976, and 1980, and who, on this island at least, is every bit as renowned as Ali or Castro.

Though part of Stevenson's reputation derives from his erstwhile power and skill in the ring (although he never fought Ali), it is also attributable to his not having succumbed to the offers of professional boxing promoters, stubbornly resisting the Yankee dollar—although Stevenson hardly seems deprived. He dwells among his countrymen like a towering Cuban peacock, occupying high positions within the government's athletic programs and gaining sufficient attention from the island's women to have garnered four wives so far, who are testimony to his eclectic taste.

His first wife was a dance instructor. His second was an industrial engineer. His third was a medical doctor. His fourth and present wife is a criminal attorney. Her name is Fraymari, and she is a girlishly petite olive-skinned woman of twenty-three who, standing next to her husband in the lobby, rises barely higher than the midsection of his embroidered guayabera—a tightly tailored, short-sleeved shirt that accentuates his tapered torso, his broad shoulders, and the length of his dark, muscular arms, which once prevented his opponents from doing any injustice to his winning Latin looks.

Stevenson always fought from an upright position, and he maintains that posture today. When people talk to him, his eyes look downward, but his head remains high. The firm jaw of his oval-shaped head seems to be locked at a right angle to his straight-spined back. He is a proud man who exhibits all of his height. But he does listen, especially when the words being directed up at him are coming from the perky little attorney who is his wife. Fraymari is now reminding him that it is getting late—everyone should be on the bus; Fidel may be waiting.

Stevenson lowers his eyes toward her and winks. He has gotten the message. He has been Ali's principal escort throughout this visit. He was also Ali's guest in the United States during the fall of 1995; and though he knows only a few words of English, and Ali no Spanish, they are brotherly in their body language.

Stevenson edges himself into the crowd and gently places his right arm around the shoulders of his fellow champion. And then, slowly but firmly, he guides Ali toward the bus.

The road to Fidel Castro's Palace of the Revolution leads through a memory lane of old American automobiles chugging along at about twenty-five miles an hour—springless, pre-embargo Ford coupes and Plymouth sedans, DeSotos and LaSalles, Nashes and Studebakers, and various vehicular collages created out of Cadillac grilles and Oldsmobile axles and Buick fenders patched with pieces of oil-drum metal and powered by engines interlinked with kitchen utensils and pre-Batista lawn mowers and other gadgets that have elevated the craft of tinkering in Cuba to the status of high art.

The relatively newer forms of transportation seen on the road are, of course, non-American products: Polish Fiats, Russian Ladas, German motor scooters, Chinese bicycles, and the glistening, newly imported, air-conditioned Japanese bus from which Muhammad Ali is now gazing through a closed window out toward the street. At times, he raises a hand in response to one of the waving pedestrians or cyclists or motorists who recognize the bus, which has been shown repeatedly on the local TV news conveying Ali and his companions to the medical centers and tourist sites that have been part of the busy itinerary.

On the bus, as always, Ali is sitting alone, spread out across the two front seats in the left aisle directly behind the Cuban driver. Yolanda sits a few feet ahead of him to the right; she is adjacent to the driver and within inches of the windshield. The seats behind her are occupied by Teófilo Stevenson, Fraymari, and the photographer Bingham. Seated behind Ali, and also occupying two seats, is an American screenwriter named Greg Howard, who weighs more than 3oo pounds. Although he has traveled with Ali for only a few months while researching a film on the fighter's life, Greg Howard has firmly established himself as an intimate sidekick, and as such is among the very few on the trip who have heard Ali's voice. Ali speaks so softly that it is impossible to hear him in a crowd, and as a result whatever public comments or sentiments he is expected to, or chooses to, express are verbalized by Yolanda, or Bingham, or Teófilo Stevenson, or even at times by this stout young screenwriter.

"Ali is in his Zen period," Greg Howard has said more than once, in reference to Ali's quiescence. Like Ali, he admires what he has seen so far in Cuba—"There's no racism here"—and as a black man he has long identified with many of Ali's frustrations and confrontations. His student thesis at Princeton analyzed the Newark race riots of 1967, and the Hollywood script he most recently completed focuses on the Negro baseball leagues of the pre–World War II years. He envisions his new work on Ali in the genre of *Gandhi*.

The two-dozen bus seats behind those tacitly reserved for Ali's inner circle are occupied by the secretary-general of the Cuban Red Cross and the American humanitarian personnel who have entrusted him with $500,000 worth of donated medical supplies; and there are also the two Cuban interpreters and a dozen members of the American media, including the CBS-TV commentator Ed Bradley and his producers and camera crew from *60 Minutes*.

Ed Bradley is a gracious but reserved individualist who has appeared on television for a decade with his left earlobe pierced by a small circular ring—which, after some unfavorable comment initially expressed by his colleagues Mike Wallace and Andy Rooney, prompted Bradley's explanation: "It's *my* ear." Bradley also indulges in his identity as a cigar smoker; and as he sits in the midsection of the bus next to his Haitian lady friend, he is taking full advantage of the Communist regime's laissez-faire attitude toward tobacco, puffing away on a Cohiba Robusto, for which he paid full price at the Nacional's tobacco shop—and which now exudes a costly cloud of fragrance that appeals to his friend (who occasionally also smokes cigars) but is not appreciated by the two California women who are seated two rows back and are affiliated with a humanitarian-aid agency.

Indeed, the women have been commenting about the smoking habits of countless people they have encountered in Havana, being especially disappointed to discover earlier this very day that the pediatric hospital they visited (and to which they committed donations) is under the supervision of three tobacco-loving family physicians. When one of the American women, a blonde from Santa Barbara, reproached one of the cigarette-smoking doctors indirectly for setting such a poor example, she was told in effect that the island's health statistics regarding longevity, infant mortality, and general fitness compared favorably with those in the United States and were probably better than those of Americans residing in the capital city of Washington. On the other hand, the doctor made it clear that he did not believe that smoking was good for one's health—after all, Fidel himself had given it up; but unfortunately, the doctor added, in a classic understatement, "some people have not followed him."

Nothing the doctor said appeased the woman from Santa Barbara. She did not, however, wish to appear confrontational at the hospital's news conference, which was covered by the press; nor during her many bus rides with Ed Bradley did she ever request that he discard his cigar. "Mr. Bradley intimidates me," she confided to her California coworker. But he was of course living within the law on this island that the doctor had called "the cradle of the best tobacco in the world." In Cuba, the most available American periodical on the newsstands is *Cigar Aficionado*.

The bus passes through the Plaza de la Revolución and comes to a halt at a security checkpoint near the large glass doors that open onto the marble-floored foyer of a 1950s modern building that is the center of communism's only stronghold in the Western Hemisphere.

As the bus door swings open, Greg Howard moves forward in his seat and grabs the 235-pound Muhammad Ali by the arms and shoulders and helps him to his feet; and after Ali has made his way down to the metal step, he turns and stretches back into the bus to take hold of the extended hands and forearms of the 300-pound screenwriter and pulls him to a standing position. This routine, repeated at each and every bus stop throughout the week, is never accompanied by either man's acknowledging that he has received any assistance, although Ali is aware that some passengers find the pas de deux quite amusing, and he is not reluctant to use his friend to further comic effect. After the bus had made an earlier stop in front of the sixteenth-century Morro Castle—where Ali had followed Teófilo Stevenson up a 117-step spiral staircase for a rooftop view of Havana Harbor—he spotted the solitary figure of Greg Howard standing below in the courtyard. Knowing that there was no way the narrow staircase could accommodate Howard's wide body, Ali suddenly began to wave his arms, summoning Howard to come up and join him.

Castro's security guards, who know in advance the names of all the bus passengers, guide Ali and the others through the glass doors and then into a pair of waiting elevators for a brief ride, which is followed by a short walk through a corridor and finally into a large white-walled reception room, where it is announced that Fidel Castro will soon join them. The room has high ceilings and potted palms in every corner and is sparsely furnished with modern tan leather furniture. Next to a sofa is a table with two telephones, one gray and the other red. Overlooking the sofa is an oil painting of the Viñales Valley, which lies west of Havana; and among the primitive art displayed on a circular table in front of the sofa is a grotesque tribal figure similar to the one Ali had examined earlier in the week at a trinket stand while touring with the group in Havana's Old Square. Ali had then whispered into the ear of Howard Bingham, and Bingham had repeated aloud what Ali had said: "Joe Frazier."

Ali now stands in the middle of the room, next to Bingham, who carries under his arm the framed photograph he plans to give Castro. Teófilo Stevenson and Fraymari stand facing them. The diminutive and delicate-boned Fraymari has painted her lips scarlet and has pulled back her hair in a matronly manner, hoping no doubt to appear more mature than her twenty-three years suggest, but standing next to the three much older and heavier and taller men transforms her image closer to that of an anorexic teenager. Ali's wife and Greg Howard are wandering about within the group that is exchanging comments in muted tones, either in English or Spanish, sometimes assisted by the interpreters. Ali's hands are shaking uncontrollably at his sides; but since his companions have witnessed this all week, the only people who are now paying attention are the security guards posted near the door.

Also waiting near the door for Castro is the four-man CBS camera team, and chatting with them and his two producers is Ed Bradley, without his cigar. There are no ashtrays in this room! This is a most uncommon sight in Cuba. Its implications might be political. Perhaps the sensibilities of the blonde woman from Santa Barbara were taken into account by the doctors at the hospital and communicated to Castro's underlings, who are now making a conciliatory gesture toward their American benefactress.

Since the security guards have not invited the guests to be seated, everybody remains standing—for ten minutes, for twenty minutes, and then for a full half hour. Teófilo Stevenson shifts his weight from foot to foot and gazes over the heads of the crowd toward the upper level of the portal through which Castro is expected to enter—if he shows up. Stevenson knows from experience that Castro's schedule is unpredictable. There is always a crisis of some sort in Cuba, and it has long been rumored on the island that Castro constantly changes the location of where he sleeps. The identity of his bed partners is, of course, a state secret. Two nights ago, Stevenson and Ali and the rest were kept waiting until midnight for an expected meeting with Castro at the Hotel Biocaribe (to which Bingham had brought his gift photograph). But Castro never appeared. And no explanation was offered.

Now in this reception room, it was already 9 P.M. Ali continues to shake. No one has had dinner. The small talk is getting smaller. A few people would like to smoke. The regime is not assuaging anyone in this crowd with a bartender. It is a cocktail party without cocktails. There are not even canapés or soft drinks. Everyone is becoming increasingly restless—and then suddenly there is a collective sigh. The very familiar man with the beard strides into the room, dressed for guerrilla combat; and in a cheerful, high-pitched voice that soars beyond his whiskers, he announces, "Buenas noches!"

In an even higher tone, he repeats, "Buenas noches," this time with a few waves to the group while hastening toward the guest of honor; and then, with his arms extended, the seventy-year-old Fidel Castro immediately obscures the lower half of Ali's expressionless face with a gentle embrace and his flowing gray beard.

"I am glad to see you," Castro says to Ali, via the interpreter who followed him into the room, a comely, fair-skinned woman with a refined English accent. "I am very, very glad to see you," Castro continues, backing up to look into Ali's eyes while holding on to his trembling arms, "and I am thankful for your visit." Castro then releases his grip and awaits a possible reply. Ali says nothing. His expression remains

characteristically fixed and benign, and his eyes do not blink despite
the flashbulbs of several surrounding photographers. As the silence
persists, Castro turns toward his old friend Teófilo Stevenson, feigning
a jab. The Cuban boxing champion lowers his eyes and, with widened
lips and cheeks, registers a smile. Castro then notices the tiny brunette
standing beside Stevenson.

"Stevenson, who is this young woman?" Castro asks aloud in a
tone of obvious approval. But before Stevenson can replay, Fraymari
steps forward with a hint of lawyerly indignation: "You mean you don't
remember me?"

Castro seems stunned. He smiles feebly, trying to conceal his confusion. He turns inquiringly toward his boxing hero, but Stevenson's
eyes only roll upward. Stevenson knows that Castro has met Fraymari
socially on earlier occasions, but unfortunately the Cuban leader has
forgotten, and it is equally unfortunate that Fraymari is now behaving
like a prosecutor.

"You held my son in your arms before he was one year old!" she reminds him while Castro continues to ponder. The crowd is attentive;
the television cameras are rolling.

"At a volleyball game?" Castro asks tentatively.

"No, no," Stevenson interrupts, before Fraymari can say anything
more, "that was my former wife. The doctor."

Castro slowly shakes his head in mock disapproval. Then he
abruptly turns away from the couple, but not before reminding Stevenson, "You should get name tags."

Castro redirects his attention to Muhammad Ali. He studies Ali's
face.

"Where is your wife?" he asks softly. Ali says nothing. There is
more silence and turning of heads in the group until Howard Bingham
spots Yolanda standing near the back and waves her to Castro's side.

Before she arrives, Bingham steps forward and presents Castro with the photograph of Ali and Malcolm X in Harlem in 1963. Castro holds it up level with his eyes and studies it silently for several seconds. When this picture was taken, Castro had been in control of Cuba for nearly four years. He was then thirty-seven. In 1959, he defeated the U.S.-backed dictator Fulgencio Batista, overcoming odds greater than Ali's subsequent victory over the supposedly unbeatable Sonny Liston. Batista had actually announced Castro's death back in 1956. Castro, then hiding in a secret outpost, thirty years old and beardless, was a disgruntled Jesuit-trained lawyer who was born into a landowning family and who craved Batista's job. At thirty-two, he had it. Batista was forced to flee to the Dominican Republic.

During this period, Muhammad Ali was only an amateur. His greatest achievement would come in 1960, when he received a gold medal in Rome as a member of the U.S. Olympic boxing team. But later in the sixties, he and Castro would share the world stage as figures moving against the American establishment—and now, in the twilight of their lives, on this winter's night in Havana, they meet for the first time: Ali silent and Castro isolated on his island.

"*Que bien!*" Castro says to Howard Bingham before showing the photograph to his interpreter. Then Castro is introduced by Bingham to Ali's wife. After they exchange greetings through the interpreter, he asks her, as if surprised, "You don't speak Spanish?"

"No," she says softly. She begins to caress her husband's left wrist, on which he wears a $250 silver Swiss Army watch she bought him. It is the only jewelry Ali wears.

"But I thought I saw you speaking Spanish on the TV news this week," Castro continues wonderingly before acknowledging that her voice had obviously been dubbed.

"Do you live in New York?"

"No, we live in Michigan."

"Cold," says Castro.

"Very cold," she repeats.

"In Michigan, don't you find many people that speak Spanish?"

"No, not many," she says. "Mostly in California, New York"—and, after a pause—"Florida."

Castro nods. It takes him a few seconds to think up another question. Small talk has never been the forte of this man who specializes in nonstop haranguing monologues that can last for hours; and yet here he is, in a room crowded with camera crews and news photographers— a talk-show host with a guest of honor who is speechless. But Fidel Castro plods on, asking Ali's wife if she has a favorite sport.

"I play a little tennis," Yolanda says, and then asks him, "Do you play tennis?"

"Ping-Pong," he replies, quickly adding that during his youth he had been active in the ring. "I spent hours boxing . . ." He begins to reminisce, but before he finishes his sentence, he sees the slowly rising right fist of Muhammad Ali moving toward his chin! Exuberant cheering and hand clapping resound through the room, and Castro jumps sideways toward Stevenson, shouting, *"Asesorame!"*—"Help me!"

Stevenson's long arms land upon Ali's shoulders from behind, squeezing him gently; and then, after he releases him, the two ex-champions face each other and begin to act out in slow motion the postures of competing prizefighters—bobbing, weaving, swinging, ducking—all of it done without touching and all of it accompanied by three minutes of ongoing applause and the clicking of cameras, and also some feelings of relief from Ali's friends because, in his own way, he has decided to join them. Ali still says nothing, his face still inscrutable, but he is less remote, less alone, and he does not pull away from Stevenson's embrace as the latter eagerly tells Castro about a boxing exhibition that he and Ali had staged earlier in the week at the Balado gym, in front of hundreds of fans and some of the island's up-and-coming contenders.

Stevenson did not actually explain that it had been merely another photo opportunity, one in which they sparred openhanded in the ring, wearing their street clothes and barely touching each other's bodies and faces; but then Stevenson had climbed out of the ring, leaving Ali to the more taxing test of withstanding two abbreviated rounds against one and then another young bully of grade-school age who clearly had not come to participate in a kiddie show. They had come to floor the champ. Their bellicose little bodies and hot-gloved hands and helmeted hell-bent heads were consumed with fury and ambition; and as they charged ahead, swinging wildly and swaggering to the roars of their teenage friends and relatives at ringside, one could imagine their future boast-ings to their grandchildren: On one fine day back in the winter of '96, I whacked Muhammad Ali! Except, in truth, on this particular day, Ali was still too fast for them. He backpedaled and shifted and swayed, stood on the toes of his black woven-leather pointed shoes, and showed that his body was made for motion—his Parkinson's problems were lost in his shuffle, in the thrusts of his butterfly sting what whistled two feet above the heads of his aspiring assailants, in the dazzling dips of his rope-a-dope that had confounded George Foreman in Zaire, in his ever-memorable style, which in this Cuban gym moistened the eyes of his ever-observant photographer friend and provoked the overweight screenwriter to cry out in a voice that few in this noisy Spanish crowd could understand, "Ali's on a high! Ali's on a high!"

Teófilo Stevenson raises Ali's right arm above the head of Castro, and the news photographers spend several minutes posing the three of them together in flashing light. Castro then sees Fraymari watching alone at some distance. She is not smiling. Castro nods toward her. He summons a photographer to take a picture of Fraymari and himself. But she relaxes only after her husband comes over to join her in the conversation, which Castro immediately directs to the health and growth of their son, who is not yet two years old.

"Will he be as tall as his father?" Castro asks.

"I assume so," Fraymari says, glancing up toward her husband. She also has to look up when talking to Fidel Castro, for the Cuban leader is taller than six feet and his posture is nearly as erect as her husband's. Only the six-foot three-inch Muhammad Ali, who is standing with Bingham on the far side of her husband—and whose skin coloring, oval-shaped head, and burr-style haircut are very similar to her husband's—betrays his height with the slope-shouldered forward slouch he has developed since his illness.

"How much does your son weigh?" Castro continues.

"When he was one year old, he was already twenty-six pounds," Fraymari says. "This is three above normal. He was walking at nine months."

"She still breast-feeds him," Teófilo Stevenson says, seeming pleased.

"Oh, that's very nourishing," agrees Castro.

"Sometimes the kid becomes confused and thinks my chest is his mother's breast," Stevenson says, and he could have added that his son is also confused by Ali's sunglasses. The little boy engraved teeth marks all over the plastic frames while chewing on them during the days he accompanied his parents on Ali's bus tour.

As a CBS boom pole swoops down closer to catch the conversation, Castro reaches out to touch Stevenson's belly and asks, "How much do you weigh?"

"Two hundred thirty-eight pounds, more or less."

"That's thirty-eight more than me," Castro says, but he complains, "I eat very little. Very little. The diet advice I get is never accurate. I eat around fifteen hundred calories—less than thirty grams of protein, less than that."

Castro slaps a hand against his own midsection, which is relatively flat. If he does have a potbelly, it is concealed within his well-tailored uniform. Indeed, for a man of seventy, he seems in fine health. His facial skin is florid and unsagging, his dark eyes dart around the room with ever-alert intensity, and he has a full head of lustrous gray hair not thinning at the crown. The attention he pays to himself might be measured from his manicured fingernails down to his square-toed boots, which are unscuffed and smoothly buffed without the burnish of a lackey's spit shine. But his beard seems to belong to another man and another time. It is excessively long and scraggly. Wispy white hairs mix with the faded black and dangle down the front of his uniform like an old shroud, weatherworn and drying out. It is the beard from the hills. Castro strokes it constantly, as if trying to revive the vitality of its fiber.

Castro now looks at Ali.

"How's your appetite?" he asks, forgetting that Ali is not speaking.

"Where's your wife?" he then asks aloud, and Howard Bingham calls out to her. Yolanda has once more drifted back into the group.

When she arrives, Castro hesitates before speaking to her. It is as if he is not absolutely sure who she is. He has met so many people since arriving, and with the group rotating constantly due to the jostling of the photographers, Castro cannot be certain whether the woman at his side is Muhammad Ali's wife or Ed Bradley's friend or some other woman he met moments ago who left him with an unlasting impression. Having already committed a faux pas regarding one of the wives of the two multimarried ex-champions standing nearby, Castro waits for some hint from his interpreter. None is offered. Fortunately, he does not have to worry in this country about the women's vote—or any vote, for that matter—but he does sigh in mild relief when Yolanda reintroduces herself as Ali's wife and does so by name.

"Ah, Yolanda," Castro repeats, "what a beautiful name. That's the name of a queen somewhere."

"In our household," she says.

"And how is your husband's appetite?"

"Good, but he likes sweets."

"We can send you some of our ice cream to Michigan," Castro says. Without waiting for her to comment, he asks, "Michigan is very cold?"

"Oh, yes," she replies, not indicating that they already discussed Michigan's winter weather.

"How much snow?"

"We didn't get hit with the blizzard," Yolanda says, referring to a storm in January, "but it can get three, four feet—"

Teófilo Stevenson interrupts to say that he had been in Michigan during the previous October.

"Oh," Castro says, raising an eyebrow. He mentions that during the same month he had also been in the United States (attending the United Nations' fiftieth-anniversary tribute). He asks Stevenson the length of his American visit.

"I was there for nineteen days," says Stevenson.

"Nineteen days!" Castro repeats. "Longer than I was."

Castro complains that he was limited to five days and prohibited from traveling beyond New York.

"Well, *comandante*," Stevenson responds offhandedly, in a slightly superior tone, "if you like, I will sometime show you my video."

Stevenson appears to be very comfortable in the presence of the Cuban leader, and perhaps the latter has habitually encouraged this; but at this moment, Castro may well be finding his boxing hero a bit condescending and worthy of a retaliatory jab. He knows how to deliver it.

"When you visited the United States," Castro asks pointedly, "did you bring your wife, the lawyer?"

Stevenson stiffens. He directs his eyes toward his wife. She turns away.

"No," Stevenson answers quietly. "I went alone."

Castro abruptly shifts his attention to the other side of the room, where the CBS camera crew is positioned, and he asks Ed Bradley, "What do you do?"

"We're making a documentary on Ali," Bradley explains, "and we followed him to Cuba to see what he was doing in Cuba and . . ."

Bradley's voice is suddenly overwhelmed by the sounds of laughter and hand clapping. Bradley and Castro turn to discover that Muhammad Ali is now reclaiming everyone's attention. He is holding his shaky left fist in the air; but instead of assuming a boxer's pose, as he did earlier, he is beginning to pull out from the top of his upraised fist, slowly and with dramatic delicacy, the tip of a red silk handkerchief that is pinched between his right index finger and thumb.

After he pulls out the entire handkerchief, he dangles it in the air for a few seconds, waving it closer and closer to the forehead of the wide-eyed Fidel Castro. Ali seems bewitched. He continues to stare stagnantly at Castro and the others, surrounded by applause that he gives no indication he hears. Then he proceeds to place the handkerchief back into the top of his cupped left hand—packing with the pinched fingers of his right—and then quickly opens his palms toward his audience and reveals that the handkerchief has disappeared.

"Where is it?" cries Castro, who seems to be genuinely surprised and delighted. He approaches Ali and examines his hands, repeating, "Where is it? Where have you put it?"

Everyone who has traveled on Ali's bus during the week knows where he hid it. They saw him perform the trick repeatedly in front of some of the patients and doctors at the hospitals and clinics as well as before countless tourists who recognized him in his hotel lobby or during his strolls through the town square. They also saw him follow up each performance with a demonstration that exposed his method. He keeps hidden in his fist a flesh-colored rubber thumb that contains the handkerchief that he will eventually pull out with the fingers of his other hand; and when he is reinserting the handkerchief, he is actually shoving the material back into the concealed rubber thumb, into which he then inserts his own right thumb. When he opens his hands, the uninformed among his onlookers are seeing his empty palms and missing the fact that the handkerchief is tucked within the rubber thumb that is covering his outstretched right thumb. Sharing with his audience the mystery of his magic always earns him additional applause.

After Ali performs and explains the trick to Castro, he gives Castro the rubber thumb to examine—and, with more zest than he has shown all evening, Castro says, "Oh, let me try it; I want to try—it's the first time I have seen such a wonderful thing!" And after a few minutes of coaching from Howard Bingham, who long ago learned how to do it from Ali, the Cuban leader performs with sufficient dexterity and panache to satisfy his magical ambitions and to arouse another round of applause from the guests.

Meanwhile, more than ten minutes have passed since Ali began his comic routine. It is already after 9:30 P.M., and the commentator Ed Bradley, whose conversation with Castro was interrupted, is concerned that the Cuban leader might leave the room without responding to the questions Bradley prepared for his show. Bradley edges close to Castro's interpreter, saying in a voice that is sure to be heard, "Would you ask him if he followed . . . was able to follow Ali when he was boxing professionally?"

The question is relayed and repeated until Castro, facing the CBS camera, replies, "Yes, I recall the days when they were discussing the possibilities of a match between the two of them"—he nods toward Stevenson and Ali—"and I remember when he went to Africa."

"In Zaire," Bradley clarifies, referring to Ali's victory in 1974 over George Foreman. And he follows up: "What kind of impact did he have in this country, because he was a revolutionary as well as . . . ?"

"It was great," Castro says. "He was very much admired as a sportsman, as a boxer, as a person. There was always a high opinion of him. But I never guessed one day we would meet here, with this kind gesture of bringing medicine, seeing our children, visiting our polyclinics. I am very glad, I am thrilled, to have the opportunity to meet him personally, to appreciate his kindness. I see he is strong. I see he has a very kind face."

Castro is speaking as if Ali were not in the room, standing a few feet away. Ali maintains his fixed facade even as Stevenson whispers into his ear, asking in English, "Muhammad, Muhammad, why you no speak?" Stevenson then turns to tell the journalist who stands behind him, "Muhammad does speak. He speaks to me." Stevenson says nothing more because Castro is now looking at him while continuing to tell Bradley, "I am very glad that he and Stevenson have met." After a pause, Castro adds, "And I am glad that they never fought."

"He's not so sure," Bradley interjects, smiling in the direction of Stevenson.

"I find in that friendship something beautiful," Castro insists softly.

"There is a tie between the two of them," Bradley says.

"Yes," says Castro. "It is true." He again looks at Ali, then at Stevenson, as if searching for something more profound to say.

"And how's the documentary?" he finally asks Bradley.

"It'll be on *60 Minutes*."

"When?"

"Maybe one month," Bradley says, reminding Castro's interpreter, "This is the program on which the *comandante* has been interviewed by Dan Rather a number of times in the past, when Dan Rather was on *60 Minutes*."

"And who's there now?" Castro wants to know.

"I am," Bradley answers.

"You," Castro repeats, with a quick glance at Bradley's earring. "So you are there—the boss now?"

Bradley responds as a media star without illusions: "I'm a worker."

Trays containing coffee, tea, and orange juice finally arrive, but only in amounts sufficient for Ali and Yolanda, Howard Bingham, Greg Howard, the Stevensons, and Castro—although Castro tells the waiters he wants nothing.

Castro motions for Ali and the others to join him across the room, around the circular table. The camera crews and the rest of the guests follow, standing as near to the principals as they can. But throughout the group there is a discernible restlessness. They have been standing for more than an hour and a half. It is now approaching 10 P.M. There has been no food. And for the vast majority, it is clear that there will also be nothing to drink. Even among the special guests, seated and sipping from chilled glasses or hot cups, there is a waning level of fascination with the evening. Indeed, Muhammad Ali's eyes were closed. He is sleeping.

Yolanda sits next to him on the sofa, pretending not to notice. Castro also ignores it, although he sits directly across the table, with the interpreter and the Stevensons.

"How large is Michigan?" Castro begins a new round of questioning with Yolanda, returning for the third time to a subject they explored beyond the interest of anyone in the room except Castro himself.

"I don't know how big the state is as far as demographics," Yolanda says. "We live in a very small village [Barrien Springs] with about two thousand people."

"Are you going back to Michigan tomorrow?"

"Yes."

"What time?"

"Two-thirty."

"Via Miami?" Castro asks.

"Yes."

"From Miami, where do you fly?"

"We're flying to Michigan."

"How many hours' flight?"

"We have to change at Cincinnati—about two and a half hours."

"Flying time?" asks Castro.

Muhammad Ali opens his eyes, then closes them.

"Flying time," Yolanda repeats.

"From Miami to Michigan?" Castro continues.

"No," she again explains, but still with patience, "we have to go to Cincinnati. There are no direct flights."

"So you have to take two planes?" Castro asks.

"Yes," she says, adding for clarification, "Miami to Cincinnati— and then Cincinnati to South Bend, Indiana."

"From Cincinnati . . . ?"

"To South Bend," she says. "That's the closest airport."

"So," Fidel goes on, "it is on the outskirts of the city?"

"Yes."

"You have a farm?"

"No," Yolanda says, "just land. We let someone else do the growing."

She mentions that Teófilo Stevenson traveled through this part of the Midwest. The mention of his name gains Stevenson's attention.

"I was in Chicago," Stevenson tells Castro.

"You were at their home?" Castro asks.

"No," Yolanda corrects Stevenson, "you were in Michigan."

"I was in the countryside," Stevenson says. Unable to resist, he adds, "I have a video of that visit. I'll show it to you sometime."

Castro seems not to hear him. He directs his attention back to Yolanda, asking her where she was born, where she was educated, when she became married, and how many years separate her age from that of her husband, Muhammad Ali.

After Yolanda acknowledges being sixteen years younger than Ali, Castro turns toward Fraymari and with affected sympathy says that she married a man who is twenty years her senior.

"Comandante!" Stevenson intercedes, "I am in shape. Sports keep you healthy. Sports add years to your life and life to your years!"

"Oh, what conflict she has," Castro goes on, ignoring Stevenson and catering to Fraymari—and to the CBS cameraman who steps forward for a closer view of Castro's face. "She is a lawyer, and she does not put this husband in jail." Castro is enjoying much more than Fraymari the attention this topic is now getting from the group. Castro had lost his audience and now has it back and seemingly wants to retain it, no matter at what cost to Stevenson's harmony with Fraymari. Yes, Castro continues, Fraymari had the misfortune to select a husband "who can never settle down. . . . Jail would be an appropriate place for him."

"Comandante," Stevenson interrupts in a jocular manner that seems intended to placate both the lawyer who is his spouse and the lawyer who rules the country, "I might as well be locked up!" He implies that should he deviate from marital fidelity, his lawyer wife "will surely put me in a place where she is the only woman who can visit me!"

Everyone around the table and within the circling group laughs. Ali is now awake. The banter between Castro and Stevenson resumes until Yolanda, all but rising in her chair, tells Castro, "We have to pack."

"You're going to have dinner now?" he asks.

"Yes, sir," she says. Ali stands, along with Howard Bingham. Yolanda thanks Castro's interpreter directly, saying, "Be sure to tell

him, 'You're always welcome in our home.'" The interpreter quotes
Castro as again complaining that when he visits America, he is usually restricted to New York, but he adds, "Things change."

The group watches as Yolanda and Ali pass through, and Castro
follows them into the hallway. The elevator arrives, and its door is
held open by a security guard. Castro extends his final farewell with
handshakes—and only then does he discover that he holds Ali's rubber thumb in his hand. Apologizing, he tries to hand it back to Ali, but
Bingham politely protests. "No, no," Bingham says, "Ali wants you to
have it."

Castro's interpretor at first fails to understand what Bingham is
saying.

"He wants you to keep it," Bingham repeats.

Bingham enters the elevator with Ali and Yolanda. Before the door
closes, Castro smiles, waves good-bye, and stares with curiosity at the
rubber thumb. Then he puts it in his pocket.

The Brave Tailors of Maida

THERE IS A CERTAIN TYPE of mild mental disorder that is endemic in the tailoring trade, and it began to weave its way into my father's psyche during his apprentice days in Italy, when he worked in the shop of a volatile craftsman named Francesco Cristiani, whose male forebears had been tailors for four successive generations and had, without exception, exhibited symptoms of this occupational malady.

Although it has never attracted scientific curiosity and therefore cannot be classified by an official name, my father once described the disorder as a form of prolonged melancholia that occasionally erupts into cantankerous fits—the result, my father suggested, of excessive hours of slow, exacting, microscopic work that proceeds stitch by stitch, inch by inch, mesmerizing the tailor in the reflected light of a needle flickering in and out of the fabric.

A tailor's eye must follow a seam precisely, but his pattern of thought is free to veer off in different directions, to delve into his life, to ponder his past, to lament lost opportunities, create dramas, imagine slights, brood, exaggerate—in simple terms, the man, when sewing, has too much time to think.

My father, who served as an apprentice each day before and after school, was aware that certain tailors could sit quietly at the workbench for hours, cradling a garment between their bowed heads and crossed knees, and sew without exercise or much physical movement, without any surge of fresh oxygen to clear their brains. Then, with inexplicable suddenness, my father would see one of these men jump to his feet and take wild umbrage at a casual comment of a coworker, a trivial exchange that was not intended to provoke. And my father would often cower in a corner as spools and steel thimbles flew around the room—and, if goaded by insensitive colleagues, the aroused tailor might reach for the workroom's favorite instrument of terror, the sword-length scissors.

There were also confrontations in the front of the store in which my father worked, disputes between the customers and the proprietor—the diminutive and vainglorious Francesco Cristiani, who took enormous pride in his occupation and believed that he, and the tailors under his supervision, were incapable of making a serious mistake; if they were, he was not likely to acknowledge it.

Once when a customer came in to try on a new suit but was unable to slip into the jacket because the sleeves were too narrow, Francesco Cristiani not only failed to apologize to the client; he behaved as if insulted by the client's ignorance of the Cristiani shop's unique style in men's fashion. "You are not supposed to put your arms *through* the sleeves of this jacket!" Cristiani informed his client, in a superior tone. "This jacket is only designed to be worn *over the shoulders!*"

On another occasion, when Cristiani paused in the Maida square after lunch to listen to the band during its midday concert, he noticed that the new uniform that had been delivered the day before to the third trumpeter showed a bulge behind the collar whenever the musician lifted the instrument to his lips.

Concerned that someone might notice it and cast aspersions on his status as a tailor, Cristiani dispatched my father, then a skinny boy of eight, to sneak up behind the bunting of the bandstand and, with furtive finesse, pull down on the end of the trumpeter's jacket whenever the bulge appeared. When the concert was over, Cristiani contrived a subtle means by which he was able to reacquire and repair the jacket.

Around this time, in the spring of 1911, there occurred a catastrophe in the shop for which there seemed to be no possible solution.

The problem was so serious, in fact, that Cristiani's first reaction was to leave town for a while rather than remain in Maida to face the consequences. The incident that provoked such panic had taken place in Cristiani's workroom on the Saturday before Easter, and it centered on the damage done by an apprentice, accidentally but irreparably, to a new suit that had been made for one of Cristiani's most demanding customers—a man who was among the region's renowned *uomini rispettati*, men of respect, popularly known as the Mafia.

Before Cristiani became aware of the accident, he had enjoyed a prosperous morning in his shop collecting payment from several satisfied customers who had come in for the final try-on of their attire, which they would wear on the following day at the Easter *passeggiata*, the most exhibitionistic event of the year for the men of southern Italy. While the modest women of the village—except for the bolder wives of American immigrants—would spend the day after Mass discreetly perched on their balconies, the men would stroll in the square, chatting with each other as they walked arm in arm, smoking and shiftily examining the fit of each other's new suits. For despite the poverty in southern Italy, or perhaps because of it, there was excessive emphasis on appearances—it was part of the region's *fare bella figura* syndrome; and most of the men who assembled in the piazza of Maida, and in dozens of similar squares throughout the south, were uncommonly knowledgeable about the art of fine tailoring.

They could assess in a few seconds the craft of another man's suit, could appraise each dexterous stitch, could appreciate the mastery of a tailor's most challenging task, the shoulder, from which more than twenty individualized parts of the jacket must hang in harmony and allow for fluidity. Almost every prideful male, when entering a shop to select fabric for a new suit, knew by heart the twelve principal measurements of his tailored body, starting with the distance between the neckline and the waist of the jacket, and ending with the exact width of the cuffs above the shoes. Among such men were many customers who had been dealing with the Cristiani family firm all of their lives, as had their fathers and grandfathers before them. Indeed, the Cristianis had been making men's clothes in southern Italy since 1806, when the region was controlled by Napoleon Bonaparte; and when Napoleon's brother-in-law, Joachim Murat, who had been installed on the Naples throne in 1808, was assassinated in 1815 by a Spanish Bourbon firing squad in the village of Pizzo, a few miles south of Maida, the wardrobe that Murat left behind included a suit made by Francesco Cristiani's grandfather.

But now on this Holy Saturday in 1911, Francesco Cristiani confronted a situation that could not benefit from his family's long tradition in the trade. In his hands he held a new pair of trousers that had an inch-long cut across the left knee, a cut that had been made by an apprentice who had been idling with a pair of scissors atop the table on which the trousers had been laid out for Cristiani's inspection.

Although apprentices were repeatedly reminded that they were not to handle the heavy scissors—their main task was to sew on buttons and baste seams—some young men unwittingly violated the rule in their eagerness to gain tailoring experience. But what magnified the youth's delinquency in this situation was that the damaged trousers had been made for the *mafioso*, whose name was Vincenzo Castiglia.

A first-time customer from nearby Cosenza, Vincenzo Castiglia was so blatant about his criminal profession that, while being measured for the suit one month before, he had asked Cristiani to allow ample room inside the jacket for the holstered pistol. On that same occasion, however, Mr. Castiglia had made several other requests that elevated him in the eyes of his tailor as a man who had a sense of style and knew what might flatter his rather corpulent figure. For example, Mr. Castiglia had requested that the suit's shoulders be cut extra wide to give his hips a narrower appearance; and he sought to distract attention from his protruding belly by ordering a pleated waistcoat with wide pointed lapels and also a hole in the center of the waistcoat through which a gold chain could be looped and linked to his diamond pocket watch.

In addition, Mr. Castiglia specified that the hems of his trousers be turned up, in accord with the latest continental fashion; and, as he peered into Cristiani's workroom, he expressed satisfaction on observing that the tailors were all sewing by hand and not using the popularized sewing machine, which, despite its speed, lacked the capacity for the special molding of a fabric's seams and angles that was only possible in the hands of a talented tailor.

Bowing with appreciation, the tailor Cristiani assured Mr. Castiglia that his shop would never succumb to the graceless mechanized invention, even though sewing machines were now widely used in Europe and also in America. With the mention of America, Mr. Castiglia smiled and said that he had once visited the New Land, and added that he had several relatives who had settled there. (Among them was a young cousin, Francesco Castiglia, who in future years, beginning in the era of Prohibition, would achieve great notoriety and wealth under the name Frank Costello.)

In the weeks that followed, Cristiani devoted much attention to satisfying the *mafioso*'s specifications, and he was finally proud of the sartorial results—until Holy Saturday, when he discovered an inch-long slash across the left knee of Mr. Castiglia's new pants.

Screaming with anguish and fury, Cristiani soon obtained a confession from the apprentice who admitted to cutting discarded pieces of cloth on the edges of the pattern under which the trousers had been found. Cristiani stood silently, shaken for several minutes, surrounded by his equally concerned and speechless associates. Cristiani could, of course, run and hide in the hills, which had been his first inclination;

or he could return the money to the *mafioso* after explaining what had happened and then offer up the guilty apprentice as a sacrificial lamb to be appropriately dealt with. In this instance, however, there were special inhibiting circumstances. The culpable apprentice was the young nephew of Cristiani's wife, Maria. His wife had been born Maria Talese. She was the only sister of Cristiani's best friend, Gaetano Talese, then working in America. And Gaetano's eight-year-old son, the apprentice Joseph Talese—who would become my father—was now crying convulsively.

As Cristiani sought to comfort his remorseful nephew, his mind kept searching for some plausible solution. There was no way, in the few hours remaining before Castiglia's visit, to make a second pair of trousers even if they had matching material in stock. Nor was there any way to perfectly obscure the cut in the fabric even with a marvelous job of mending.

While his fellow tailors kept insisting that the wisest move was to close the shop and leave a note for Mr. Castiglia pleading illness, or some other excuse that might delay a confrontation, Cristiani firmly reminded them that nothing could absolve him from his failure to deliver the *mafioso*'s suit in time for Easter and that it was mandatory to find a solution now, at once, or at least within the four hours that remained before Mr. Castiglia's arrival.

As the noon bell rang from the church in the main square, Cristiani grimly announced: "There will be no siesta for any of us today. This is not the time for food and rest—it is the time for sacrifice and meditation. So I want everybody to stay where you are, and think of something that may save us from disaster."

He was interrupted by some grumbling from the other tailors, who resented missing their lunch and afternoon nap; but Cristiani overruled them and immediately dispatched one of his apprenticed sons to the village to tell the tailors' wives not to expect the return of their husbands until sundown. Then he instructed the other apprentices, including my father, to pull the draperies across the windows and to lock the shop's front and back doors. And then for the next few minutes, Cristiani's entire staff of a dozen men and boys, as if participating in a wake, quietly congregated within the walls of the darkened shop.

My father sat in one corner, still stunned by the magnitude of his misdeed. Near him sat other apprentices, irritated at my father but nonetheless obedient to their master's order that they remain in confinement. In the center of the workroom, seated among his tailors, was Francesco Cristiani, a small wiry man with a tiny mustache, holding his head in his hands and looking up every few seconds to glance again at the trousers that lay before him.

Several minutes later, with a snap of his fingers, Cristiani rose to his feet. Though he was barely five feet, six inches tall, his erect carriage, fine styling, and panache lent substance to his presence. There was also a gleam in his eye.

"I think I have thought of something," he announced slowly, pausing to let the suspense build until he had everyone's total attention.

"What is it?" asked his most senior tailor.

"What I can do," Cristiani continued, "is make a cut across the *right* knee that will exactly match the damaged left knee, and—"

"Are you crazy?" interrupted the older tailor.

"Let me finish, you imbecile!" Cristiani shouted, pounding his small fist on the table. "And then I can sew up both cuts of the trousers with decorative seams that will match exactly, and later I will explain to Mr. Castiglia that he is the first man in this part of Italy to be wearing trousers designed in the newest fashion, the knee-seamed fashion."

The others listened with astonishment.

"But, maestro," one of the younger tailors said in a cautious tone of respect, "won't Mr. Castiglia notice, after you introduce this 'new fashion,' that we tailors ourselves are not wearing trousers that follow this fashion?"

Cristiani raised his eyebrows slightly.

"A good point," he conceded, as a pessimistic mood returned to the room. And then again his eyes flashed, and he said: "But we *will* follow the fashion! We will make cuts in *our* knees and then sew them up with seams similar to Mr. Castiglia's." Before the men could protest, he quickly added: "But we will *not* be cutting up our own trousers. We'll use those trousers we keep in the widows' closet!"

Immediately everyone turned toward the locked door of a closet in the rear of the workroom, within which were hung dozens of suits last worn by men now dead—suits that bereaved widows, not wishing to be reminded of their departed spouses, had passed on to Cristiani in the hope that he would give the clothing away to passing strangers who might wear them in distant villages.

Now Cristiani flung open the closet door, pulled several pairs of trousers off the suit hangers, and tossed them to his tailors, urging a quick try-on. He himself was already standing in his white cotton underwear and black garters, searching for a pair of trousers that might accommodate his slight stature; and when he succeeded, he slipped them on, climbed up on the table, and stood momentarily like a proud model in front of his men. "See," he said, pointing to the length and width, "a perfect fit."

The other tailors began to pick and choose from the wide selection. Cristiani was now down from the table, the trousers off, and was beginning to cut across the right knee of the *mafioso*'s pants, duplicating the already damaged left knee. Then he applied similar incisions to the knees of the trousers he had chosen to wear himself.

"Now, pay close attention," he called out to his men. With a flourish of his silk-threaded needle, he applied the first stitch into the dead man's trousers, piercing the lower edge of the torn knee with an inner stitch that he adroitly looped to the upper edge—a bold, circular motion that he repeated several times until he had securely reunited the center of the knee with a small, round, embroidered wreathlike design half the size of a dime.

Then he proceeded to sew, on the right side of the wreath, a half-inch seam that was slightly tapered and tilted upward at the end; and, after reproducing this seam on the left side of the wreath, he had created a minuscule image of a distant bird with spread wings, flying directly toward the viewer; a bird that most resembled a peregrine falcon. Cristiani thus originated a trouser style with wing-tipped knees.

"Well, what do you think?" he asked his men, indicating by his off-hand manner that he did not really care what they thought. As they shrugged their shoulders and murmured in the background, he peremptorily continued: "All right now, quickly, cut the knees of those trousers you'll be wearing and stitch them together with the embroidered design you've just seen." Expecting no opposition, and receiving none, Cristiani lowered his head to concentrate entirely on his own task: finishing the second knee of the trousers he would wear, and then beginning, meticulously, the job on Mr. Castiglia's trousers.

In the latter case, not only did Cristiani plan to embroider a winged design with silk thread that matched exactly the shade of the thread used on the buttonholes of the jacket of Mr. Castiglia's suit, but he also would insert a section of silk lining within the front part of the trousers, extending from the thighs to the shins, that would protect Mr. Castiglia's knees from the scratchy feel of the embroidered inner stitching and would also diminish the friction against the knee seams when Mr. Castiglia was out promenading at the *passeggiata*.

For the next two hours, everyone worked in feverish silence. As Cristiani and the other tailors affixed the winged design on the knees of all the trousers, the apprentices helped with the minor alterations, button sewing, the ironing of cuffs, and other details that would make the dead men's trousers as presentable as possible on the bodies of the tailors. Francesco Cristiani, of course, allowed none but himself to handle the *mafioso*'s garments; and as the church bells rang, signaling the end of the siesta, Cristiani scrutinized with admiration the stitching he had done, and he privately thanked his namesake in heaven, Saint Francis di Paola, for his inspired guidance with the needle.

Now there was the sound of activity in the square: the jingles of horse-drawn wagons, the cries of the food vendors, the voices of shoppers passing back and forth along the cobblestone road in front of Cristiani's doorstep. The window draperies of the shop had just been opened, and my father and another apprentice were posted beyond the door with instructions to call in with words of warning as soon as they caught a glimpse of Mr. Castiglia's carriage.

Inside, the tailors stood in a row behind Cristiani, famished and fatigued, and hardly comfortable in their dead men's trousers with wing-tipped knees; but their anxiety and fear concerning Mr. Castiglia's forthcoming reaction to his Easter suit dominated their emotions. Cristiani, on the other hand, seemed unusually calm. In addition to his newly acquired brown trousers, the cuffs of which touched upon his buttoned shoes with cloth tops, he wore a gray lapelled waistcoat over a striped shirt with a rounded white collar adorned by a burgundy cravat and pearl stickpin. In his hand, on a wooden hanger, he held Mr. Castiglia's gray herringbone three-piece suit, which, moments before, he had softly brushed and pressed for the final time. The suit was still warm.

At twenty minutes after four, my father came running through the door, and, in a high voice that could not betray his panic, he announced: *"Sta arrivando!"* A black carriage, drawn by two horses, clangorously drew to a halt in front of the shop. After the rifle-toting coachman hopped off to open the door, the dark portly figure of Vincenzo Castiglia descended the two steps to the sidewalk, followed by a lean man, his bodyguard, in a wide-brimmed black hat, long cloak, and studded boots.

Mr. Castiglia removed his gray fedora and, with a handkerchief, wiped the road dust from his brow. He entered the shop, where Cristiani hastened forward to greet him and, holding the new suit high on its hanger, proclaimed: "Your wonderful Easter costume awaits you!" Shaking hands, Mr. Castiglia examined the suit without comment; then, after politely refusing Cristiani's offer of a bit of whiskey or wine, he directed his bodyguard to help him remove his jacket so that he could immediately try on his Easter apparel.

Cristiani and the other tailors stood quietly nearby, watching as the holstered pistol strapped to Castiglia's chest swayed with his movements as he extended his arms and received over his shoulders the gray lapelled waistcoat, followed by the broad-shouldered jacket. Inhaling as he buttoned up his waistcoat and jacket, Mr. Castiglia turned toward the three-sectioned mirror next to the fitting room. He admired the reflection of himself from every angle, then turned toward his bodyguard, who nodded approvingly. Mr. Castiglia commented in a commanding voice: *"Perfetto!"*

"Mille grazie," responded Cristiani, bowing slightly as he carefully removed the trousers from the hanger and handed them to Mr. Castiglia. Excusing himself, Mr. Castiglia walked into the fitting room. He closed the door. A few of the tailors began to pace around the showroom, but Cristiani stood near the fitting room, whistling softly to himself. The bodyguard, still wearing his cloak and hat, sat comfortably in a chair, his legs crossed, smoking a thin cigar. The apprentices gathered in the back room, out of sight, except for my nervous father, who remained in the showroom busily arranging and rearranging stacks of material on a counter while keeping an eye focused on the fitting room.

For more than a minute not a word was spoken. The only sounds heard were made by Mr. Castiglia as he changed his trousers. First there was the thump of his shoes dropping to the floor. Then the faint whishing rustle of trouser legs being stepped into. Seconds later, a loud bump against the wooden partition as Mr. Castiglia presumably lost his balance while standing on one leg. After a sigh, a cough, and the creaking sound of shoe leather—more silence. But then, suddenly, a deep voice from behind the door bellowed: "Maestro!" Then louder: "MAESTRO!"

The door bolted open, revealing the glowering face and crouched figure of Mr. Castiglia, his fingers pointing down toward his bent knees, and the winged design on the trousers. Waddling toward Cristiani, he yelled: "Maestro—*che avete fatto qui?*"—what have you done here?

The bodyguard jumped, scowling at Cristiani. My father closed his eyes. The tailors stepped back. But Francesco Cristiani stood straight and still, remaining impassive even when the bodyguard's hand moved inside his cloak.

"What have you done?" Mr. Castiglia repeated, still squatting on bent knees, as if suffering from locked joints. Cristiani watched him silently for a second or two; but finally, in the authoritarian tone of a teacher chiding a student, Cristiani responded: "Oh, how disappointed I am in you! How sad and insulted am I by your failure to appreciate the honor I was trying to bestow upon you because I thought you deserved it—but, sadly, I was wrong . . ."

Before the confused Vincenzo Castiglia would open his mouth, Cristiani continued: "You demanded to know what I had done with your trousers—not realizing that what I had done was introduce you to the modern world, which is where I thought you belonged. When you first entered this shop for a fitting last month, you seemed so different from the backward people of this region. So sophisticated. So individualistic. You had traveled to America, you said, had seen the New

World, and I assumed that you were in touch with the contemporary spirit of freedom—but I greatly misjudged you. . . . New clothes, alas, do not remake the man within . . ."

Carried away by his own grandiloquence, Cristiani turned toward his senior tailor, who stood closest to him, and he impulsively repeated an old southern Italian proverb that he regretted uttering immediately after the words had slipped out of his mouth.

"Lavar la testa al'asino è acqua persa," Cristiani intoned. Washing a donkey's head is a waste of water.

Stunned silence swept through the entire shop. My father cringed behind the counter. Cristiani's tailors, horrified by his provocation, gasped and trembled as they saw Mr. Castiglia's face redden, his eyes narrow— and no one would have been surprised if the next sound were the explosion of a gun. Indeed, Cristiani himself lowered his head and seemed resigned to his fate—but strangely, having now gone too far to turn back, Cristiani recklessly, repeated his words: *"Lavar la testa . . ."*

Mr. Castiglia did not respond. He sputtered, bit his lips, but said not a word. Perhaps, having never before experienced such brazenness from anyone, and particularly not from a tiny tailor, Mr. Castiglia was too wonderstruck to act. Even his bodyguard now seemed paralyzed, with his hand still inside his cloak. After a few more seconds of silence, the eyes in Cristiani's lowered head moved tentatively upward, and he saw Mr. Castiglia standing with his shoulders slouched, his head hanging slightly, and a glazed and remorseful look in his eyes. He then looked at Cristiani and winced. Finally, he spoke. "My late mother would use that expression when I made her angry," Mr. Castiglia confided softly. After a pause, he added, "She died when I was very young . . ."

"Oh, I am so sorry," Cristiani said, as the tension subsided in the room. "I do hope, however, that you will accept my word that we *did* try to make you a beautiful suit for Easter. I was just so disappointed that your trousers, which are designed in the latest fashion, did not appeal to you."

Looking down once again at the knees, Mr. Castiglia asked: "*This* is the latest fashion?"

"Yes, indeed," Cristiani reassured him.

"Where?"

"In the great capitals of the world."

"But not here?"

"Not yet," Cristiani said. "You are the first among the men of this region."

"But why does the latest fashion in this region have to begin with me?" Mr. Castiglia asked, in a voice that now seemed uncertain.

"Oh, no, it has not really begun with you," Cristiani quickly corrected him. "We tailors have *already* adopted this fashion." And holding up one of his trouser knees, he said: "See for yourself."

Mr. Castiglia looked down to examine Cristiani's knees; and then, as he turned to survey the entire room, he saw the other tailors, one after another, each lift a leg and, nodding, point to the now familiar wings of the infinitesimal bird.

"I see," Mr. Castiglia said. "And I see that I also owe you my apologies, maestro," he went on. "Sometimes it takes a while for a man to appreciate what is fashionable."

Then after shaking Cristiani's hand, and settling the financial account—but seemingly not wanting to linger a moment longer in this place where his uncertainty had been exposed—Mr. Castiglia summoned his obedient and speechless bodyguard and handed him his old suit. Wearing his new suit, and tipping his hat, Mr. Castiglia headed toward his carriage through the door that had been pulled wide open by my father.

Origins of a Nonfiction Writer

I COME FROM AN ISLAND and a family that reinforced my identity as a marginal American, an outsider, an alien in my native nation. But while this may have impeded my assimilation into the mainstream, it did guide me through the wayward yet interesting path of life that is familiar to many searching people who become writers.

My origins are Italian. I am the son of a dour but debonair custom tailor from Calabria and an amiably enterprising Italian-American mother who successfully operated our family dress business. I was educated by Irish-Catholic nuns and priests in a poor parish school on the Protestant-controlled island of Ocean City, off the southern coastline of New Jersey, where I was born in 1932.

This breezy, sand-swept community had first been established as a religious retreat in 1879 by Methodist ministers wishing to secure the presence of God on the beach, to shade the summer from the corrupting exposure of the flesh, and to eliminate the temptations of alcohol and other evil spirits they saw swirling around them as freely as the mosquitoes from the nearby marshlands. While these sober ministers did not achieve all of their virtuous ambitions, they did instill on the island a sense of Victorian restraint and hypocrisy that exists to this day.

The sale of liquor remains forbidden. Most businesses are closed on the Sabbath. The steeples of churches rise prominently in an unpolluted sky. In the center of town are white gingerbread houses with large porches, turrets, and finials that retain the look of late-nineteenth-century America. In my youth a voluptuous young woman who strolled on the beach wearing a slim bikini would often prompt mild frowns from the town's proper matrons, if not from the middle-aged men concealing their interest behind dark sunglasses.

In this setting where sensuality and sin are always in delicate balance, I cultivated a rampant curiosity that coexisted with my nun-numbed sexuality. Often I went clam digging after supper with my boyhood friends, but at times I strayed alone toward the beachfront bulkheads behind which the island's most amorous teenaged couples necked every night; later, however, I conformed to the bedtime rules of my parochial school: I slept on my back, with my arms across my chest, and my hands resting on opposite shoulders—a presumably pious posture that made masturbation impossible. At dawn I served Mass as the acolyte to a whiskey-scented priest, and after school I worked as an errand boy in my family's dress shop that catered to decorous women of ample figures and means. These were the ministers' wives, the bankers' wives, the bridge players, the tale bearers. They were the white-gloved ladies who in summer avoided the beach and the boardwalk to spend considerable amounts of time and money along the main avenue in places like my parents' shop, where, amid the low humming of the fans and the attentive care of my mother in the dressing rooms, they would try on clothes while discussing their private lives and the happenings and misadventures of their friends and neighbors.

The shop was a kind of talk show that flowed around the engaging manner and well-timed questions of my mother; and as a boy not much taller than the counters behind which I used to pause and eavesdrop, I learned much that would be useful to me years later when I began interviewing people for articles and books.

I learned to listen with patience and care, and never to interrupt even when people were having great difficulty in explaining themselves, for during such halting and imprecise moments (as the listening skills of my patient mother taught me) people often are very revealing—what they hesitate to talk about can tell much about them. Their pauses, their evasions, their sudden shifts in subject matter are likely indicators of what embarrasses them, or irritates them, or what they regard as too private or imprudent to be disclosed to another person at that particular time. However, I also overheard many people discussing candidly with my mother what they had earlier avoided—a reaction that I think had less to do with her inquiring nature or sensitively posed questions than with their gradual acceptance of her as a trustworthy individual in whom they could confide. My mother's best customers were women less in need of new dresses than the need to communicate.

Most of them were born of privileged Philadelphia families of Anglo-Saxon or Germanic stock, and they were generally tall and large-sized in a way typified by Eleanor Roosevelt. Their suntanned, leathery, handsome faces were browned primarily as a result of their devotion to gardening, which they described to my mother as their favorite summertime hobby. They acknowledged not having gone to the beach in years, wearing during those years what I assume were bathing suits too modestly designed to prompt a lifeguard's second look.

My mother had been reared in a Brooklyn neighborhood populated primarily by Italian and Jewish immigrant families, and while she had acquired a certain worldliness and fashion consciousness during the four premarital years she had worked as a buyer for the borough's largest department store, she had known very little about Protestant America until she married my father. He had left Italy to live briefly in Paris and Philadelphia before residing on the white-bread island of Ocean City, where he started a tailoring and dry cleaning business, and later, in partnership with my mother, the dress boutique. Although my father's reserved and exacting manner, and the daily care he attached to his appearance, gave him a semblance of compatibility with the town's most scrupulous leading men, it was my convivial mother who established our family's social ties to the island's establishment, doing so through the women she cultivated first as customers and eventually as friends and confidantes. She welcomed these women into her shop as if into her home, guiding them to the red leather chairs outside the dressing rooms while offering to send me out to the corner drugstore for sodas and iced tea. She did not permit telephone callers to interrupt her discussions, relying on my father or one of the employees to take messages; and while there were one or two women who abused her forbearance as a listener, droning on for hours and ultimately inducing her to hide in the stockroom when she next saw them coming, most of what I heard and witnessed in the shop was much more interesting and educational than what I learned from the black-robed censors who taught me in parochial school.

Indeed, in the decades since I have left home, during which time I have retained a clear memory of my eavesdropping youth and the women's voices that gave it expression, it seems to me that many of the social and political questions that have been debated in America in the second half of the twentieth-century—the role of religion in the bedroom, racial equality, women's rights, the advisability of films and publications featuring sex and violence—all were discussed in my mother's boutique as I grew up during the war and postwar years of the 1940s.

While I remember my father listening late at night to the war news on his shortwave radio in our apartment above the store (his two younger brothers were then in Mussolini's army opposing the Allied invasion of Italy), a more intimate sense of the conflict came to me from a weeping woman who visited our shop one afternoon with word of her son's death on an Italian battlefield, an announcement that drew my mother's deepest sympathy and compassion—while my troubled father remained behind the closed door of his tailoring room in the rear of the building. I recall other women complaining during these years of their daughters leaving school to "run off" with servicemen, or to do volunteer work in hospitals from which they frequently did not return home at night, and of middle-aged husbands who were seen barhopping in Atlantic City after attributing their absences from home to their supervisory jobs in Philadelphia defense plants.

The exigencies of the war, and the excuses it provided, were of course evident and available everywhere; but I think that large events influence small communities in ways that are uniquely illuminating with regard to the people involved, for the people *are* more involved in places where almost everybody knows everybody else (or think they do), where there are fewer walls behind which to hide, where sounds carry farther, and where a less-hurried pace allows a longer look, a deeper perception, and, as personified by my mother, the leisure and luxury of listening.

From her I not only learned this first lesson that would be essential to my later work as a nonfiction writer pursuing the literature of reality, but I also gained from my store-centered upbringing an understanding of another generation, one that represented a variety in style, attitude, and background beyond what I could have encountered in my normal experiences in school or at home. In addition to my mother's customers and their husbands who occasionally accompanied them, the place was frequented by the female employees who helped my mother with the selling and bookkeeping during the busy summer months; the elderly semiretired tailors who worked with my father in the back room altering suits and dresses (and, not infrequently, trying to remove whiskey stains from the clothes of the town's many furtive drinkers); the high school senior boys who drove the plant's delivery trucks; and the itinerant black men who operated the pressing machines. All the pressers were flat-footed and had been rejected for military service during World War II. One of these was a militant Muslim who first made me aware of black anger in this period when even the U.S. Army was racially segregated. "Draft or no draft," I heard him say often, "they never gonna get *me* to fight in this white man's war!"

Another presser who then worked in the shop, a massive man with a shaved head and knife-scarred forearms, had a small, feisty wife who regularly entered the steaming back room to berate him loudly because of his all-night gambling habits and other indiscretions. I was reminded of her aggressiveness many years later, in 1962, while I was researching an article for *Esquire* on the ex-heavyweight champion Joe Louis, a man with whom I had cavorted through several New York nightclubs on the evening before our flight back to his home in Los Angeles. At the baggage claim area in Los Angeles, we were met by the fighter's wife (his third), and she promptly provoked a domestic quarrel that provided me with the opening scene of the magazine article.

After my colleague Tom Wolfe had read it, he publicly credited it with introducing him to a new form of nonfiction, one that brought the reader into close proximity to real people and places through the use of accurately reported dialogue, scene-setting, intimate personal details, including the use of interior monologue—[my mother would inquire of her friends: *What were you thinking when you did such-and-such?* and I asked the same question of those I later wrote about]—in addition to other techniques that had long been associated with fiction writers and playwrights. While Mr. Wolfe heralded my Joe Louis piece as emblematic of what he called "The New Journalism," I think his complimenting me was undeserved, for I had not written then, or since then, anything I consider to be stylistically "new," since my approach to research and storytelling had evolved out of my family's store, drawing its focus and inspiration primarily from the sights and sounds of the elderly people I saw interacting there every day like characters in a Victorian play—the white-gloved ladies sitting in the red leather chairs, indulging in midafternoon chats while gazing be-

yond the storefront awning out into the hot, sun-burnished business
district in a time that seemed to be passing them by.

I think of them now as America's last generation of virgin brides. I
see them as representing nonactive statistics in the Kinsey Report—
women who did *not* partake in premarital sex, or extramarital sex, or
even masturbation. I imagine that most of them have now departed from
the planet, taking with them their old-fashioned values laced tight by
bindings of restraint. At other times I feel something of their reincar-
nated vitality (together with the vigilance of my parochial school's nuns)
in the spirit of 1990s neo-Victorianism—their hands in the writing of the
Antioch College dating code, their voices in harmony with antiporn fem-
inism, their presence hovering over our government like a governess.

But my memory of the white-gloved ladies remains benign, for
they and the other people who patronized or worked in my parents'
store (plus the curiosity transferred by my mother) sparked my early
interest in small-town society, in the common concerns of ordinary
people. Each of my books, in fact, draws inspiration in some way from
the elements of my island and its inhabitants, who are typical of the
millions who interact familiarly each day in stores and coffee shops
and along the promenades of small towns, suburban villages, and
urban neighborhoods everywhere. And yet, unless such individuals
become involved in crimes and horrible accidents, their existence is
generally ignored by the media as well as by historians and biographers, who tend to concentrate on people who reveal themselves in
some blatant or obvious way, or who stand out from the crowd as leaders, or achievers, or are otherwise famous or infamous.

One result is that "normal" everyday life in America is portrayed
primarily in "fiction"—in the works of novelists, playwrights, and
short-story writers such as John Cheever, Raymond Carver, Russell
Banks, Tennessee Williams, Joyce Carol Oates, and others possessing
the creative talent to elevate ordinary life to art, and to make memo-

rable the commonplace experiences and concerns of men and women worthy of Arthur Miller's plea in behalf of his suffering salesman: "Attention must be paid."

And yet I have always believed, and have hoped to prove with my efforts, that attention might also be paid to "ordinary" people in nonfiction, and that *without changing the names or falsifying the facts,* writers might produce what in this anthology is called the "Literature of Reality." Different writers, of course, reflect differing definitions of reality. In my case, it reflects the perspective and sensibilities of a small-town American outsider whose exploratory view of the world is accompanied by the essence of the people and place I left behind, the overlooked nonnewsworthy population that is everywhere, but rarely taken into account by journalists and other chroniclers of reality.

My first book, *New York—a Serendipiter's Journey,* published in 1961, presents the small-town character of New York neighborhoods and reveals the interesting lives of certain obscure individuals dwelling within the shadows of the towering city. My next book, *The Bridge,* published in 1963, focuses on the private lives and loves of steelworkers as they link a bridge to an island, altering the character of the land and its inhabitants. My first best-seller in 1969, entitled *The Kingdom and the Power,* describes the family backgrounds and interpersonal relationships of my former colleagues on the *New York Times,* where I worked from 1955 through 1965. This was my only full-time job, and I spent all my years there in the main newsroom on Forty-third Street off Broadway. This newsroom was my "store."

My next best-seller, *Honor Thy Father,* was written in reaction to my defensive father's embarrassment over the prevalence of Italian names in organized crime. I grew up hearing him claim that the American press exaggerated the power of the Mafia and the role of Italian gangsters within it. While my research would prove him wrong, the book that I completed in 1971 (having gained access to the Mafia through an Italian-American member whose friendship and trust I cultivated) was less about gun battles than about the islandlike insularity that characterizes the private lives of gangsters and their families.

In response to the sexual repression and hypocrisy that was evident in my formative years, I wrote, almost in dedication to the patrons of my mother's boutique, *Thy Neighbor's Wife*. Published in 1980, it traces the definition and redefinition of morality from my adolescence in the 1930s through the sexually liberating pre-AIDS era that continued into the 1980s—a half century of social change that I described in the context of the ordinary lives led by typical men and women around the country.

The final chapter in that book refers to the research I did among nude sunbathers at a private beach located twenty miles downstream from my native island—a beach I visited without clothing and on which I would soon discover myself being observed by voyeurs standing with binoculars aboard the several anchored vessels they had sailed over from the Ocean City Yacht Club. In my earlier book about the *Times*, *The Kingdom and the Power*, I had referred to my one-time profession as voyeuristic. But here on this nudist beach, without press credentials or a stitch of clothing, my role was suddenly reversed. Now *I* was being observed, rather than doing the observing. And there is no doubt that my next and most personal book, *Unto the Sons*, published in 1991, progressed from that final scene in *Thy Neighbor's Wife*. It is the result of my willingness to expose in a book of nonfiction myself and my past influences, without changing the names of the people or the place that shaped my character. It is also a modest example of what is possible for nonfiction writers in these times of increased candor, of more liberal laws with regard to libel and the invasion of privacy, and of expanding opportunities to explore a wide variety of subjects even, as in my case, from the narrow confines of an island.

I left the island in the autumn of 1949 to attend the University of Alabama. I was then seventeen, acne-scarred, and socially insecure in ways I had not been when younger. The comfort I had found among my elders during my errand-boy days in my parents' shop, and the polite and highly personalized "store manners" that I had inherited from my mother and that had ingratiated me with the elite women who patronized her boutique in summertime, had provided me with no headstart advantages during the previous damp and deserted months of the off-season when I had attended high school. To most of the teenagers with whom I spent four scholastic years in a chilly brick building two blocks from the ocean, I was a classmate in name only.

I was variously looked upon as "aloof," "complicated," "vague," "smug," "quirky," "in another world"—or so I was described by a few former students years later at a class reunion I attended. They also recalled that during our school days I had somehow seemed to be "older" than the rest of them, an impression I attribute partly to my being the only student who came to class daily wearing a jacket and tie. But even if I appeared to be older, I did not feel senior to anyone, and certainly never a leader in any of those areas by which we judged one another—athletically, socially, or academically.

In sports I was too slightly built and insufficiently fast to make the football team; in basketball I was a bench-warming substitute guard; and in baseball I was a fair contact hitter and a shortstop with "good hands" but an erratic throwing arm, and I was inserted into the starting lineup by the coach hesitantly and irregularly. My main athletic contributions usually came *after* the games, when I returned home and used the store's typewriter to write about the contests for the town's weekly newspaper, and sometimes for the daily paper published in nearby Atlantic City. This was not an assignment I had initially sought. It had long been the obligation of one of the assistant coaches to phone-in to the press the scores and accounts of those games that the editors deemed too unimportant to be covered by any of their own personnel. But one afternoon during my junior year, the assistant coach of our baseball team protested that he was too busy to perform this chore; and for some reason the head coach asked me to do it, possibly because at the time he saw me standing nearby in the locker room doing nothing, and because he also knew that I subscribed to sports magazines (which he frequently borrowed and never returned). On the mistaken assumption that relieving the athletic department of its press duties would gain me the gratitude of the coach and get me more playing time, I took the job and even embellished it by using my typing skills to compose my own accounts of the games rather than merely relaying the information to the newspapers by telephone. Sometimes this resulted in my receiving bylines on articles in which I was obliged to acknowledge my inadequacies as an athlete: *The game got out of hand in the eighth inning when, with the bases loaded, Talese's wild throw from shortstop bounced beyond the first baseman's reach and rolled under the stands . . .*

Although there were many young women in high school to whom I was attracted, I was too self-conscious, especially after my bout with acne, to ask any of them out on dates. And while I devoted hours every evening to my schoolbooks, what most engaged my interest in those books were ideas and observations that my teachers invariably considered inconsequential and never included in the questions they formed for our quizzes and examinations. Except for my excellent marks in typing class, taught by a buxom, flaxen-braided opera buff who was a friend of my mother's—and who sent my spirits soaring one day when she compared my nimble-fingered hands to those of a young classical pianist whom she admired—my grades were below average in almost every subject; and in the late spring of 1949, I graduated from high school in the lower third of my class.

Adding to my dismay later that summer was being rejected by each of the dozen colleges to which I had applied in and around my home state of New Jersey. After I had contacted our principal's secretary, seeking the names and addresses of additional colleges to which I might apply, the principal himself paid a rare and unexpected visit to my parents' shop. At the time I was up in my father's balcony office that overlooked the main room of the shop, seated at his desk reviewing the list of late-afternoon delivery stops I was about to make in connection with my summertime job as a driver of one of the dry cleaning trucks. I was not aware of the principal's presence until I heard his familiar stentorian voice greeting my mother, who was standing at a dress rack putting price tags on some of the new fall merchandise I had earlier unpacked.

While I watched anxiously, crouching behind one of the potted palms placed along the ledge of the balcony, I saw my father coming out from the tailoring room to shake hands with the principal before joining my mother in front of a counter while the principal cleared his throat loudly, as he always did in our assembly hall prior to making announcements. A lean and bespectacled man with curly gray hair, he was dressed as usual in a white round-collared shirt adorned with a polka-dot bow tie, and hung from a gold watch-chain strung across the vest of his three-piece beige suit was his diamond-studded Phi Beta Kappa key, which I could see sparkling from a distance of thirty feet. My custom-tailored father, being his own best customer, was also nattily attired, but there was a lofty bearing about the principal that somehow diminished my father, or so it seemed to me, and it made me uncomfortable even though it had no apparent effect upon my father. He stood there calmly next to my mother with his arms crossed, leaning ever-so-lightly back against the counter waiting for the principal to speak.

"I'm really sorry to burden you both with this," he began, not sounding sorry at all, "for I know your son is a fine young man. But I'm afraid he is not college material. He persists in sending out applications, which I've always advised him against, and now I'm appealing to you to try to discourage him." He paused, as if expecting some objection. When my parents remained silent, he continued in a softer tone, even sympathetically: "Oh, I know you both want the best for your son. But you both work very hard for your money. And I would hate to see you waste it on his tuition. I really think it would be better for you, and for your son as well, if you would keep him here in your business, and perhaps prepare him to take it over one day, rather than to entertain any thoughts of his going on to college, and . . ."

As my parents continued to listen quietly, I stared down at the three of them, humiliated but not surprised by what I was hearing, and yet I was disappointed that my parents had said nothing on my behalf. It was not that I resented the idea of taking over their business. As their only son, and the older of their two children, I sometimes thought of it as inevitable and perhaps my best prospect. But I was also eager to escape the familiarity of this island that in wintertime especially was so forlorn; and I had looked upon college as a way out, a destination toward which I had always saved my store earnings and to which my parents had also promised to provide whatever I lacked financially. Still, I was not sure how a college education would serve my career, since I was uncertain I would ever have a career—except, as the principal was cogently suggesting, within the boundaries of the shop.

In recent weeks, perhaps in reaction to my mounting rejection mail, my father had often repeated an offer he had first made months earlier about sending me to Paris to study tailoring on the classical level it was practiced by his Italian cousins on the Rue de la Paix. I might ultimately develop into a high-fashion designer of suits and dresses for women, my father explained, zestfully adding: "Ah, *there's*

where the money is!" The renowned dress designer Emanuel Ungaro
had once worked as a tailoring apprentice in the firm of my father's
cousin, and I myself had not dismissed the idea of seeking such an ap-
prenticeship during this uncertain summer after high school.

Another possible option for me existed in journalism. In addition
to the sports reporting I did for the town weekly, I had volunteered
during my junior year to do a nonathletic feature called "High School
Highlights," a column devoted to student programs and activities in
drama, art, music, community work, and such social events as the class
dances and proms I had always avoided. The editor liked my idea and
accepted it on the condition that I expect no higher payment than our
already established sports rate, which was ten cents for every inch of
my writing as measured within the newspaper's published pages. From
the "Highlights" column and sportswriting combined, I soon was receiving weekly checks in the range of two to four dollars—a sum far
below what was paid even to the lowest apprentice tailor in Paris, my
father reminded me; but I was being rewarded in extra ways that were
privately satisfying.

Although I continued to forgo asking young women to dances, I
sometimes did go alone in my new role as a social columnist. For individuals who were as shy and curious as myself, journalism was an
ideal preoccupation, a vehicle that transcended the limitations of ret-
icence. It also provided excuses for inquiring into other people's
lives, asking them leading questions, and expecting reasonable answers; and it could as well be diverted into serving any number of hidden personal agendas.

For instance, when my pet mongrel ran away one day while I was at
school during my senior year—despite my mother's insistent denials,
I've always believed that she gave my dog away, or had him "put away,"
because of my repeated failures at keeping him out of the store—I persuaded the editor to let me write a feature article about the local animal

shelter, an idea inspired entirely out of my wishful thinking that I would find my dog there, or at least confirm there my worst suspicions about my mother, whose graciousness toward customers did not extend to animals. After three prolonged visits to the shelter, however, where I discovered no evidence of my dog's life or death, I did learn for the first time about the "power of the press"—or rather about the many privileges and courtesies that could be accrued by self-interested people like myself while masquerading as an objective journalist. The town's leading animal rights advocates, including the philanthropists who helped to support the shelter financially, welcomed me cordially every time I arrived there to examine each howling and vibrating steel cage bearing newly arrived animals; and I was also given access (unattended) to the office filing cabinets that contained not only public documents and statistics about lost-and-found pets but also several unpaid parking tickets tagged to the dogcatcher's private car, along with a few fading, mistakenly filed love letters received long ago by one of the shelter's deceased volunteer secretaries. In the files I found mortuary records pertaining to a pet cemetery that I never knew existed on the outskirts of Atlantic City; and when I mentioned this to the shelter's director, he insisted on driving me there—filling me with renewed hope and fear that I might at last discover the final destiny of my missing mongrel.

But after being introduced to the head groundskeeper of the sprawling, tree-shaded burial grounds jutted with stone statuary, crosses, and other monuments honoring the memory of some 800 pets—dogs, horses, cats, monkeys, guinea pigs, canaries, parrots, goats, mice—I was assured that no mongrel matching my description had recently been brought there. Yet my interest in the pet cemetery continued unabated, and with the groundskeeper's permission I subsequently returned several times alone, driving my dry cleaning truck after work to the site, which was ten miles inland beyond the island's bridge. Remaining until twilight to stroll past the gravestones, which often displayed the pet's pictures along with their names and their owner's words of affection, I was no longer searching for signs of my own dog but was responding instead to the vast sadness and sense of loss that now allied me to this place.

Here were mourners lamenting the death of their animals in human terms, decorating the gravesites with flowers, and, as the groundskeeper told me, often interring their pets in white lambskin caskets within concrete vaults, and placing silk handkerchiefs over their animal's faces while services were said, services accompanied at times by funeral processions, pallbearers, and requiem music. Many affluent and famous people whose pets had died while the owners were visiting or working in Atlantic City had chosen this place for the burial, and among those who did this were the financier J. P. Morgan, the songwriter Irving Berlin, and the film actress Paulette Goddard. Some of the buried animals had achieved distinction on their own: Here were the remains of "Amaz the Wild," a celebrated show dog reputed to be the last of the great Russian wolfhounds raised by the Romanoff family; "Cootie," the revered mascot of Infantry Company 314 of World War I history; and "Rex," a dog that performed for years on stage in Atlantic City and throughout the nation.

The cemetery had been founded in the early 1900s by an animal-loving couple who resided in the Atlantic City area and whose practice of providing their dead pets with funeral rites and gravestones in their backyard had gained the approval of their pet-owning neighbors, and then the desire of these neighbors to share the space and the cost of its upkeep. After the original couple's death, the cemetery was bought and enlarged upon by a woman who was in her midseventies when the groundskeeper introduced me to her; and from her—after a minimum of coaxing—I obtained all the cooperation I needed to write what I hoped would be a lengthy and poignant article about the cemetery.

This story had the elements that appealed to me. I was connected to it personally. It had enduring human appeal. And it was centered on an obscure place that until now had eluded the attention or interest of other writers and journalists. Since I had already satisfied my obligation to my editor regarding the island's animal shelter—I had written a brief unsigned piece announcing the director's latest fund-raising campaign—I was free to submit this more interesting story in a place where I might attract more readers, namely the *Atlantic City Press*. From a *Press* copyreader that I knew from my sports assignments, I obtained the name of the Suburban Editor to whom I should submit the article; and two weeks after I had mailed it to him, I received a note of acceptance together with a check in a sum sufficiently awesome to impress my father temporarily—twenty-five dollars.

The 2,000-word piece was run with my byline at the top of the suburban section under a double-decked four-column headline accompanied by a large picture of the burial grounds taken by a staff photographer. While I was then years away from the understated literary style I would aspire to during my *Esquire* magazine-writing period, the cemetery piece showed early signs of my continuing interest in providing readers with precise details (. . . *Mr. Hillelson gave his dog, Arno, a funeral with six pallbearers and a three-car procession through the streets . . .*) although it also came with a bit of bathos that the cemetery owner had recounted to me and that I could not resist (. . . *as the old blind man's dog was lowered into the ground, he rose and cried, "Oh God! first you take away my eyes, and then my dog"*).

The response to the article was immediate. I received many complimentary telephone calls and letters from readers as far away as Trenton and Philadelphia, along with comments from both the Suburban Editor and my island editor indicating that I might have a future in some aspect of reporting or writing. Neither of these men had attended college, which were facts I had elicited from them when it began to seem that this would also be my fate. But it had not been "fate" in their cases, they had emphasized; they had eschewed college by choice, as had many journalists of their generation, believing that it induced an effeteness in a tough profession then smitten by the flamboyant spirit of the "Front Page," of reporters who talked like big-city detectives, and who typed, if at all, with two fingers.

I do not know if I was finding consolation in this imagery as I sat eavesdropping in the balcony while my principal was characterizing me as ill prepared for university life. All I recall, as I mentioned earlier, was a certain recurring shame about my lowly academic status, and disappointment that my parents had not challenged the principal's assessment of me, leading me to wonder if perhaps they might even be secretly relieved; insofar as the store was concerned, the question of succession was now resolved.

After the principal had departed, and while my parents now began communicating quietly at the counter, I sank softly into my father's chair and listlessly glanced at my delivery route spread out on the desk. I remained there for several minutes, not knowing what to do next, not even knowing if my parents were aware that I was up there—until I suddenly heard my father's voice calling from the bottom of the staircase.

"Your principal is not very smart," he announced, removing an envelope from his breast pocket and summoning me down to read it. And with a slight smile he added, "You're going to college."

The envelope contained a letter of admission from the University of Alabama. Unknown to me until it was later explained, my father had discussed my difficulties a month earlier with a fellow Rotarian for whom he made suits—an Alabama-born physician who had practiced medicine on the island since the mid-1920s. He was also our family doctor and, lucky for me, an influential graduate of the University of Alabama. In addition to this, his sister-in-law was my typing teacher, whose limited but laudatory view of my talents represented the most impressive vote of confidence I could ever hope to get from the local faculty; and she, together with the doctor, apparently had written so positively and persuasively about me to the Alabama dean, contending that I had a growth potential beyond what was indicated by my school grades, that I was admitted into the university's freshman class.

Also in my favor perhaps was the desire of many southern colleges in those days to bring to their then lily-white and heavily home-bred campuses some out-of-state diversity that might include students with backgrounds that were Slovak, Greek, Italian, Jewish, Muslim, or anything but black. Long before the terms *affirmative action* and *mi-nority quotas* came into use, such sentiments existed unofficially in places like Alabama with regard to the offspring of people that the Klan might define as marginally white; and I think I was a beneficiary of this slow-moving trend toward tolerance. When I read my father's letter, however, I realized that I did not know where Alabama *was;* and after locating it on a map, I felt some anxiety about attending a college so far away from home. But during the Labor Day weekend, as many of my fellow graduates from high school were preparing to leave the is-land for campuses within the state, or within neighboring New York and Pennsylvania, I was happy that I would be far away from them. Where I was going no one would know me. No one would know who I was, who I had been. My high school records were as good as burned. I would have a fresh start, a second chance. As my parents and young sister escorted me on a balmy fall afternoon in early September of 1949 past the stone columns of the Philadelphia train station, where I would soon board one of the silver-paneled railcars across which was painted a dark streamline-lettered sign reading *The Southerner,* I imagined that I was feeling what my father had been feeling twenty-five years before when he left Europe at seventeen for America. I was an immigrant starting a new life in a new land.

The train moved slowly and jerkily through the night down past the Shenandoah Valley of Virginia into the Carolinas and Tennessee and the northwestern tip of Georgia. The car was filled with attractive, friendly, and neatly dressed young men and women who chatted amiably and laughed often, and who traveled with their tweed jackets and camel's hair coats folded carelessly up in the overhead racks next to suitcases plastered with stickers announcing: "Duke," "Sweet Briar," "Georgia Tech," "LSU," "Tulane"—and none, I was happy to note, "Alabama." I was still pursuing a singular route.

I did not linger in the club car, where a crap game was being conducted on the floor by several shouting men in their midtwenties who were students on the GI Bill. I learned this from overhearing two black porters complaining to one another about the ruckus; since neither made any attempt to stop it, it continued through the eighteen hours I remained on board. I spent most of that time staring out the window at a blurred nocturnal landscape, trying to memorize some of the strange and faintly lit station names of the small towns we raced through; and, since I could not sleep, I read a few chapters from *The Young Lions* by one of my favorite authors, Irwin Shaw—I think my being seen on two occasions carrying novels by Irwin Shaw and John O'Hara into senior English had not endeared me to the Virginia Woolf–loving woman who taught the class—and on the train I also perused the Alabama registration catalog that had arrived on the eve of my departure. I planned to major in journalism. Although I still was not convinced that this would become my career, I believed that taking journalism would challenge me the least in an academic sense. I wanted every chance to remain in school and protect my student-deferment status from the clutches of my draft board.

After the train had arrived at a town in central western Alabama called Tuscaloosa, where I was the single departing passenger, I handed the two cracked leather suitcases I had borrowed from my

father down to a top-hatted black jitney driver, who soon trans-
ported me into what could have been a movie set for *Gone With the
Wind*. Stately antebellum buildings loomed wherever I looked from
the jitney's windows, structures that were part of the older section of
the University of Alabama. Some had been restored after the campus had been attacked and torched by Union soldiers during the
Civil War. Now all of them were being put to use for classroom study
or as social or residential centers for students, faculty, and alumni.

My dormitory was a half mile beyond, built on lowlands near a
swamp that had become an expanding locale of postwar building re-
sulting from the student increase magnified by the GI Bill. My quarters
were small, dank, and, as I would discover soon enough, penetrated
regularly by windblown musky odors emanating from a papermill located outside the school grounds off the main highway. The dormitory
was also invaded by the nightly return of ex-GI students from the beer
halls that flourished beyond the "dry" county that encompassed the
campus—serenading revelers eager to begin playing cards and shooting dice with the vigor I had seen exhibited by those other veterans on
the club car.

But far from being disturbed by the nightly commotion—though I
contributed very little to it even as I began making friends during the
succeeding weeks—I became drawn to these older men more than to
my contemporaries. In my comfortable role as an observer and listener, I liked watching the veterans playing blackjack and gin rummy,
and hearing their war stories, their barracks language, their dirty
jokes. Up half the night, and rarely cracking a book, they rose daily to
attend classes, or cut classes, with no apparent fear of ever failing a
course—an attitude that left some of them open for surprises. Not all
the survivors of the war survived their first college year.

I of course did not follow their example, lacking the confidence at
this point to be casual about anything; but being around these men

loosened me up a bit, spared me from having to compare myself exclusively and perhaps unfavorably with my age group, and it seemed to have a favorable effect on my health and schoolwork. My acne had all but vanished within six months of my arrival, a cure I could attribute to the festive atmosphere of the dorm and maybe even the salubrious, if foul-smelling, fragrance that floated in from the papermill. I made passing grades in all of my freshman courses, and near the end of the term I had my first coffee date, then movie date, then first French kiss with a blonde sophomore from Birmingham. She was studying journalism but would have a career in advertising.

As a journalism student I was usually ranked in the middle of the class, even during my junior and senior years when I was active on the college weekly and worked as the campus correspondent for the Scripps-Howard daily, the *Birmingham Post–Herald*. The faculty tended to favor the reportorial style of the conservative though very reliable *Kansas City Star*, where some of them had previously worked as editors and staff writers. They had definite views of what constituted "news" and how news stories should be presented. The "five *W*s"—who, what, when, where, why—were questions they thought should be answered succinctly and impersonally in the opening paragraphs of an article. Since I sometimes resisted the formula and might try instead to communicate the news through the personal experience of the single person most affected by it—being doubtless influenced more by the fiction writers I preferred reading to the practitioners of "objective" nonfiction—I was never a faculty favorite.

It should not be inferred, however, that there was any unpleasantness between us or that I was a rebellious student. They were reflecting an era that predated the rise of television as the dominant force in spot-news reporting. I was reflecting my own peculiar background in my ambivalence about who and what was important. In reading through old newspapers and other antiquated periodicals in the school library and elsewhere, as I sometimes did in my leisure time, it seemed that most of the news printed on the front pages was historically and socially less revealing of the time than what was published in the classified and the display advertising spread through the middle and back pages. The advertising offered detailed sketches and photographs showing the then-current fashion in clothing, the body styles of cars, where rental apartments were obtainable and at what cost, what jobs were available to the white-collar and the laboring classes; while the front pages were largely concerned with the words and deeds of many seemingly important people who were no longer important.

Throughout my college days, which ended in 1953, and in the years following at the *Times*, I sought assignments that were unlikely candidates for page one. Even when I specialized in writing about sports, whether it was at Alabama or at the *Times*, the final results interested me less than who played the game; and if given the choice of writing about people who personified the Right Stuff or the Wrong Stuff, I would invariably choose the latter. When I became the sports editor of my college newspaper in my junior year, I took full advantage of my position to describe the despair of the infielder whose errant throw lost the game; of the basketball benchwarmer who saw action only during scrimmages; and of many other ill-starred characters on the fringes of the playing field. One of the sports features I wrote for the college paper concerned a big, seven-foot student from the backwoods hill country who did not know how, and did not want to learn how, to play any games. I also wrote about an elderly black man, the grandson of slaves, who was the athletic department's chief locker-room attendant; and how in this time and place where there was no interracial contact in sports, the all-white 'Bama football team began each game by stroking the black man's head for good luck. If I wrote more compassionately about losers than winners during my sports-writing days, it was because the losers' stories to me were more inter-

esting, a view I retained long after leaving the Alabama campus. As a
Times sportswriter I became enamored of a heavyweight fighter, Floyd
Patterson, who was constantly being knocked down, but who kept getting up. I wrote more than thirty different pieces about him in the
daily paper and the *Times Sunday Magazine*, and finally did a long
piece about him in *Esquire* entitled "The Loser."

This was done when I was engaged in what Tom Wolfe called the
"New Journalism," but, as I hope is obvious, it is founded in old-
fashioned legwork, hanging out with the story's subject day after day
(just as I had hung out in my parents' shop as a juvenile observer and
listener)—the "Art of Hanging Out," I've sometimes called it—and it
is an indispensable part of what motivates my work, together with
that other element that I have maybe mentioned too much already,
that gift from my mother: curiosity. My mother also knew that there
is a difference between curiosity and nosiness, and this distinction
has always guided me with regard to the people I interviewed and how
I presented them in print. I never wrote about anyone for whom I did
not have at least a considerable measure of respect, and this respect
is evident in the effort I take with my writing and the length I will go
in trying to understand and express their viewpoints and the social
and historical forces that contributed to their character—or lack of
character.

Writing for me has always been difficult, and I would not invest
the necessary time and effort on people merely to ridicule them; and
I say this having written about gangsters, pornographers, and others
who have earned society's disapproval and contempt. But there was
in these people also a redeeming quality that I found interesting, a
prevailing misconception that I wanted to correct, or a dark streak
upon which I hoped to cast some light because I believed it would
also illuminate a larger area in which a part of us all live. Norman
Mailer and Truman Capote have achieved this in writing about mur-

derers, and other writers—Thomas Keneally and John Hersey—show it to us out of the gas chambers of Nazi Germany and the fatal fumes of Hiroshima.

Nosiness represents mainly the interests of the mean-spirited, the one-night-stand temperament of tabloid journalists and even mainstream writers and biographers seizing every opportunity to belittle big names, to publicize a public figure's slip of the tongue, to scandalize every sexual dalliance even when it bears no relevance to that person's political or public service.

I have avoided writing about political figures, for so much about them is of temporary interest; they are dated people, victims of the recycling process of politics, doomed if they openly say what they truly think. My curiosity lures me, as I've said, toward private figures, unknown individuals to whom I usually represent their first experience in being interviewed. I could write about them today, or tomorrow, or next year, and it will make no difference in the sense of their topicality. These people are dateless. They can live as long as the language used to describe them lives, *if* the language is blessed with lasting qualities.

My very first writing in the *Times*, in the winter of 1953 following my June graduation from Alabama, dealt with an obscure man who worked in the center of "the Crossroads of the World," Times Square. I was then a copyboy, a job I had gotten after walking into the paper's personnel department one afternoon and impressing the director with my fast and accurate typing and my herringbone tailored suit (she later told me). Some months after I had gotten the job, I was on my lunch hour, wandering awkwardly around the theater district, when I began to concentrate on the five-foot-high electric light sign that rotated in glittering motion the world's latest headlines around the tall, three-sided building overlooking Forty-second Street. I was not really reading the headlines; I was wondering instead: *How does*

that sign work? How do the words get formed by those lights? Who's behind
all this?

I entered the building and found a staircase. Walking up to the top,
I dicovered a large, high-ceilinged room, like an artist's loft, and
there on a ladder was a man putting chunks of wooden blocks into
what looked like a small church organ. Each of these blocks formed
letters. With one hand he held a clipboard on which the latest headline bulletins were attached—the headlines changed constantly—and
in the other hand he held blocks that he inserted into the organ that
created lettering along the exterior wall's three-sided sign containing
15,000 twenty-watt bulbs.

I watched him for a while, and when he stopped I called to him,
saying I was a copyboy from the *Times*, which was located a half block
away but which also owned this smaller building with the sign. The
man greeted me, and, taking a coffee break, he came down the ladder
and talked to me. He said his name was James Torpey, adding that he
had been standing on that ladder setting headlines for the *Times* since
1928. His first headline was on the night of the presidential election,
and it read: "Hoover Defeats Smith!" For twenty-five years this man
Torpey had been on that ladder, and even with my limited experience
in New York journalism I knew that *that* was some kind of story. After
writing some notes about Mr. Torpey on the folded paper I always kept
in my pocket, I returned to the main office and typed a short memo
about him and put it in the mailbox of the City Editor. I wasn't being
paid to write, only to run errands and perform other menial tasks; but
within a few days, I received word from the editor that he would welcome a few paragraphs from me on the high life of the lightbulb man—
and this was published (without my byline) on the second day of
November in 1953.

That article—and also by bylined piece in the *Times*'s Sunday travel
section three months later about the popularity of the three-wheeled

rolling chairs that people rode on the Atlantic City boardwalk—brought me to the attention of the editors. Other pieces followed, including a Sunday magazine article that the *Times* published in 1955 while I was on leave with the army. The piece was about a woman old enough to be one of my mother's most venerable customers—a silent-screen actress named Nita Naldi, who had once been Valentino's leading lady in Hollywood. But in 1954, decades after Nita Naldi's exit from the film business, it was announced that a new musical called *The Vamp*, inspired by the actress's life, and starring Carol Channing, would soon be coming to Broadway.

I had read this item in a tabloid's theater column one morning while riding the subway to work, months before leaving for the army. The column mentioned that Nita Naldi was then living as a recluse in a small Broadway hotel, but the hotel was not named. New York then had close to 300 small hotels in the Broadway area. I spent hours looking in the yellow pages in the *Times* newsroom when I was not otherwise occupied; then I jotted down the hotel numbers and later began placing calls from one of the rear phones that copyboys could use without being in visual range of the City Editor's desk clerks, who liked to assert their authority over copyboys.

I phoned about eighty hotels over a four-day period, asking each time to be connected to Miss Naldi's suite, speaking always in a confident tone that I hoped might convey the impression that I *knew* she was staying there. But none of the hotel people had ever heard of her. Then I called the Wentworth Hotel, and, to my amazement, I heard the gruff voice of a man say, "Yeah, she's here—who wants her?" I hung up. I hurried over to the Wentworth Hotel in person.

The telephone, to me, is second only to the tape recorder in undermining the art of interviewing. In my older years, especially while doing publicity tours for one of my books, I myself have been interviewed by young reporters carrying tape recorders; and as I sit answering their questions I see them half-listening, relaxing in the knowledge that the little plastic wheels are rolling. But what they are getting from me (and I assume from other people they talk to) is not the insight that comes from deep probing and perceptive analysis and much legwork; it is rather the first-draft drift of my mind, a once-over-lightly dialogue that too frequently reduces the exchanges to the level of talk radio on paper. Instead of decrying this trend, most editors tacitly approve of it, because a taped interview that is faithfully transcribed can protect the periodical from those interviewees who might later claim that they had been damagingly misquoted—accusations that, in these times of impulsive litigation and soaring legal fees, cause much anxiety, and sometimes timidity, among even the most independent and courageous of editors. Another reason editors are accepting of the tape recorder is that it enables them to obtain publishable articles from the influx of facile freelancers at pay rates below what would be expected and deserved by writers of more deliberation and commitment. With one or two interviews and a few hours of tape, a relatively inexperienced journalist today can produce a 3,000-word article that relies heavily on direct quotation and (depending largely on the promotional value of the subject at the newsstand) will gain a writer's fee of anywhere from approximately $500 to slightly more than $2,000—which is fair payment, considering the time and skill involved, but it is less than what was being paid for articles of similar length and topicality when I began writing for some of these same national magazines, such as the *Times Sunday Magazine* and *Esquire*, back in the 1950s and 1960s.

The telephone is another inadequate instrument for interviewing, because, among other things, it denies you from learning a great deal from observing a person's face and manner, to say nothing of the surrounding ambience. I also believe people will reveal more of themselves to you if you are physically present; and the more sincere you are in your interest, the better will be your chances of obtaining that person's cooperation.

The house phone of the Hotel Wentworth, which I knew I had to use in announcing myself to Nita Naldi, did not present the same obstacles that a regular phone might have: I would, after all, be calling within her own building; *I was already there*, an undeniable presence!

"Hello, Miss Naldi," I began, having asked the operator to be directly connected without my having first announced myself to one of the hotel's desk clerks, a courtesy that—suspecting their mercenary nature—might have boomeranged to my disadvantage. "I'm a young man from the *Times*, and I'm downstairs in your hotel lobby, and I'd like to meet you for a few minutes and talk about doing an article for the *Sunday Magazine*."

"You're *downstairs?*" she asked, in a dramatic voice of mild alarm. "How did you know where I lived?"

"I just called all the Broadway hotels I could."

"You must have spent a lot of money, young man," she said, in a calmer voice. "Anyway, I don't have much time."

"May I just come up to introduce myself, Miss Naldi?"

After a pause, she said: "Well, give me five minutes, then come up. Room 513. Oh, the place is a perfect mess!"

I went up to the fifth floor and will never forget the place. She occupied a small suite with four parrots, and the suite was decorated like a turn-of-the-century movie set. And she was dressed in a style that would have no doubt appealed to Rudolph Valentino himself, and perhaps *only* to him. She had dark arched eyebrows and long earrings and a black gown, and jet-black hair which I'm sure she dyed daily. Her gestures were very exaggerated, as in the silent-screen era they had to be; and she was very amusing. I took notes, went back to my apartment after finishing work that day, and I wrote the story, which probably took three or four days, or even longer, to complete. I turned it in to the Sunday editor who handled show business subjects, and asked if he would be kind enough to read it.

A week later, he called to say he would like to use the article. His response marked one of the happiest days of my young life. The magazine would definitely publish it, he repeated, adding he did not know exactly when. It lay in type for a few months. But finally it did appear, on October 16, 1955, while I was serving in the tank corps in Fort Knox, Kentucky. My parents sent me a telegram. I called them back from a telephone booth, collect, and my mother read the published article to me over the telephone. It began:

> In order that Carol Channing be flawlessly vampish, beguiling and pleasingly unwholesome as the star of the musical on the silent movie era which comes to Broadway Nov. 10 and is called, not unexpectedly, "The Vamp," she has had as a kind of adviser, aide de camp, critic and coach, that exotic former siren named Nita Naldi. When it comes to vamping roles, no one is a more qualified instructor than Miss Naldi. In her heyday, in the Twenties, Nita Naldi was the symbol of everything passionate and evil on the silent screen.

And it ended:

> . . . still very dark and buxom, Miss Naldi is recognized surprisingly often as she travels about. "Women don't seem to hate me anymore," she says with satisfaction. She is often stopped in the street and asked, "What was it really like kissing Valentino?" Young people will remark, "Oh, Miss Naldi, my father has told me so-o-o much about you!" to which the actress manages to respond graciously. Not too long ago a man approached her on

*the corner of Forty-sixth Street and Broadway and exclaimed in wonder,
"You're Nita Naldi, the Vampire!" It was as if he had turned the clock
back, restoring Miss Naldi to the world she had inhabited thirty years ago.
Eager to live in the present, the actress replied in a tone that mixed resentment and resignation, "Yes, do you mind?"*

My mother ordered several dozen copies of the magazine and
mailed them out to all the customers who had known me as a boy in
the store, and she included in her package my address at the base. In
the fan mail I later received from them was also a letter from the City
Editor of the *Times* informing me that, after I was discharged and
had returned to the paper, I would no longer be employed as a copyboy. I was being promoted to the writing staff and assigned to the
Sports Department.

In a postscript, he added, "You're on your way."

When I Was Twenty-five

WHEN I WAS TWENTY-FIVE, I was chasing stray cats around Manhattan. I trailed them while they foraged for food in the city's garbage dumps, in the fish markets and poultry centers, and in the rat-infested docks along the Hudson River; and I remember marking my twenty-fifth birthday in a dark tunnel under Grand Central Terminal observing dozens of hissing cats battling one another for the edible leftovers that had been jettisoned earlier in the day from the lunch pails of the subway's track workers.

The year was 1957. It was a bad time for New York's 400,000 stray cats. They were victims of their own overpopulation and the dearth of garbage cans in the city's newly constructed apartment buildings; and I was researching my first full-length article for the *New York Times Sunday Magazine* about the cats' citywide struggle for survival. Other people were worrying at this time about the Dodgers leaving Brooklyn, or the lingering presence of the "Mad Bomber," or the fact that the Soviets had just launched a dog into space. But I was concentrating on cats, and when my 4,000-word article was published on May 12, 1957—under the headline "Journey into the Cat Jungle"—I confiscated about thirty copies from the *Times*'s printing plant and mailed them to my relatives and friends around the nation. It was my first fling with what Andy Warhol would later identify as a fifteen-minute fame buzz, and yet, like the initiation to love in early youth, its sweet memory can be sustained privately forever. That is how I recall the publication of that article about hungry cats by a hungry young writer.

I had recently arrived in New York after two years in the army and four years as a student at the University of Alabama, and I was mes-

merized by New York, and intensely curious about the things that relatively few people cared about (like the nocturnal dusting habits of the
city's skyscraper charwomen, and what the doormen in apartment
houses knew about the tenants' marital lives, and, of course, the di-
etary needs of freelance cats). But until I got a job in journalism I
knew of no way to indulge my peculiar interest in the natural and un-
natural order of city life.

I came from a small town. My perceptions were rather provincial.
I possessed a sense of wonder about what others saw as ordinary. But
I thought that the ordinary, the everyday happening in an average person's routine, was worthy of writing about, especially in a newspaper,
if it was written well.

There were *Times* editors, to be sure, who did not like what I was
writing; they called them "ragpicker" stories and we would have polite
but stubborn confrontations. To dissuade me they assigned me to the
political beat in Albany to cover the New York State legislature, there
to listen to the lies and pointless pronouncements of the politicians
and to report this as "news." I could not do it. There was a rule on the
Times in those days that reporters' bylines usually accompanied articles that were at least eight paragraphs in length. During my time in
Albany, I never wrote a political story longer than seven paragraphs. I
did not want my byline on an article that was limited to the rulings and
railings of the Albany legislators, and as a consequence, the *Times* editors discharged me and thought they were punishing me by bringing
me back to the home office and assigning me to write obituaries. I was
never happier. Obituary writing was in the realm of personal history,
biography, a summation of an individual's worth and consequence,
and anyone who commanded an obituary in the *Times* was doubtless
an individual of distinction and singular achievement—which was
considerably more than I had seen during my brief career as a twenty-
five-year-old political correspondent.

It was during my obituary-writing period that I also began to concentrate on writing for the *Times Sunday Magazine*, for I was in the
"doghouse" with the daily edition. After my cat story I did about thirty
more *Times* magaziners in the months that followed. I wrote about
silent-screen actresses in an age of sound, about old men who rang
the bells during boxing matches at Madison Square Garden, about the
river captains of the Staten Island ferries, about the window design-
ers of Fifth Avenue boutiques and the sculptures of the plastic but
nonetheless alluringly realistic female mannequins.

I was then living in Greenwich Village, in a brick building across
from the city's first café-espresso house and also a late-night bar that
catered to homosexual men. It was very common on my street to see
interracial couples walking hand-in-hand, and to hear the poets in
the cafés protesting in a manner one usually associates with the
1960s, but I think that the 1950s in Greenwich Village was really the
1960s—it was a decade ahead of the rest of the city, and it was in the
Village that I also fell in love. She was a magazine editor uptown, but
she joined me downtown for dinner every night, and in 1959 we
eloped in Rome and have been married ever since.

Advice to young writers? The one essential quality is curiosity, in my
opinion, and the energy to get out and learn about the world and about
people who lead unique lives, who dwell in obscure places. I've subsequently expanded this thinking into writing books about Mafia wives
(*Honor Thy Father*), love advocates (*Thy Neighbor's Wife*), immigrant tailors (*Unto the Sons*), and high-altitude steelworkers (*The Bridge*).

There are stories everywhere within view, within range; and the
only other advice I might offer (following my own father's advice to
me): "Never write anything for money." It is perhaps strange advice in
this age of bottom-line rationalizing, greed, and gluttony; but it is the
advice that has guided me through these forty years since back in 1957
(in the company of cats) I turned twenty-five.

Walking My Cigar

EACH EVENING AFTER DINNER, ACCOMPANIED by my two dogs, I stroll onto Park Avenue to walk my cigar. My cigar is the same color as my dogs, and my dogs are also drawn to its smell; they leap up my legs as I light it, prior to our walk, with their nostrils widened and their eyes narrowly focused with the same greedy stare I see whenever I offer them milk bones or a tray of spicy canapés left over from one of our cocktail parties. Were my cigar not so expensive, and were I not certain that they would eat it, I might offer them a puff, for I'm sure they would appreciate the after-dinner pleasure much more than most of my friends. Too many of my friends, including my wife—who, incidentally, smokes cigarettes—have been swayed in recent years by the insidious campaign against cigar smoking, and this has affected my otherwise admirable disposition. It has made me defensive at times, argumentative, even an activist against America's antismoking lobby—which is really ridiculous, because I'm basically a nonsmoker myself except for my single after-dinner cigar.

I look forward all day to my nightly cigar, much as I looked forward to dating Scandinavian airline stewardesses, back in my early days of bachelorhood in the 1950s. In those days, nearly all stewardesses were beautiful, and the Scandinavians were additionally reputed to be sexually adventuresome (except for those stalwart moralists that I unfortunately came to know). This was also a period of such widespread tolerance for tobacco that it was even lawful to smoke cigars on airplanes. While I was not a smoker back then, I recall inhaling and enjoying the rich aromatic fragrance of other men's cigars as I sat on airplanes and in restaurants; and from these men's expensive style in dress, and their self-assurance, I saw them as part of a privileged breed that, only because they were much older than me, did I experience no envy.

Not only were they older, but they tended to be portly and jowly, although such characteristics in the 1950s were somewhat in fashion among male members of the power elite. The most respected among the elite's portly, jowly, cigar-smoking clubmen in those days was Sir Winston Churchill, England's Second World War leader, a crusty old gent who stood before cheering crowds with his hands in the air, waving his cigar along with his V-sign, which his fellow cigar smokers could well have interpreted to be the twin symbols of the free world over the brutal forces of regimentation.

Cigar smoking took on a more youthful and romantic image after 1960 with the elevation to the presidency of John F. Kennedy, who often appeared in public puffing on one of his favorite Havanas; and this was when I, and some of my colleagues in the newspaper business, also indulged for the first time. From a journalist friend of mine who covered politics in Washington, I was able to obtain the best in Cuban cigars before and during America's lengthy embargo on all Cuban products. I especially remember the gift box of Havana Churchills my friend sent me after the birth of my first daughter, in 1964, and a second box after the arrival of my second daughter, in 1967. Even more fondly do I recall in later years how my little girls would argue each night over whose turn it was to wear the "ring" after I had removed it from one of my after-dinner cigars—a ritual that not only introduced them to the blissful effluvium of a superior smoke but also inculcated within them an appreciation and respect for the pleasure it brought me.

That their loving response toward me and my cigars continues to this day, decades after their final fight over paper rings, makes me wonder if some women's repugnance of cigar smoking might have less to do with a cigar's smoke or smell than with their personal relationships with the first man in their lives who indulged in the habit. Since the public outcry against cigar smoking, which is an all-but-exclusive male practice, has been accelerated during these recent decades that have also witnessed the increased emphasis on women's rights, it has occurred to me that there might be some connection.

This could well be the case in my own home. My wife of thirty-plus years, who never complained of cigar smoke during the first half of our marriage, has, since her subsequent promotions in the business world, shown an assertiveness against my nightly habit that has driven me out into the streets, there to seek acceptance and tolerance in the polluted evening air of New York, with my dogs.

And yet even the streets do not guarantee a green light for cigar smokers. I was made aware of this one recent evening as I passed a sidewalk café on Madison Avenue and suddenly noticed that two female diners were not only holding their noses but were waving their hands over their plates of food and wine glasses as ways of nullifying what they presumably feared to be the floating poison of my cigar smoke. And, just as I passed their table, one of the women exclaimed, "Ugh."

"Are you referring to my cigar, madam?" I asked, pausing to remove my seven-dollar Macanudo Vintage No. 1 while pulling back on the leash of my growling Australian terriers.

"Yes," she said. "I find it offensive. In fact, it stinks."

She was a blondish woman in her early thirties, bespectacled and of a lean and dour mien, but hardly unattractive; she wore a pair of Indian beads draped over her slender neck, dangling halfway down her yellow gingham blouse, and she had on a beige linen jacket with a button on the lapel reading, "Pro-Choice."

"This is a public street, you know," I said.

"Yes," she said, "and I'm part of the public."

I was tempted to inhale and blow smoke in her direction, which hardly would have downgraded the air quality of the avenue, where the soot from the uptown buses and cars had already turned the café's white tablecloths toward shades of battleship gray and navy blue. But I noticed that the woman's companion, who had not ceased waving her hands over her dinner, had now drawn the attention of the waiter and some people at the next table; and suspecting I would have few allies in this crowd, I allowed my dogs to pull me farther uptown.

Puffing deeply on my cigar, which now seemed to have turned into a hotter smoke, I thought more about the social ostracism confronting cigar smokers.

Was it indeed motivated by female sexism? Have some angry members of the women's movement defined cigars as a vestige of that bygone male era of male clannishness and exclusivity? Are some of these women getting back at their cigar-chomping, tough-minded, sexist fathers who, refusing to pass on the lucrative family business to a worthy daughter, favored instead an incompetent son? What would Sigmund Freud, an inveterate cigar smoker, say to all this? Would he identify the cigar as a phallic symbol that contemporary women both envy and loathe?

No, no, I decided; in my case I could not blame women entirely for the cool receptions accorded to my cigars. Just as many men have groused about my cigars: for example, many doormen whose hostile stares I've seen whenever I've paused to relight my cigar under the marquees of their apartment houses or hotels; and those taxi-cab drivers who, spotting me on rainy nights waving toward them with my cigar extended, have sped past me while giving me the finger. And I should also mention that New York's restaurants, which are overwhelmingly owned and operated by men, have led a vigilant campaign against cigar smokers that contrasts with their relative permissiveness toward cigarette smokers, who are allowed to light up in designated areas. The restaurateurs' strict boycott of cigars extends also to those who smoke pipes, I might add. But what do I care about pipe smokers?

And yet there is one famous New York restaurant that (in addition to "21") does welcome cigar smokers, and this is owned and operated by a woman! She is Elaine Kaufman, the proprietress and social lioness of Elaine's on Second Avenue, a bastion of democracy that is favored by writers and other advocates of freedom. As long as her patrons do not criticize the food, Elaine allows them to do pretty much as they wish in her restaurant; and if anybody complains to her about the cigar smoke, she promptly points them in the direction of a doorway leading into a side room, which the regulars call Siberia.

Still, the liberty available to cigar smokers at Elaine's and a few other restaurants hardly refutes the fact that the cigar is becoming increasingly a less portable pleasure; and, in my view, this is but one symptom of a growing neo-Puritanism and negativism that has choked the nation with codes of correctness, and has led to greater mistrust between the sexes, and has finally, in the name of health and virtue and fairness, reduced options and pleasures that, in measured amounts, had once been generally accepted as normal and natural.

"When America is not fighting a war, the puritanical desire to punish people has to be let out at home," the writer Joyce Carol Oates explained years ago, referring to literary censorship. But this applies to restrictions of every kind, including the current edicts against my humble cigar—out of whose smoke my paranoia rises each night and does not evaporate even when I take a final puff and toss the butt into the street, signaling to my dogs that our nightly walk in the outdoors is over.